Benjamin Rush Davenport

The Crime of Caste in Our Country

Americans enforce equality

Benjamin Rush Davenport

The Crime of Caste in Our Country
Americans enforce equality

ISBN/EAN: 9783744727433

Printed in Europe, USA, Canada, Australia, Japan

Cover: Foto ©ninafisch / pixelio.de

More available books at **www.hansebooks.com**

THE CRIME OF CASTE
IN OUR COUNTRY

AMERICANS ENFORCE EQUALITY

Sham Aristocracy of Wealth Permitted by the People

Lesson of 1892 Taught Imitators of English Aristocracy

HISTORY OF THE POWER OF PEOPLE RE-TOLD

Records for Three Thousand Years Searched for Examples

Bullets, 1861—Ballots, 1892

By BENJAMIN R. DAVENPORT

PHILADELPHIA:
KEYSTONE PUBLISHING CO.
1893

Copyright by
JOSEPH W MORTON, Jr.
1892

THIS BOOK IS DEDICATED TO ALL AMERICAN CITIZENS,

WHO BELIEVE

THAT PATRIOTISM, HONESTY, VIRTUE, AND MERIT

ALONE ~~CONSTITUTE~~ INEQUALITY IN MANKIND;

WHO OBJECT TO AND RESENT ARROGANCE AND PRESUMPTION
UPON THE PART OF

THE POSSESSORS OF WEALTH

AND TO THOSE TO WHOM

"CASTE" AND FOREIGN MANNERISMS ARE OBNOXIOUS.

THE AUTHOR.

DEFINITION OF "CASTE."

The word "Caste," we derive from a Portuguese word, which means "a race;" the Portuguese being the early voyagers to the East Indies, where they found the distinction of classes of society established under the Brahminical regime of India. Thence it came to be applied as a term of distinction of society in other countries. There were four castes in India: 1, the Priests; 2, military; 3, merchants; 4, the servile classes.

Members of the lowest caste were forbidden to marry those of the upper. Children of such unions were outcasts and irredeemably base; they could not accumulate property, nor change or improve their conditions. Along with many other senseless and inconvenient rules for the conduct of the different castes, were such as those forbidding members of different castes from using the same springs or running streams, sitting at the same table, eating with the same utensils, or preparing food in the same vessels. It was contamination for those of the first class to even mingle in the public highway with those who were of the lower castes. For convenience, and in the interest of the commercial prosperity of India, the British, after much exertion, have been able to eradicate many of these absurd distinctions, and the habits that resulted therefrom.

The attempt to create class distinctions in Free America, upon the basis of wealth or assumed social superiority, is a crime, and as such will be punished by the Common People.

INDEX.

	PAGE.
INTRODUCTION	11

CHAPTER I.
Vox Populi, Vox Dei 33

CHAPTER II.
The Alleged General Discontent 65

CHAPTER III.
November 8, 1892 79

CHAPTER IV.
Society as the People Found It November 8, 1892 . 91

CHAPTER V.
Some Reasons for Wrath 111

CHAPTER VI.
The Aristocratic "Chappie" vs. Abraham Lincoln . 145

CHAPTER VII.
Hon. John Brisben Walker, on Homestead 161

CHAPTER VIII.
Surrender at Homestead.—Organized Labor Defeated 183

CHAPTER IX.
Possible Fruits of Victory 204

CHAPTER X.
The Cause of Bullets, '61; Ballots, '92.—Abraham Lincoln, the People's Choice in '60 225

CHAPTER XI.
Andrew Jackson, 1828 241

CHAPTER XII.
Thomas Jefferson, 1800 249

CHAPTER XIII.
The Revolution in 1776 257

CHAPTER XIV.
The French Revolution 278

CHAPTER XV.
England, 1645 295

CHAPTER XVI.
The German Empire, 1520–1525 307

CHAPTER XVII.
Switzerland, 1424 312

CHAPTER XVIII.
Russia 315

CHAPTER XIX.
Patricians and Plebeians in Rome 320

CHAPTER XX.
Greece.—Venice.—The Rule of "Caste" 324

CHAPTER XXI.
Egypt, 4235 B. C. 330

CHAPTER XXII.
Christianity 333

CHAPTER XXIII.
Not a Democratic Party Victory.—Democracy is Not the Name of a Party, but of a Principle . . . 346

CHAPTER XXIV.
Not a Defeat of Abraham Lincoln's Republican Party 390

CHAPTER XXV.
The Populist: the "Allies."—Elected by the People; therefore, with the "Common People" . . . 409

CHAPTER XXVI.
"Flabbyism" and the Income Tax 417

CHAPTER XXVII.
Conclusion 428

ILLUSTRATIONS.

	PAGE.
Abraham Lincoln	Frontispiece.
Grover Cleveland	32
James B. Weaver	64
John D. Rockefeller	105
Ward MacAllister	110
"The Public be D—d"	115
Mrs. Benjamin Harrison	127
Benjamin Harrison	131
American Queen	136
American Duchess	137
Jay Gould	143
Abe, "The Rail-Splitter"	154
"Chappie" on Fifth Avenue	155
Andrew Carnegie	160
Henry C. Frick	162
The Mistake at Homestead	182
William H. Vanderbilt	219
W. Seward Webb	223
Andrew Jackson	240
Thomas Jefferson	248

INTRODUCTION.

HAD a Johnstown flood, a Charleston earthquake, a war with Chili, or a Homestead strike occurred on November 8, 1892, instead of an election, those Napoleons of journalism, James Gordon Bennett, of the New York *Herald*, Joseph Pulitzer, of the New York *World*, and Whitelaw Reid, of the *Tribune*, would have had a score of representatives on the scene at once, without thought of expense; would have had every detail in its most minute particular investigated, and reproduced every statement, embellished by the pencils of a host of artists, utterly regardless of expense, keeping, as these magnificent journals ever have, good faith with the public and their readers, making lasting monuments of their wonderful papers for coming generations of journalists to gaze upon.

But a revolution occurred on November 8, 1892, a revolution of the American people, so overwhelming, so decisive, and so pronounced as to absolutely stupefy even the genius of the press. Instead of corps of reporters, artists, special correspondents, speeding over the land to ascertain the cause—not the result; the cause, the origin, —of this stupendous surprise, all the great journals of the country, having each nailed to its flag-staff some theory or text utterly inconsistent with the result, utterly disproportioned to the overwhelming revolution, that they have sought by vain endeavor to make an overwhelming result compatible with and agreeable to some one part or portion of the cause thereof.

To loudly proclaim, as did the New York *Sun*, that an exhibition of the will of the people, so pronounced as that of November the 8th, was occasioned by the Force Bill, is as utterly unreasonable as to ascribe the magnificent volume within the banks of the Mississippi to some little trickling rivulet flowing from the plains of Nebraska. To say, with the *Tribune*, that the grand result pronounced in the mighty voice of the people was produced by the misunderstanding of the McKinley Bill, is as groundless as to ascribe the echoing thunder tones of heaven to the swelling throat of a canary bird. To herald over the land, "Pauper emigration did it," with the New York *Herald*, is about as pregnant with truth as would be the assumption that the foundation and everlasting strength of Christianity has for its basis the misguided vaporings of a negro preacher in Richmond, who proclaims, "The sun do move." To announce, as did the *World*, that "Tariff reform and WE, the Democrats, achieved this victory," is entitled to as much respect as would be given the utterances of a drummer boy of the Federal Army at Gettysburg.

It was not any one nor all of these causes that moved the people. Each newspaper, Democratic or Republican, has selected some nail upon which it hangs the laurel wreath of victory, inscribed with its own puny text for which it has fought its little battle, and each newspaper of the Republican press has covered, with the tattered garments of defeat, its little text wherein it had proclaimed that the Republican party would be victorious, and labeled its tattered garment of lack of judgment with some phrase like, " Disloyalty of Platt," " Incapacity of Carter," "Want of Organization," " Lack of Popularity and Magnetism of our Candidate," " The Voters didn't come out." Had the press no part of its own reputation at stake, they would have searched and delved into the bosoms of men ; yes, neither space nor distance, time nor expense, would have been spared by the magnates of the newspaper world to ascertain the true cause. But in ascertaining that true cause, it would have been necessary, in announcing the same, to stultify themselves in what they had been predicting, proclaiming, foretelling, and advising, for months and years.

The truth is in the air ; was in the air before the election. 'Twas breathed ; it was thought ; yea, better, it was *felt*, by the great throbbing, aching heart of the men and women of the Union. From the hovel to the palace, the insidious, poisonous vapor of a supposed affected, sham aristocracy, with the noxious slime of a half-proclaimed doctrine of the inequality of man and woman, by reason of non-possession of wealth, had crept. The air of freedom was polluted by the emanations arising from the imported English decaying corpse of aristocracy. It was everywhere. In blindness and self-delusion, the press made its battle ; in the very air of it, howling against Protection and for Protection, against Force Bill and for Force Bill, while the wretched, cankerous ulcer was eating into the pride of every free-born man and woman in the land. The very silence of the people, the general apathy, was evidence of but one of the symptoms of the insidious disease with which the body politic was being consumed.

A scene that has been described in Washington just prior to the late Civil War best illustrates the condition of the people. The city of Washington was filled with silent, sullen, suspicious men. A sombre air pervaded the Capital. South Carolina had seceded ; the Union was disintegrating. All that had been, was being forgotten. Old ties were breaking ; old friendships becoming strange. Each man viewed his neighbor and his friend of yesterday, with a doubt in his mind as to whether they would fight side by side, or be at each other's throats to-morrow. Men paced their rooms in the various hotels, anxious and careworn, sleepless and fearful. Yet, the surface was still, a dangerous state of general apathy obtained, if silence and murmuring, without action, can be called apathy.

It was night, yet the streets were not deserted. Suddenly a window of the Ebbitt House was raised, a man stepped on to the balcony out of the window, and in clear, vigorous, and manly tones began to sing "The Star-Spangled Banner." Windows were raised; the crowd collected around the Ebbitt House. It was the signal for the breaking of a dam. A flood of patriotism burst from the hearts of the hearers; it was the bugle note, calling upon Americans to save their country. Where there had been silence, were now outspoken vows of fidelity and loyalty to the Union. The battle was won that night; not at Gettysburg and Vicksburg*.

Just so with the people of America in 1892; for years they have endured in silence, murmuring and thinking, heart to heart speaking by responsive heart throbs ; not by word. The rich, who had accumulated their wealth by reason of monopolies which were the necessary consequence of the Civil War, men who had laid the foundation

---

*This story has frequently been related, verbally, but the Author has never seen it in print Its authenticity, however, is fully established.

of their fortunes by speculating upon the necessities of the government while contending for the very existence of the Union, had, year by year, by a stealthy, yet ever-increasing presumption, begun to assume the possibility of a class distinction, presuming that the possession of wealth entitled them to privileges, and arrogating to themselves mannerisms of the titled classes of Europe, adopting crests, coats of arms, claiming descent from titled foreigners, an exclusiveness in their social relations, disregarding the laws of morality. The women of this would-be aristocratic class, flaunting their jewels and laces in the faces of their poorer sisters, with elevated noses, and garments drawn aside, feared to touch or gaze at the poor but honest mothers and wives of America.

It was not much : it was rank presumption ; it was nonsense, absurd. "There's no such thing possible in America as class distinction ; in fact, it does not exist, cannot exist ; the 'Four Hundred' of New York is a joke, a by-word, a stupendous folly."

But, good people of the said "Four Hundred," remember that while the American is neither a Socialist nor an Anarchist, when you presume to make a distinction, socially, between the poor man, his wife, children, and mother, you touch him in the most sensitive part of his being. You may have your villas at Newport, you may ape the English fashionable season in London by a similar one in New York; you may have your steam yachts; you may ride to hounds; your women may marry divorced dukes and puppified sons of lords; but, mark you, claim no privilege, attempt no distinction between yourselves and the poorest honest man and woman in the land. Equality is the jewel that every true American holds most dear. No free son of our Republic will sell this treasure for gold, whether it be offered directly as a bribe or shrewdly tendered under the guise of "protected" wages.

It did not do for the Republican press of the country to demonstrate that Protection brought higher wages to the workingman. They might have proved that by voting the Republican ticket the workingman's pay would have been a hundred dollars a day; they might have shown him that in point of pocket he would be eternally blest by supporting the party which he deemed identified with those who attempted to force "caste" upon our country. It is not a question of money; the equality of man is the American's birthright. For it, our fathers sought these shores, contending with privation, enduring untold labor, dangers, and death. For it, our forefathers fought the most powerful nation on earth, when they were but a scattered handful of colonists, scattered from

Massachusetts to Georgia. When the attempt was made—that it was attempted, there can be no doubt—to buy the American's birthright by preaching to him "increased wages," it failed.

Take every speech of every Republican orator, every bit of Republican literature, every editorial in the Republican papers, all speak from but one text, viz.: "Workmen, farmers, in fact, all ye good people of America, you can make more money under Protection;" which plainly means, "Let Protection and the Republican party (which you designate in your hearts as The Rich Man's party) continue in power, accumulating wealth, creating class distinctions, and you can have better wages."

In other words, "Sell us the right to create a Republic like that of Venice, wherein the rich became the privileged class, and we will give you better pay."

The Democratic press, orators, and literary bureau were no better. They no more understood the feeling of the people, for their continual cry was, "Free Trade, and you will be better off in pocket." They excoriated trusts, monopolies; they talked of corruption and what would be done to benefit, IN POCKET, the poor man, if the Democratic party came in power; just as blind as their brothers of the Republican party, they appealed to the American pocketbook.

While every Democratic orator knew that he felt the sting of the venomous and growing reptile, "caste," in no place in the literature of the Democratic party, in no paper, can be found one single reference to the pride of the American in his citizenship, in his equality. It seemed as if each man thought that he alone endured a pang upon the subject of "caste" and social distinction ; for, bear in mind, the man with one million will feel the slight and attempted distinction between his family and the family with ten millions, just as keenly as the cashier of a bank will feel the distinction that the president attempts to make between their social positions; the farmer with ten acres feels towards the farmer with a hundred acres, exactly the same as the farmer with a hundred does towards the farmer possessed of a thousand acres.

This disease was not confined to the horny-handed sons of toil ; the heart in the hovel was not the only one that ached. It was not confined to the follower of the plow ; but its pestilential breath pervaded every home in the land, leaving everyone below the multi-millionaire unhappy. The clerk of the dry-goods store was hurt because the floor walker assumed a superiority; the floor walker, because the proprietor assumed it ; the proprietor, because the importer from whom he purchased goods assumed a distinction ; **and so it** continued, from the longshoreman up, until it reached our millionaire would-be princes, who ape and mimic English life and manners, leaving, as it arose, a sting of increasing bitterness ; but each man felt too proud to give utterance to what he thought it shamed him even to recognize as a sensation.

Hence the apathy on the surface, the sentiment confessed only to themselves and in the closet of the voting booth. Because the people had identified the Republican party with the class of men who were striving to create this class distinction, and because of the very charm of the word Democracy to their aching hearts, they voted the Democratic ticket—not Democrats alone in a political sense, but men who believe in democracy in the broad sense, that St. Paul preached on Mars Hill at Athens, in the broad sense that Christ's life demonstrated.

It was useless, against this first overmastering, powerful emotion in the American breast, to call upon the old veterans of the Civil War, to whom the Republican party had given increased pensions. It was useless to cry even to the negro, to whom the Republican party had given freedom. He, too, had become imbued with the spirit of equality. The wealthy could not purchase the birthright of the veteran by appealing to his pocketbook, any more than they could that of the laborer. He had shed his blood in the cause of equality, resisting then the assumed superiority of blood and birth so often flaunted in his face by gentlemen from the South.

In 1861, the "mudsills" of the North and West, the tillers of the soil, had shouldered their muskets at the call of that great man of the people, Abraham Lincoln, leaving home and loved ones to face unknown dangers and diseases in the cause of EQUALITY. Down in their hearts then was a sentiment which is revived in 1892. That thing which had been the hardest to bear, for the laboring settler of the West and the workman of the North, was the existence of "caste" in the South, and the supposed superiority of the Southerners In the halls of Congress. Love of the Union was the outspoken, pronounced cause of their coming at Lincoln's call; but there was something behind and beneath all of that, that had been growing for years; it was resentment, because of the South's assumption of "caste" in our country.

The question was settled, by these very veterans, from 1861 to '65 with bullets, and it was utterly unavailing to call upon them for ballots in 1892 against the cause for which they fought in 1861.

The very negro said to himself: "You gave us freedom, the Republican party, but the

Republican party of Abraham Lincoln was purely a Democratic party, in a broader sense." To the negro's mind, no three Presidents of the past will more thoroughly represent a picture pleasing to the eye of the enslaved or the lower classes, than Jefferson, Jackson, and Lincoln. All were Democrats—men who believed in the people and labored for the people, leading lives of pure simplicity, affecting no superiority of rank or position. It was useless to attempt to hold the negro vote.

The very name of the "People's Party," so strongly did it indicate and describe this sentiment of the people, enabled that party, with all its incongruous doctrines, to carry the electoral votes of some States of the Union.

How frivolous seemed the claim of the Democratic papers and politicians, that the popularity of Grover Cleveland, and the confidence that people had in his rectitude and honesty, caused this revolution. How it appears to be trifling with truth to ascribe the victory of the people, the true Democracy, to the "masterly manner in which Mr. Harrity managed the campaign." Mr. Whitney's diplomacy, Mr. Dickinson's energy and ability, Mr. Sheehan's shrewdness, sink into utter insignificance, and become as a grain of sand upon the seashore, where they have happened to be tossed by the mighty wave of the ocean of feeling, full of resentment, that filled the hearts of the people. Their little all was but the piping of a penny whistle in a gale of wind. W. H. Vanderbilt's four words, "The public be damned," uttered from the pedestal of $150,000,000, made a greater impression, and became more indelibly impressed upon the minds of the whole people, ranging in wealth from $10,000,000 to less than a cent, than all the management of Harrity, the diplomacy of Whitney, the skill of Sheehan, or the energy of Dickinson. The reported expression of Mr. Russell Harrison, when asked, while in London, what his position was in America, as son of the President,—"Oh, about what the Prince of Wales is here,"—was thought of and resented to greater purpose than was produced by all the speeches of the eloquent Cockran.

The women of the land made more speeches, and effective speeches, to the voters of the land when they thought of the much-advertised American Duchess. They had felt most keenly—for woman's life is social much more than man's—the attempted social distinction ; and, strange as it may appear to some of the skillful politicians that they had never recognized it, the women of America had become largely Democratic, and in them the Democratic party had its most powerful orators ; for even the most brutal, neglectful, and unloving husband resents in a vigorous manner the least slight or insult offered to his wife. Upon every occasion, gathering, entertainment, charitable undertaking, some wife had been slighted. Because of the attempted creation of "caste," she became a powerful factor, at once, in the campaign of the people. It mattered not whether her husband was a millionaire or not, no matter in what portion of society,—the clerk in a dry-goods store, the farmer, the banker, the millionaire,—the same result would follow. Some would attempt to arrogate to themselves a better position, and claim certain superiority over her. The banker's wife feels as keenly the slight of the wife of a railroad president, as the wife of a longshoreman does any assumed difference in social position on the part of the wife of the retail grocer.

This all-prevailing crime of "caste" does not, like most crimes are supposed to do, originate in the gutter, but it permeates the mass of the population, like the source of a great river, starting at the very top of the mountain, and dripping constantly downward.

The example of the rich in imitating the immoralities of the privileged classes of Europe, presents a spectacle of presumed immunity from the consequences of their crimes which would be as detrimental to the continuation of the purity of American homes, as the increase of the feeling of "caste" would be to the happiness of the people. A most beautiful illustration of corruption in high places was presented in the disgusting and nauseating Drayton-Borrowe affair, wherein the daughter of an Astor, a multi-millionaire, one of the members of the supposed upper "caste," is paraded before the public as imitating the vices and immoralities of the Court of Charles II. Yet these same Astors would claim, by reason of their assumed position, some exemption from the result of the crime, which would not be accorded to the wife of a farmer, clerk, or a bank cashier, to say nothing of the fact that, had this beautiful sample of America's sham aristocracy been a laborer's wife, she would, by the peculiar ethics adopted by the corrupt English aristocracy, have been a fit subject for the police court.

Another of the disgusting apings of foreign vices, along with the foolish claim of "caste," is exhibited in the delightful Deacon assassination in France. Another representative of American aristocracy, so-called, would play the part of a French Countess. Fortunately for the world, the man Deacon had left remaining a few drops of American blood in his veins, and rid the world of a brute, as any honest American laboring man would have done. The class which the shameless imitators pretend to represent in America assumed the privilege abroad (in Europe) to indulge in drunkenness, debauchery, gambling, and general immorality; leaving the virtues, sobriety, honesty, and purity to the lower classes. In America, there being but one class, those who assume to imitate the manners of the immoral, to carouse and debauch, render themselves obnoxious to the mass of the people, and that political party which becomes identified in the minds of the people with any set, or "caste," possessing such distorted principles, becomes correspondingly objectionable. There can be but one law of morals in America. Debauchery, drunkenness, and dishonesty, though sheltered by a palace, are as odoriferous to the senses of the people as the polluted air from a sewer.

There are many able and learned men of America who think seriously and have thought intently for years upon this subject, but hesitated to utter sentiments that falsely and absurdly are called socialistic and anarchical. There is no desire upon the part of Americans to deprive any citizen of his property and his freedom to enjoy the same as he will, so long as he has due appreciation of and respect for the rights of others. No man in the Republic can possess any right, by reason of his wealth, greater than the poorest in the land. Each citizen of a republic, in consideration of the liberty that he enjoys, surrenders all claim to be anything except one of the people, and any assumed immunity from the consequences of his acts is objectionable, and will be visited upon his head. The roistering sons of millionaires, though clad in evening dress and drunk with champagne, are no less disgusting rowdies than the sons of the laborer, hilarious as the result of gin drunk in a groggery. Unfortunately for the Republican party, in looking over the row of America's money princes (?), we find "Republican" written behind almost every name. The villa at Newport, the castle in Scotland, the Tally Ho coach, is generally owned by a Republican. In fact, our would-be aristocrats began to assume that it was almost a disgrace to be anything else than a Republican; one would lose "caste" thereby.

The Republican party, of course, is not responsible for this. The Republican candidate, Benjamin Harrison, than whom there is no better example of a patriotic, earnest, honest American, Christian, father, husband, son, gentleman, and soldier, is worthy to be an example to the young men of our country. He was not responsible for the impression made by this excrescence that has grown like some hideous and poisonous fungus upon the stalwart oak planted by Abraham Lincoln. The decay has arisen from this polluting attachment. The McKinley Bill and Protection, while possessing many points of excellence it behooves the country to examine with care before erasing from the statute-books, are not responsible for the natural animosity of the people toward this child, deformed, misshapen, Sham Aristocracy, clinging to the skirts of the Republican party. The attack was upon this hideous tumor, and, by its amputation by the people, the life-blood of the Republican party has become exhausted ; for the operation necessarily was made painful, deep-felt, and severe. The Democratic party derived all the benefit from the defeat of the Republican party, at the hands of the people, without having contributed thereto to any amazing extent.

The result of the election of 1892 should be as the warning written on the wall was to Belshazzar. The rich must understand, and learn now in time, that they hold their lives, their liberty, and their property in this Republic only by the will of the people ; that the people, Democratic always in the broad sense of democracy, are long-suffering ; but retribution, as surely as night doth follow day, may come, if this warning be not heeded, in some more terrible shape than an overwhelming defeat, at the polls, of that party to which the rich attach themselves. It is not well to flaunt riches or claim privileges or "caste" before the face of a free people.

It would be well for the rich to learn this lesson. It was taught by the people under the name of the Republican party when they elected Lincoln ; under the name of the Democratic party when they elected Andrew Jackson ; under the name of the Democratic party when they elected Thomas Jefferson. It was taught to rich and powerful England when she lost a continent in 1776 ; it was taught to Anglo-Saxon England when Charles I. lost his head ; it was taught to France when the long-suffering peasantry and poor broke down the barriers of "caste," and flooded her fair fields with the tide of blood.

It has been taught in every nation—Rome, Greece, Egypt. The people will suffer long and much, but the resentment occasioned by "caste" and social distinction far outweighs any advantages that money can buy them.

November 8, 1892, showed that the workmen couldn't be bought, the farmer couldn't be bought, the veteran couldn't be bought, the negro couldn't be bought, by all the fair promises held out by the party of Protection, because this cup of nectar was poisoned by the deadly essence of "caste," which means extinction of all that the people hold dear. Should the Democratic party create, cause, or have arise under its administration, and become attached to that party, any set, or "caste," claiming any superiority over their fellow-citizens, the Democratic party would be killed, though the eternal sun might never shine again upon America should that party be defeated.

The purpose and object for which this book is written is not for the instruction of the people as to how they *are* to do, but it is, if possible, to put notes to the music that has been singing in the hearts of the Common People,—for we are all Common People. That song which echoes our own sentiments, even though we cannot sing the song, is always the sweetest. The man who tells the story we have thought and felt, is the greatest writer to us. Dickens is dear to the hearts of us all because he echoes and puts in words the sentiments of our own souls. If this book tell, in words, that which has been throbbing in the breasts of the people, it but articulates that which they have spoken silently for themselves. The author is one of the people, but he has felt what he believes others have felt. The book is not intended to aid or to harm either the Democratic or the Republican party. The writer is a supporter of ANY party, call it what you will, that represents the BEST INTERESTS, THE HONOR, DIGNITY, VIRTUE, of AMERICANS and American homes.

> " Is there, for honest poverty
>   That hangs his head, and a' that;
>   The coward-slave, we pass him by.
>   We dare be poor, for a' that;
>   For a' that, and a' that,
>   Our toil's obscure, and a' that,
>   The rank is but the guinea's stamp;
>   The man's the gowd for a' that.

" What though on homely fare we dine,
　　A prince can make a belted knight,
　A marquis, duke, and a' that;
　　But an honest man's aboon his might
　Guid faith he manna fa' that,
　　For a' that, and a' that,
　The pith o' sense and pride o' worth
　　Are higher ranks than a' that.

" Then let us pray that come it may,
　　As come it will for a' that,
　That sense and worth, o'er a' the earth,
　　May hear the gree, and a' that,
　That man to man, the world o'er,
　　Shall brothers be for a' that."

GROVER CLEVELAND.

Selected by the "Common People," November 8, 1892,
to Represent the Interests of the Masses
against the Classes.

CHAPTER I.

VOX POPULI, VOX DEI.

THE voice of the people, is indeed, the voice of God, and in grand and tremendous tones has that voice resounded through the land. The 8th of November, 1892, will long be remembered in the history of our country as one which stands in the annals of time as a monument to the might of the people, upon which might be carved in letters of everlasting durability, "Do not tread on me." The tidal wave, so often referred to by the newspapers, has come with unexpected momentum, washing aside the puny politicians as thistledown on the mighty stream of the Mississippi.

That mirror of public opinion, so generally correct, so apt to be accurate, is absolutely stupefied by the tremendous character of the uprising of the people. Even those who fondly hoped for victory, among the Democratic journalists, stand in reverential awe before the stupendous results so noiselessly and irresistibly effected by the masses. They vainly seek, like one bereft of sight, for the delusive cause of this great outpouring of Democratic sentiment.

That most preëminent and respectable organ of mugwump principles, the New York *Times*, of November 9, 1892, sounds the praises of Cleveland and his popularity as the cause; which is pardonable, as the *Times* has consistently closed its eyes before the blinding light of Cleveland's preëminence and brilliancy, and refused to see anything else or any other issue in the campaign, arguing that by the magic of the one word, "Cleveland," victory could be attained. Its leader on the result of the people's resentment to the crime of "caste" in our country, is a sounding eulogy upon Cleveland, with here and there a glimmer of light breaking upon the vision.

"Meanwhile the victory of Mr. Cleveland is the most signal since the re-election of Lincoln in the last year of the war for the Union."

It is noticeable in this paragraph that Cleveland's preëminence so overshadowed, in the mind of the *Times*, Lincoln, that the prefix of " Mr." is used before Cleveland's name, while just plain "Lincoln" is good enough for the man who preserved the Union. One would hardly expect, therefore, that the *Times* would do more than shout the praises of Cleveland, and give no credit to the sense of the people for their victory. Quoting from their article:—

"The nomination of Mr. Cleveland was dictated by the general sentiment of the party, inspired wholly by confidence in his integrity, purity, firmness, and sound sense. It was unaided by any organization, promoted by no machine, advocated by no literary bureau, appealed to no base passion. * * * * * * His election is due to the recognition by hundreds of thousands of sound-hearted American citizens, who had not before acted with the Democratic party, that under his guidance, with its avowed policy, that party was a fit depository of the powers of the Government. It is, moreover, preëminently a victory of courage and fidelity to principle. The Chicago Convention, in taking Mr. Cleveland as its candidate, planted itself firmly on the ground of principle."

It is perfectly plain to be seen that, from a source where the wreath of victory dangles, inscribed with but one word, and that "Cleveland," one could hardly expect to find information as to the cause that brought about this revolution in the minds of the people. Not that there is any objection to the praises of Cleveland, because all that they say of him is believed by thousands throughout the country, and the same thing is believed to be true of thousands of other men whom the Democratic party might have nominated. Horace Greeley, could he have been taken from his tomb and reanimated, would just as surely have been elected upon the Democratic ticket, had the people believed, as they did, that that ticket represented that "caste," moneyed aristocracy, to which **they were bitterly in their heart of hearts opposed.**

The New York *World*, controlled by one of the brightest, keenest, and shrewdest of men in the journalistic field, in an excellent editorial of November 10, 1892, proceeds to tell what the victory means. And one sentence particularly would be significant, if followed by a little definition of "plutocracy." Were this word significant enough to cover the objectionable features of the peculiar kind of "caste" which had become identified with the Republican party, it would be sufficient, but such is not the understanding of the word.

New York *World*, November 10th: "The President elect is the very embodiment of conscientious caution. He is preëminently conservative. His administration will mean economy, reform, retrenchment in every branch of the Government. The victory does mean putting a stop to riot, extravagance, profligacy, and corruption."

Few, very few, men who voted the Democratic ticket believe that there had been corruption, profligacy, under the Republican administration. The people were not directly affected by the aforesaid charges. The victory did not mean that.

The people are no longer political drones; they are thinking men, moved by sentiments and forces which have not as yet been explained by the most laborious newspaper articles written in the heat of the campaign, actuated in many cases by partisan interests, party journalists, aristocratic tendencies, and political affiliations. Each would see only his side of the party shield, and that was sure to be golden.

Mr. Cleveland, in his speech at the Manhattan Club, New York, commenting on this fact, states: "The American people have become political, and more thoughtful, and more watchful than they were ten years ago. They are considering now, vastly more than they were then, political principles and party policies, in distinction from party manipulation and distribution of rewards for political services and activities."

The reason for this is obvious. The country has been flooded of late years with newspapers, brought down to a nominal price; the people have read them thoughtfully; have written to them for explanations of difficulties and doubts arising in their minds, and have profited by these explanations. They have seen paraded in the newspapers the exhibitions of the pride of "caste"; they have seen chronicled the doings of the American Duchess with her divorced duke; they have learned to hate that which the Republican party would have preached to them as the source of all their happiness and prosperity. The Republican party, viewing it only as a means whereby fortunes were accumulated, espoused the principles which created a desire in the minds of divorced dukes, puppified lords, and degenerate descendants of English nobility, from cupidity, to marry America's fair daughters. The cheapness of the newspapers placed within the reach of the poorest the information upon which he based his faith. The penny paper is the great leveler of the land.

The New York *Herald*, of November 13th, commenting on the recent election, takes a biblical text as its theme: "Then were the people of Israel divided into two parts. Half of the people followed Tibni and half followed Omri; but the people that followed Omri prevailed against the people that followed Tibni: so Tibni died and Omri reigned," and says:—

"In those days, questions in dispute were settled by pitched battles. In these modern times, the arbitrament of war has become wellnigh obsolete, and national policies are decided by ballots instead of bayonets. We doubt if the history of the world records a spectacle as inspiring or instructive as that presented by the American people on Tuesday last, when by an orderly revolution they sent one class of political ideas to the rear, and another class to the front. The party leaders on both sides may have gone into the conflict for personal emolument, or some advantage for their followers, which is scarcely concealed under the words, 'Patronage and Purposes,' but the body of the people were the rank and file—the merchant, mechanic, artisan, and farmer; they cast their votes for the greatest good to the greatest number, because the prosperity of the whole means the prosperity of each."

In other words, 65,000,000 people have made themselves acquainted with the principles which underlie their government; have learned, through innumerable newspapers, which fall on hill and prairie as thick as snowflakes in December, the value and effect of the differing national policies, and on election day, expressed an intelligent and honest opinion.

In his work on "The American Commonwealth," James Bryce put the matter in terse and brilliant language, as follows:—

"The parties are not the ultimate force in the conduct of affairs. Public opinion—that is, the mind and conduct of the whole nation—is the opinion of the persons who are included in the parties, for the parties taken together are the nation, and the parties, each claiming to be its true exponent, seek to use it for their purposes. Yet, it stands above the parties, being cooler and larger-minded than they are. It awes party leaders, and holds in check party organization. No one openly ventures to resist it. It is the product of a greater number of minds than in any other country, and it is more indisputably sovereign. It is the central point in the whole American policy."

The people have spoken. Democracy is triumphant. Democratic principles have prevailed.

They are rooted in the hearts of the common
people. The voice of God has spoken. To you,
Mr. Cleveland, is entrusted a great task. You
took the enemy in flank, you invaded his own
territory; you put him upon the defensive, and
the defence was unsuccessful, while his offensive
operations against the Democratic stronghold
crippled and embarrassed. You have the love of
the American people. Nourish it; cherish it as
the apple of your eye, and your name will go
down into history, linked with the name of Jackson, Jefferson, and Abraham Lincoln.

Mr. Thomas Dolan, a well-known manufacturer, of Philadelphia, told some plain truths in an
impromptu speech at the Clover Club banquet in
that city, shortly after the election. Some parts
of it have become public. Mr. Dolan was asked,
jokingly, why "it snowed the next day." His
answer had the pungent, incisive, trenchant quality characteristic of the man. "You ask me," he
said, "why it snowed the next day. If you want
an answer, I will give it to you; but I must give
it in plain terms, for I can speak in no other way.
It 'snowed the next day' because there was the
most stupendous lying in this campaign of any
that I have ever known. It has been said here
this evening, that this was a campaign without
personality and without mud-flinging. That may
have been so in the treatment of candidates, but

in reference to others, it was a campaign of shameless lying, vituperation, and calumny. The manufacturers of the country, some of those here to-night, were held up as thieves and robbers who are stealing what belongs to labor. The very men who are giving labor its employment, and are seeking to assure it good wages, were assailed and denounced as its worst enemies. The Democratic press was full of abuse of those who have done their best to build up the prosperity of the country. There never was more unscrupulous lying than there has been in the dishonest and demagogic attempt to array class against class, and it is because of this persistent lying, imposed upon the people for the time being, that 'it snowed the next day.' " This is, of course, an explanation by a *representative* Republican, of Republican defeat.

The New York *World*, of November 20th, gives a better explanation, though not a true one :—

Republican politicians are searching in all manner of out-of-the-way corners for the causes of their party's defeat. They are carefully overlooking the actual cause which lies open to less prejudiced view. The Republican party was defeated because its politicians have strayed away from honest and patriotic courses. They have worshiped strange gods; they have allied themselves and their party with the plutocratic interests of the country ; they have betrayed the people to the monopolists ; they have sought to substitute money for manhood as the controlling power; they have tried to buy elections ; they have squandered the substance of the country, in order that there might be no reduction in oppressive taxes, which indirectly, but enormously, benefit a favored class. The party is punished for its sins. It has forfeited popular confidence by its misconduct. It has ceased to deserve power, and the people have taken power from it.

Murat Halstead, a deep thinker, wielding a forceful pen, writing about the recent mistakes of the Republican party, says :—

"There was too much 'Tariff Reform' and too little attention to practical politics in the conduct of the recent Republican campaign. The mistakes of the Republican party were many. They attempted too much tariff reform and too much ballot reform and too much civil service reform, and strangely mingled too little and too great attention to practical politics. The high character of the Harrison administration was not of the 'fetching' sort. There were strong and distinguished Republicans sharply opposed to another Harrison administration, in California, Nevada, Colorado, Kansas, Illinois, Indiana, Michigan, Ohio, Pennsylvania, New York, Maine, and several of the Southern States. In some States, there was grief because he did too much for Senators and too little for Representatives, and in others, the Senators suffered because the Representatives were especially recognized ; and there were scores of personal irritations that were nothing in themselves, but in the aggregate, became an element of mischief that was magnified into disaster. The ranks seemed solid toward the close of the campaign, but there were weaknesses, here and there, known to those whose information was from the interior. There were three things that seemed to give assurances of Republican success: First, the country was prosperous, and the economic value of protection seemed to be demonstrated, and nowhere more clearly than in the Homestead strike. Second, it was the testimony of home statistics and foreign news that the McKinley tariff was helping our workingmen, and had a powerful tendency to the transfer of industries to our shores, while the reciprocity treaties were aiding our manufacturers and food producers alike to new markets. Two of the grandest steamships on the Atlantic, one the swiftest ever built, were to hoist the stars and stripes and be transferred from the British navy to our own, and this was understood to be the dawn of an era of restoration of our lost strength on the seas. Third, President Harrison was revealed to the nation in his administration as a man of the highest order of ability, of industry that never wavered, and will that was unflinching and executive, while he was the readiest, most varied, and striking public speaker of his time. We have had no President with more influence with his own administration than he wielded. The Republicans have so long been accustomed to holding at least a veto on the Democratic party, that they could not be aroused to the full appreciation of the danger of giving that party the whole power of Government. The masses of men declined, in this fast age and rapidly-developing country, to be warned by the events of more than thirty years ago. The first surprise was public apathy. There were few displays. It was not a great summer and autumn for brass bands and torches. It was not a great year for newspapers. Those that largely increased their circulation did it outside of presidential excitements and political attractions. The second surprise was the immense registration. Then it was seen that comparative public quietude did not mean lack of interest. Everybody knew something was going to happen. Republicans were cheered, and said: 'This means the quiet vote. The secret ballot is with us. Times are good. There'll be a big vote, on the quiet, to let well enough alone. Harrison is a great President, and it is the will of the people that he shall continue his good works.' The Democrats said: 'The secret ballot is with us this time. The workingman is dissatisfied. He gets more wages than he does abroad, but he holds that he is robbed of his share of the riches of the land, and the quiet vote is with us. The workshops are for a change.' There was much in what they said. The workingmen gave the Democrats New York, New Jersey, Connecticut, Indiana, Illinois, and the election; but was there ever such a combination of antagonisms gathered into an opposition force, to carry the Government by storm, as that which the Democracy was enabled to make? Contrast the Democratic platforms of Connecticut and Kentucky. They are more flagrantly opposed to each other than the Minneapolis and Chicago papers. Connecticut is rankly Protection, and Kentucky rabidly Free Trade. Both are for freedom. The Democrats joined with the Populists in several States to give Weaver votes, and in other States terrorized, threatened, assaulted, and cheated his opponents.

"Take the money matters; we find the Democracy are red dog, wild cat, rag baby, silver pig, or gold bug, according to the local demands. They are all for Cleveland, however. The very ferocity of the personal factions of the Democratic party in New York was converted into steam power to drive the Cleveland machine. There was emulation in his service, between his old friends and enemies; and the enemies of other days exceeded the friends in the competitive struggle. The Democrats who hoped he would be defeated, and there were many thousands of them, were the most particular of men to vote for him because they felt their future in the party depended upon their 'record.' What they wanted was to be beaten in the 'give-a-way game,' and they trusted to the last to be able to say: 'There, you see how it is; we told you he was impossible. We've done all we could, and it is just as we said.'

"When the shriekers of calamity are able to harness the prosperity of the country and turn it against the Government; when the beneficiaries of a great policy turn against it and vote it down; when those who lick the cream of good times, hunger and thirst for experimental changes; when opposing interests and factions, principles and purposes, personalities and all the potencies of all the fads, can be united for a common purpose, there are surprises for citizens who have held in a commonplace way, but the unreasonable and inconsistent, the unwarrantable and the illogical, must also be the impracticable.

"It has been remarked of St. Petersburg, that in case of the occurrence of, first, a great flood in the Neva ; second, extraordinary high tide ; third, a long, strong blow from the gulf, the city must be overwhelmed. The years, the decades, and the centuries come and go without the disaster. It was long understood in the Ohio valley that there would be a flood beating all in history, and competing with Indian tradition, if there happened, in the order set down, these events : (1) during a wintry night, a sudden general rain, followed quickly by a freeze, covering Western New York and Pennsylvania, West Virginia, Kentucky, West North Carolina, Tennessee, Ohio, and Indiana with a sheet of ice ; (2) if, upon this vast glassy surface, there should fall a series of heavy snows ; (3) if, upon the snow, there should come rain, beginning near the Mississippi, which should be full and filling all the streams, locking them from the mouths against speedy discharge ; (4) and if there followed rain-storms for a week, so distributed as to boom all the rivers in order from west to east ; (5) culminating with three tremendous downpours over all the mountain regions, sweeping from the glazed earth the whole accumulation of snows, and so timed as to tumble all the floods at once into the Ohio, whose channel has been obstructed by the piers of many bridges, and a habit of encroaching upon it, then the river would make a demonstration memorable and marvelous. All this took place, just as we have set it down, five winters ago, and the high-water-mark at Cincinnati is seventy feet above low-water-mark. Up to this, the boast of the old folks in the valley was, that they had seen 'the flood of '32,' and there could never be anything like it. The world did not now-a-days afford such spectacles as they had beheld in '32! A few dingy old houses had incredible high-water '32 marks upon it. If the river looked angry, and rushed through a few low streets, the veterans would say: 'You should have seen the flood of '32. 'Twas the biggest thing we ever had, or ever will have. But they do say the Indians said, they once hitched canoes to walnut trees away above the '32 mark; but them Indians was such liars.' The flood of 1885 beat that of 1832 two feet, and the flood of 1887 was nearly seven feet above the old high-water-mark. Averaging the chances, it will not happen again for one hundred years. The river Rhine has a way of rising at the same time with the Ohio, and was higher in 1885 than it had been in two hundred years. There was favoring the Democratic party this year, such a combination of circumstances as that which made an Ohio flood seem a prodigy. The high-water-mark is astounding. The country is still here. There is something to eat, and even to drink. Such a Democratic disaster will not be due again for a generation."

John Russell Young, the brilliant journalist, writing in the Philadelphia *Evening Star*, quoted by the New York *Press*, of November 19th, has his explanation for the defeat ready : " Communities are like men, like women, like children, like dogs. Why do they do it? Why does a man buy wildcat stocks? Why does a woman rave over a bonnet, or marry a student of divinity? Why? Because we are more or less fools, even as the good Lord made us fools, and if we were not fools, it would be a teasing, tiresome world. Why does a boy go to bed as cross as the roaring forties after his Christmas dinner? He has had too much mince pie. The country has had too much mince pie. It kicks. It kicked after Quincy Adams, the best of all Presidents. It kicked after Van Buren, who was as downy as an Angora cat. It kicked after Arthur, whose administration was sunshine. It kicks after Harrison, the radiant, prosperous Government. Too much mince pie! Cleveland comes in because of his medicinal properties. We must take to our herbs now and then."

The practical politicians of the Republican party feel it incumbent upon them to give their version of the great defeat. James S. Clarkson, who, for many years, has been a guiding spirit among Republican leaders, of the late verdict says: "It is an order from the American people for a change in the industrial economic policy of the Government." He charges that the Republican party has lost strength and votes among the rich and among the people of independent means, who now want cheap labor; also among the workingmen, who have come to believe that free trade will cheapen the expense of living, while the Trades-Unions will still keep up their wages. He says: "The result is not a personal defeat of President Harrison, nor really a defeat of the party. It was a Protection defeat, a repudiation of high tariff, a Republican reverse in a field where it put aside all the nobler issues, and staked everything on economic and mercenary issues."

The surprising overturn of affairs in the distinctly Republican State of Illinois is accounted for by Senator Cullom by distinctive issues other than the McKinley and Force Bills: "Our losses in this State are mainly due to the school question, but in the nation at large they are due, in my judgment, to the passage of the McKinley law, and the impression in the minds of the masses in regard to it. When it was passed, the people expected us to revise the tariff, and revise it in the direction of reducing duties, and, while we did make reductions, they were dissatisfied because so many increases were made. When the bill came to the Senate from the House, we cut many of these in pieces, but, when it went back to the House and got into the Conference Committee, enough of them were restored to put us on the defensive and at a great disadvantage. Yes, I think our defeat can fairly be attributed to the McKinley Bill," and Senator Cullom represents the State of Abraham Lincoln. The prairies that gave breath to the typical champion of the people, produced this statesman, who, representing the State of a man who stands first in the minds of the people as their representative, sees only the indications of the mercenary spirit of the people. How Abraham Lincoln would have gauged correctly, instinctively, the heart-throbs of the people whom he assumed to represent in the councils of the nation!

Senator Cullom, in his opinion, mirrors only the reflection, cast upon the surface of his mind, by the aristocratic and multi-millionaired Senate of the Union, in which he occupies a seat. He sees only the cold, hard dollars and cents at issue.

He does nôt appreciate, as Abraham Lincoln would have done, the feeling of the people whom he pretends to represent. In every prairie home of Illinois there was an insulted wife or mother by the assumed distinctions made by the would-be aristocrats of the Republican party. Stevenson's speeches awakened no echo in their hearts, except that it gave an opportunity for the exhibition of the old, old story, written by the swords of the Anglo-Saxon people, "Caste is a crime." That the State of all States, Illinois, which gave to the

Federal Union Abraham Lincoln, should be presented in the sedate Senate of the Union, by a man whose views are so narrowed by the horizon of his own thoughts as to express a sentiment like the foregoing; namely, that the people were governed in their selection of their representative, the Chief Magistrate, by the power of the pocketbook; to be so unresponsive to the throbbing hearts of his constituency, is most disappointing.

Editors can be at times epigrammatic, and this election has brought forth some keen and trenchant opinions on the causes of defeat. Here are a few of them. All of them seek, as a child playing blind-man's-buff, in darkness, for that which, had the bandage which blinds them been removed from their eyes, would have been made plain, and which was occasioned by their own presumption in assuming to measure the depths and power of the people's feelings and impulses:—

Clark Howell, in the Atlanta *Constitution*, says: "Now, after thirty-one years, since Buchanan's Democratic administration, another political revolution has taken place, and, as a result, the election of 1852, which destroyed the Whig party, is repeated in the Waterloo defeat of the Republican party, and the question is, will this defeat finish the career of that party? The probability is that it will."

The Atlanta *Constitution*, of November 17th, in a brisk editorial, states that "Colonel J. B. McCullagh, the esteemed editor of the St. Louis *Globe-Democrat*, is not very happy. Naturally, he has his regrets and his hours of gloom, but he is not so miserable that he is unable to appreciate a mystery that crosses and recrosses his path in broad daylight. He cannot, for instance, understand the post-mortem talk of his party leaders. 'Curiously enough,' he says, 'they are now claiming that Harrison was defeated by the very things which they then said must insure his success.' Of course, these statements have a humorous twang, but it seems to us that a Republican as prominent as Colonel McCullagh would be willing to drop a veil over these gibbering evidences of human frailty. After all is said, there is but one trouble with the Republicans. They have but one regret. Editor Grubb, of Darien, outlined the situation very aptly when he said that the only thing that the Republicans desired, was the opportunity to steal a State. They are perfectly willing to see Harrison defeated; they are perfectly willing to retire from the control of the government; the only bitterness they feel is the realization of the fact that they failed to steal a State. They stole three Southern States in 1876. They stole two Northern States in 1890, and they stole a Western State last year, but they have failed to steal a single one in 1892. It is no wonder they are going about talking wildly and rolling their eyes. These are the symptoms of paresis, and, under the circumstances, Senator McCullagh ought to forgive them. The grief and disappointment of the Republican leaders are natural; a general election, and not a State stolen! Surely, their hands have lost their cunning. They made a tremendous effort to keep up their record. They tried to steal Delaware and West Virginia and Connecticut, but everywhere the Democrats met them and exposed their plans. The result was, that they failed to steal even one State. Under the circumstances, we think editor McCullagh should treat his brethren gently; he should not make satellite allusions to their troubles. Let them gibber."

Thank God, with our Australian Ballot system, each free-born American citizen carries with him into the voter's booth, if he be at all sensitive, and clothed with an enlightened conscience, the same awful sense of responsibility with which the enlightened and tender-conscienced Catholic enters the sacred realm of the confessional-box. Tremendous issues are at stake. He feels their force, and arises to the occasion, as he ever has done when the exercise of worth, virtue, or virility has been required upon his part, and of the great mass of the common people, Daniel Webster,

Henry Clay, Abraham Lincoln, furnish fair samples of the people's worth, virtue, and virility.

The Buffalo *Commercial*, than which there is no paper in the State of New York in possession of more perspicacity and political common-sense, in speaking of Senator Allison, a Republican leader of the Senate, states that just before leaving for Europe he intimated that the McKinley Bill was too strong a specific for the Republican party. "You remember," he said, "that epitaph on the tombstone of the young man who died before his time: 'I was well; medicine made me ill, and here I lie.'"

The Illinois *State Journal* remarks : " Until the post-mortem is held, it is, perhaps, just as well not to be certain what it was that hit the G. O. P. last Tuesday. It may have been the McKinley Bill, or the Homestead matter, or the Lutheran business, or the naturalized vote, or several other things, and then it may have been a complication of all these diseases." Thou wise physician, who would lose sight of the most important evidence of the disease, the discontent of the people, the artificial class distinction created by the sham aristocracy of America, the diagnosis of the disease, called discontent, as made by the press generally, is as faulty and erroneous as would be the opinion of the quack who would call measles, smallpox. Every symptom of the displeasure of the people at the prevalence of the crime of "caste" in our country was evident; yet, apparently, the most learned failed to discern it.

The Toledo *Bee* says: "The Republican party is dead. The step backward has been taken, and it was a step back that led the party over the precipice of power into the depths of oblivion. The Democratic party has relegated the boodlers, the spoilsmen, and the factional leaders to the rear. What is there left for us to live for?"

Says the Louisville *Courier-Journal*: "The people will have none of its high tariffs, and none of its Force Bills; but without its high tariffs and its Force Bills, it is only an organized hunt for official plunder. The people will not support it in its old course, and will not believe its brittle promises of reform."

" 'High tariff did it,' said Mr. Harrison ; but in taking satisfaction for his defeat out of the Napoleonic McKinley, the President is less than just to the magnetic Blaine; for, if high tariff caused the explosion, despite the 'reciprocity attachment,' what might it not have done without that little Pan American vent-hole?" This from the Philadelphia *Record*.

The President, had he combined the magnetism of Blaine, the Napoleonic ability of McKinley,— yea, had he, in fact, borne the magical name of Lincoln,—could not possibly have been re-elected, for the people were opposed to the ideas of "caste," fostered with such care by the members of the Republican party, in whom, in some mystical manner, have become concentrated the wealth and objectionable characteristics which tended to make the Southern cavalier so unpopular in 1860. The people, in their wrath, would have risen against any party so besmeared with the slime of that noxious crime.

The Atlanta *Constitution*, of November 17th, claims that "the leaders of the two great parties have had a good deal to say during the past few months about 'the campaign of education.' In the main, this phrase very correctly describes the work of both parties. Republican speakers and journalists work night and day to convince the people of the benefits of high Protection. On the other hand, the Democrats are equally active in exposing the true inwardness of McKinleyism and class legislation. This educational literature covered the country, and the average voter got a clearer insight of the questions at issue than he ever had before. One effort of this campaign of education was to eliminate personalities ; principles and measures were discussed, and the candidates escaped the usual mudslinging. Another result is seen in the sweeping and decisive nature of the vote. The revolution was so complete that the defeated side realized the utter absurdity of indulging in any bitter complaints, with the great mass of American people arrayed against them. Our victory was so crushing, that it absolutely restored something like good feeling ; and we find Whitelaw Reid and Chauncey Depew saying pleasant things to Mr. Cleveland at a banquet, and speaking of their defeat in a humorous fashion. This would not have been the case, had the election been close and only a bare majority of electoral votes for the successful ticket. Altogether, the country has good reason to be satisfied with its campaign of education. It has purified our politics, wiped out sectional lines, and made our people more thoroughly American than ever."

And for the erasure of sectionalism, God be thanked! but that a man of Mr. Clark Howell's preëminent ability should have wandered around so near to the object of his search, the cause of the Republican party's defeat, and not found it, is astonishing. In his own home, the State of Georgia, the Empire State of the South, and as editor of the leading paper in the State, that he should be so oblivious to the fact that the election, by the votes of the people, was a protest upon the part of the people against the assumption by the rich, that such a thing as "caste" could be possible in America.

Georgia, of all the Southern States, is preeminently industrial. Oglethorpe, when he first settled on the banks of the Savannah river, was himself surrounded by the poor debtors of England. The Salzburgers, who sought the shores of the uninhabited, uncivilized, new colony, were poor, uncultured people. Georgia never possessed, as a colony or as a State, the aristocratic tendencies of its neighbor, South Carolina. The foremost men have ever been essentially of the people; her settlers largely of the Democratic masses; the names preëminent in her history are the names of industrial New England. So Democratic is and was the State of Georgia, that her most eminent son, Alexander H. Stevens, had to be weaned away reluctantly from the doctrine of which Abraham Lincoln was the personification. Since the war, the State of Georgia more readily adapted herself to the new condition created by the result of the struggle. It was never a State of tremendous landed proprietors. The influx of emigration from the crowded Northern States found readier assimilation in the State of Georgia than in any other Southern State. In that State, the negro sooner realized his responsibilities as a citizen of the South, sooner became convinced that his best and wisest course was to merge himself into the large class of toilers and laborers in the commonwealth. That a man with the opportunity, ability, and brilliancy of Clark Howell, should become so utterly befogged by the mists arising from the marsh of old party cries and principles, should fail to recognize that the tremendous majority accorded the Democratic candidate, was but an exhibition of that spirit which has pervaded the State of Georgia from its embryonic existence on the Savannah river ; that Mr. Howell should have forgotten the lesson taught by the forefathers of the Georgians of to-day, that Democracy was one of the essential elements to the happiness of the citizens, settlement, colony, commonwealth, and State, is passing strange. The very negro, upon becoming a Georgian and a citizen, became a Democrat, almost as a matter resulting from the atmosphere he breathed. Georgia's vast majority for the Democratic nominee was not rolled up except by the aid of the negro, who, in his heart of hearts, is a Democrat, and the appeals of the Republican party to his gratitude, claiming that they were the emancipators of his race, were as futile as was the waving of the bloody shirt in the face of the veterans of the North. The negroes of the State of Georgia joined with their fellow-laborers of the Anglo-Saxon race, to give added weight to the opposition of the masses against " caste " in our country.

The *Mail and Express*, in an editorial of November 9th, says : " If Benjamin Harrison is defeated, the people of this country, by their ballots yesterday, decided again to try the experiment of the Democratic administration. It is most extraordinary and unusual for the American people to seek a change in administration at a time of unwonted prosperity; to render a verdict in favor of a change, while the working masses are everywhere busily employed, while farmers are reaping their richest harvests, factories running day and night, and building extensions and our foreign trade growing with rapid strides, all under the beneficent influences of Republican policy, wisely and faithfully administered by a President whose conduct of affairs has been conspicuously conservative, successful, acceptable, and clean. If Grover Cleveland has been elected, a change in administration has been ordered. What shall we get in return? We shall see! The triumph of Democracy would mean a radical change in our economical policy. It would mean the selection for Vice-President of a man whose political record has stamped him as unsafe, untrustworthy, and conspicuously unfit for the high office to which he has been called. An ardent advocate of the unlimited issue of greenbacks and fraudulent silver; a bitter opponent of National Banks, and the advocate of State Banks issue; outspoken in his demand for the imposition of the abandoned and inquisitorial income tax, Mr. Stevenson would, after the 4th of March, occupy a place separated from the Executive head of this Government by the frail tenure of a single life. In the Senate, the highest legislative body in the land, over which Mr. Stevenson, as Vice-President, would preside, a Senate which may possibly have a Democratic majority, his influence in favor of economic and financial heresies would be potential. Let the people bear in mind the peace, the happiness, and the prosperity they now enjoy. When anxiety and unrest come, as they speedily would, with the renewed agitation in the next Congress, of an attack upon our protective tariff; when the spindles of our mills are silent, the forges black with ashes, our looms yellow with rust, and unemployed men clamor here as they are clamoring to-day in the streets of London and Lancashire against the reduction of wages, let them listen to the plausible excuses and fine-spun prevarications of the Free Trade tariff reformers, who will be responsible. And if, as Vice-President, he should do the evil he can do by aiding the meddlers with our financial and taxation systems, the honest money men of New York and New England, of Illinois and Indiana, who voted for him because he was associated with their idolized free trade candidate, would have only themselves to thank for the prospect of disaster and panic they might face. They would then pay the penalty of their reckless inconsideration. Protection for American homes, for American workingmen and American farmers, an honest dollar for honest men, and a policy of free trade extension by the beneficent influences of reciprocity, may all suffer assaults in the four years to come, but we can trust the sober, second judgment of the American people, in the light of another but recent experience with the free trade and fraudulent silver Democracy, to do again in 1896 what it did with that party at the close of the first Cleveland experiment, and turn the incompetents out."

It *is* most extraordinary and unusual for the American people to seek a change in the administration at a time of unwonted prosperity, but the inward agitation of soul at the thought of great wrongs committed by a pretended beneficent party led to the revolution of '92, in very much the same manner as inward agitation on another subject brought about that which placed Abraham Lincoln in the Presidential Chair. The American workman is above the American dollar !

The New York *World*, in an editorial of November 16th, says: " The *Iron Trade Review* is putting the manufacturers up to a dodge in order to make the people sorry that they voted for Mr. Cleveland. Its advice is that the manufacturers reduce the wages of their workingmen 'to fortify themselves in advance in view of the increasing probabilities of destructive foreign competition.'

Is this an indication of the kindly feeling entertained by the Protectionists for their workingmen? They have professed that their tax policy was maintained for the purpose of increasing wages. They have been charged with misrepresentation; and they are now advised by one of their organs to prove that the charge is true, by making the wage-earners suffer in order that revenue reform may become unpopular. Nothing could better show the dishonesty of the Protection claim that the tariff exists for the workingman. If that claim were true, the manufacturers would resist every tendency toward downward wages, instead of pushing them down in order to gain an advantage for themselves in a political controversy. The wages of labor are regulated by the supply and demand of the labor market, and the people who would cut down wages, not because they must, but because they want to revenge themselves for a Democratic victory by making the workingman suffer, are the people who have been insisting that the McKinley law repealed the law of supply and demand, and that they are the true and unselfish benefactors of the workingmen. Happily, the next President is a Democrat."

General JAMES B. WEAVER.
Presidential Candidate of the People's Party, 1892.

CHAPTER II.

THE ALLEGED GENERAL DISCONTENT.

THE workmen of our country, it is true, want better times, cheaper clothing, the doing away with trusts, and many other desirable changes; but far more than this, they feel the need of the absolute crushing out of the last vestige of "caste." They at last realize that "caste" is a crime; and the common people have, at heart, no sympathy with criminals, and especially criminals of that class. The common people stay at home, work hard, and very seldom have need to "go to Canada," or take a flying trip to Southern Europe. Their sins are mainly those of passion. At their best, they are kindly disposed to their fellows; but they are *human.* They feel a snub from their employer or employer's son as keenly as their honest, hard-working wives and daughters feel the haughty stare and condescending patronage of Madame Crœsus and her bejewelled daughters. Here we offer our readers some explanations, given by the common, average American citizen, for the defeat of the Republican party at the polls on November 8th. The article is taken from the pages of the New York *Tribune,* November 21,

1892, the official organ of the Republican Vice-Presidential candidate, and therefore entitled to more than ordinary consideration. The article is headed " The General Discontent." It consists of talks with the people about the recent election in New York State and Vermont. It is, largely, the observations of a correspondent who has walked through the State, asking farmers and workingmen why they voted for Cleveland. Let it not be forgotten that Whitelaw Reid is the editor of this paper.

"The politician who attempts to explain defeat is 'crying over spilt milk.' The newspaper which tells 'how it was done' is 'whining.' The writer of a political obituary has hardly an enviable task. A defeated party is supposed to accept with philosophical resignation the rejection of pet policies, and with the calmness of the fatalist, tell itself that it 'was to have been.' The reasons given for the result of the recent election are as numerous as there are differences in the minds of the two parties. Some say that the desire for free trade is the cause of the Republican overthrow. Others, that the thing that did it is the McKinley bill; others again, that the people want the 'repeal of the Bank Tax law'; but to him that looks beneath the surface, there is ample evidence that the defeat of the Republican party is not mainly due to the 'unpopularity' of its candidates, nor to the love which the people are said to bear for Grover Cleveland; not to the McKinley bill, nor to any 'desire on the part of the people for free trade;' not because free silver is or is not wanted. Not through the 'superb generalship' of the Democratic National Committee was a victory gained, nor was the battle lost through the 'lamentable incompetency' of the Republican leaders. The chief cause of Republican defeat and Democratic victory is the modern tendency toward socialism.

"This statement by no means implies that the socialistic

propaganda has taken a firm hold upon the citizen of the United States, or that its tenets have but to be sowed in American soil to bear an abundant harvest. The people have not subscribed to the mild doctrines of Henry George, nor to the more radical and incendiary plans of John Burns, nor do they place confidence in the ability or stability of the leaders of the 'New Order of Things.' They have not the slightest desire to overturn existing government; the ravings of the Anarchists they repudiate altogether.

"But since 1873, on Black Friday, political and social conditions in the United States have been those of unquiet and discontent among certain thousands. The Greenback party then had its origin. It is within the last decade, however, that social discontent has manifested itself more markedly in the formation of political parties, all of which, according to the leaders of them, were destined to glorious futures, when the Democratic and Republican parties should be wiped out of existence.

"This unsettled state of affairs showed itself in the formation of the Greenback party, the Labor party, the Socialistic party, the Farmers' Alliance, and, finally in the People's party.

THE RISE OF THE PEOPLE'S PARTY.

"The true reason for the formation of the Alliance, or People's party, in the North, West, and South, is not difficult to find. When the tide of immigration and settlement turned toward the great wheat and corn fields of Iowa, Nebraska, North and South Dakota, every natural condition was favorable to the growing of abundant crops, which brought the farmer a golden return for his labor. But beginning with 1884 the crops in many sections of the Northwest were failures. This unfavorable condition lasted until 1890, when a great demand for cereals from Europe, and enormous crops harvested in America, turned the flood of prosperity back again to the farmer, who had for six years suffered because of poor crops. During these years of hard times the farmer had encumbered himself with numerous and necessary debts, so that the profits of the prosperous years of 1890 and 1891, as well as those of this year, have gone in payment of accrued interest and the liquidation, in part, of a vast mortgage indebtedness. After having been obliged to stint himself for several years, it is but natural that when a chance presented itself he should desire to surfeit upon the plenty, rather than be obliged because of his indebtedness to pay out the first money which had come to him from several years of toil to those whom he owed. It is but natural, too, under such conditions, that he should have embraced a project which, as he understood it, was to lift the burden from his shoulders and put it upon the back of the Government, to make money 'easy,' and to render indebtedness not a hardship, but rather something which might be wiped out as easily as it could be incurred.

THE DISCONTENT IN THE EAST.

"The result in Wisconsin shows clearly that the wounds received in the battle over the Bennet law had not yet healed, and the agitation over the repeal of the Edwards law is the cause of Republican disaster in Illinois; but no such issues as perverted the minds of Republicans in the Northwest, and in Wisconsin and Illinois, were matters of controversy in the old line Republican States of Ohio and New Hampshire.

"The political veteran who has battled in these States for many campaigns is puzzled where to seek the cause of such overwhelming disaster. To cry 'boodle' is to bring ridicule upon the party, but to give the McKinley bill as the only or main cause is to show only a superficial knowledge of the existing condition of affairs.

" To find out why the people voted as they did, one must ask them. It is they that have piled up these great majorities, and, seemingly, have repudiated Republican doctrines, and put the seal of disapproval upon what the Republican party believes has given this country unexampled prosperity. Let any man who believes that the 'popularity' of Grover Cleveland, the demand for free trade, or any policy which is shown in the Democratic platform, other than that which embodies the general statement that the Democrats will give the country better times, is the cause of Republican defeat, ask the people why they voted as they did, and he will find that it is this tendency, unconscious and entirely undeveloped, toward socialism which has given the Democrats victory. It is not permanent nor lasting, so far as it exists in seeming antagonism to Republican policies. In 1896 a cyclone of disapproving votes is just as likely to sweep over the Democratic camp as it has this year devastated the Republican stronghold.

"But it is one thing to make a statement, and another to prove it. In order to ascertain what it was that brought defeat to the Republican party, I took a trip through the States of New York and Vermont, and in five days interviewed several hundred laboring people and men who are in business in a small way in various mercantile pursuits, and who voice the opinion and sentiments of thousands in similar walks of life. Talk with many was profitless. They had nothing against President Harrison, nothing in particular that they knew of against Protection. They did not vote the Democratic ticket because they were impressed with the greatness of Mr. Cleveland, or with the soundness of his views, or with the policy of the party as presented in the Chicago platform. They said they wanted better times and more money. They wanted cheaper clothing, cheaper fuel, cheaper everything; but they wanted to sell what they had to sell, whether it be labor or goods, at the highest possible price. They did not, because they could not, deny that the country as a whole had grown vastly prosperous under Republican administrations.

"They were not sure that the McKinley bill or previous tariffs had had anything to do with the hard times which they declared exist. The laborer could not say but what the cost of store articles had decreased largely in the last quarter of a century. In fact, many of them could remember when articles of common consumption and use cost much more than they do to-day; while the products of the farmer and the stocks of the shopkeeper, so the farmer and the tradesman were obliged to affirm, were sold not many years ago at a lower price and with less profit than to-day.

"The farmers acknowledge that perhaps the elements may have had something to do with poor crops, that the opening of the vast farming territory of the Northwest, and the inexorable enforcement of the law of supply and demand, may have had something of a disastrous effect upon the farmers of the East. But these were not looking for reasons. They did not want reasons. They did not wish to consider causes. They did not think that they and their affairs have anything to do with causes, effects, policies, or platforms. All they know is that times are bad—with them. All they want is better times. 'Figures don't prove anything,' they say. 'We are hard up, and have been for years; we do not know what causes hard times, nor do we care, if the future only brings prosperity. The Republicans are in power, and have been since 1862, with the exception of four years; therefore, if they have not given and cannot give us better times, who can but the Democrats? We are going to try them.'

"This is what a part of that vote which gave the Democratic majority in New York thought. They would have voted just as readily for Populist, Prohibition, or Socialist candidates had they thought that any of these parties had the power to better their condition. But this element was not large enough alone to give Mr. Cleveland a majority in New York State. It was the smaller tradesman, the farmer, and the laborer. These are the ones, and such the element whose vote gave success to the Democratic party, and in voting thus they had no intention of rejecting any particular Republican, or of approving any particular Democratic policy.

AN EXAMPLE OF POPULAR REASONING.

"A tailor who lives in a little town not far from Albany, and whose entire stock in trade does not amount in value to the cost of one bolt of goods owned by his more fashionable brother who does business in Broadway, voted on November 8th his first Democratic ticket. I asked him why he did so, after having voted for four Republican candidates, and having all his life approved the Republican policy of Protection. He said: 'I voted for Mr. Cleveland, not for anything Mr. Cleveland or the Democratic party have done, but rather for what he and his party have said they would do. Nor did I vote against Mr. Harrison because I do not like him, nor against the Republican party because it has always stood for Protection, but more with a view of making an experiment than anything else. I do not believe that times are good with a majority of people; I know they are not with me. This does not seem to be the day for the man who is in business in a small way. I don't know anything about the condition of affairs in free-trade England, but I know that here we have Standard Oil trusts, a sugar trust, a rubber trust, and a trust in almost every line, and if a small dealer attempts to compete with a large dealer, the weaker man is crushed. The great clothing company, with its millions of capital, undersells me, and I am compelled to meet its prices or go out of business and get into something else.

" 'All the business of the country seems to be getting into the hands of a few people and a few big corporations. I don't like such a state of affairs. I don't want to be crushed out of existence for attempting to compete with the millionaire clothing dealer. In order to live and conduct my business I must make a profit on my goods. I do not say that the tariff or that any Republican legislation is responsible for this condition of affairs. It may be that no legislation can eradicate the evil, but legislation certainly can prohibit trusts.

" 'What I do know is that I, and such men as I am, cannot do business in competition with these combinations of capital. What I want is a living. In this I am not unreasonable ; the world owes me a living, but I am willing to work and work hard to get it. All that I want is a fair chance. Maybe I made a mistake when I voted the Democratic ticket. Perhaps Protection is just what we have needed and yet need. Perhaps Free-Trade will make things better. I don't know how this is, but when I voted I was willing to run my chances in order to find out. I am a Republican still, and if the Democrats cannot make things better I shall try to take life as it comes and do the best I can.'

"This is, in a measure, the reasoning of most of the smaller tradesmen. They want better times; they want centralization of capital done away with; they want trusts prohibited, and combinations of all kinds destroyed. They want more money, money more easily obtained, with a less rate of interest.

"The intelligent laborer is giving much thought to the condition of himself and his fellows. He is as yet not enough of a student to dive into theories, to analyze policies ; nor is he able, at the present, to plan for himself any legislation which shall better his condition. A group of laborers, some of whom worked on the railroad and some in the quarries, in

Washington County, acknowledged to me that they voted on the 8th of November, for the first time, the Democratic ticket. I was not able, after exhaustive questioning, to get from any one of them a reason why he had voted as he had done. The answer one gave me is the answer all gave: He wanted less hours of work, better pay, cheaper necessities. A boss of one of the gangs of quarrymen, a man who in his time had been a day laborer himself, a person of good, hard common sense, an out-and-out Republican, told me that, although the men under him had always before voted the Republican ticket, so far as he knew, yet at this election they had voted for Cleveland, more because they were dissatisfied with their condition, to a certain extent, and the Republicans were in power, and because the Democrats had repeatedly made the general statement that their policies would bring good times, when the laborer should work few hours for large pay, the necessities of life be much cheaper than they are to-day, and the luxuries of the rich taxed to support the general government.

"'I tried to reason with them,' said the boss; 'but you might as well have tried to reason with a drove of mules, they are so stubborn. I told them they might better leave well enough alone; that the country had never been so prosperous as it was to-day; that wages were good, and that the cost of store articles had been steadily decreasing for years, and had never been so low as they were to-day. But no, they did not believe that; they did not want to believe it; they said they were overworked; that they were not getting good pay—although their wages have never been larger—and they want, well, I don't believe any one of them can tell what he does want. They said the Republican party was in power and times were not good, and if the Democrats were able to make good times, why, they wanted them in power and would vote the Democratic ticket.'

OBSERVATIONS OF ONE WHO VOTED THE REPUBLICAN TICKET.

"A shoemaker in the town of Granville, Washington County, a good deal of a philosopher in his way, with plenty of good horse-sense showing in his rugged face, a man whose language was refined, and whose conversation showed him to be a reader as well as a reasoner, gave me the best exposition of the causes of the Republican defeat that I have yet heard any one make. 'I am a Republican,' said he; 'I always have been and I always shall be. I hoped the party would win, but yet when I talked with the people around this place, and in other towns which I sometimes visit, those people who do a great deal of thinking, and who vote as their reason, wrong or right, tells them to vote, I was mightily afraid the fight would go against us. I do not think very much of Anarchistic ideas, or of the theories of the Socialist, nor of the golden promises made by Weaver and the People's party. No human being can ever make a paradise out of this world, and at no one time will everyone in it be satisfied and happy. This nation of ours has grown so rapidly, and there are so many foreigners here who have become citizens, and we print so many cheap and silly books, that I am not surprised that the Republican party was defeated. If a party of angels had made up the Government, the result would have been just the same. The same causes that led to Republican defeat in 1892 will overthrow the Democratic Government in 1896. Ever since the Greenback party was started, and ever since the Socialistic and the hundred other 'istic' agitators have been telling the people how they are abused, how they are robbed, that the rich are growing richer and the poor poorer, everything has been in such an unsettled condition that I do not wonder at the result of the election. It could not have been otherwise.

"'I believe the Administration has been everything it should be; that General Harrison has been a splendid President; that his policy has been for the good of the people; but I don't believe that the best man that ever lived, if he had been a Republican and in power, could have been elected to the Presidency of the United States this year. Up in all this section of the country, and throughout the State, for that matter, the man who had always before voted the Republican ticket in an independent way cast a Democratic ballot, more because he wanted to make an experiment than anything else. It is funny how unreasonable people are. They don't sit down and calmly figure for themselves, but they jump at conclusions, and because with some of us times are hard, they don't stop to think who or what is responsible.

I was talking with just such a man only the other day. He was hard up, so he claimed, but I know he has been doing business here ever since I can remember, and has always lived and looked and acted just about the same as he does now. He keeps a store. As near as I could get at it, he wanted to sell everything he had to sell at a good deal better price than it is fetching now, but he wanted everybody else to sell to him what stuff he wanted to buy a good deal cheaper than what he is paying for it now. He would not listen to me when I told him that that is what everybody else wants to do; to buy everything cheap and sell everything dear; but I told him that if people did not buy until they could get things at their own price, or sell until they could sell things at their own figure, it would take but a mighty little while for everybody to starve to death. He said he was going to vote the Democratic ticket just to see what would happen in the next four years.

"'Many of the quarrymen bring their boots here to be mended. They tell me they want more money and fewer work hours. They have not much of an idea how they are going to get them, other than that the Democrats have told them that if Cleveland was elected they would get what they wanted and everybody would be happy.

"'Therefore, they voted the Democratic ticket. But, I believe,' continued the shoemaker, 'that after all this election will turn out mighty well for the Republican party. In the end, the new way of voting is going to help us. Before this the boss or the politician could take his men or his gang and vote them as he wished. Now this is, to a certain extent, changed. The half-way independent man who before was led to the polls and voted, goes to the polls and votes for himself. Before this he was part of the machine, gave election matters but little thought, and was enthusiastic only because others were so. Now, he must either vote blindly or he must think for himself, and in the end he is going to think it out and is going to do the right thing. He will then see that the Republican policy has been and is for his benefit; that it has contributed more than any other one thing to make this country great and prosperous, and the people happy and contented.'

"One of the head workmen in a Troy factory possesses

similar ideas. He is a man of more than ordinary intelligence, and says that many of his acquaintances voted the Democratic ticket more because they were uneasy and wanted something, they did not know what, than because they had any particular liking for Cleveland and the Democracy, or dislike for Harrison and the Republican party. This opinion is held by many of the skilled workmen of the factories in both Albany and Troy, and in the smaller towns between New York and Plattsburg.

A FARMER'S REASONS FOR HIS VOTE.

"It was a more difficult matter to get any Republican farmer to acknowledge that he voted the Democratic ticket. One was finally found who admitted that he had.

"'What were your reasons?' I asked.

"'Well, I don't know as I can exactly tell you,' he answered; 'we have not had a very easy time of it, we farmers, for the last eight or ten years.'

"'But don't you think,' said I, 'that the opening of the farming lands in the West has a great deal to do with the decrease of farm values in the East?'

"'Well, perhaps so,' he replied. 'It is hard for a man who is not a political economist and who doesn't make a business of keeping track of such things to give any reason for the hard times, or to choose between the reasons given by Democrats and Republicans. So far as I know, the Republican party has always kept its promises made to the farmers. Since the McKinley tariff we have been getting better prices for our potatoes and other produce in Northern New York, for before, we had not been able to compete with Canada. Yet, we don't make much of a living, even at this. You say that statistics prove that this country, as a Nation, is vastly more prosperous than any other, and that we are a good deal richer than we were ten years ago; yet I am not any better off, and most of the farmers around here are not any better off, and I made up my mind that if, as the Democrats promise, a change of Administration would make good times, why, I wanted a change; if Free Trade will make things better, I want Free Trade; if State banks will give us money, and more of it, I want State banks put on equal terms with

National banks. If these changes are brought about, it may make things a good deal worse than they are now. At any rate, I am willing to try it. If I find that the Democrats have deceived me, in 1896 I shall vote the Republican ticket again.'

"These interviews show the state of mind among people who are enough in number to turn overwhelmingly a majority for either the Republican or the Democratic party. In them is ample evidence that the people whose votes defeated the Republican party are not dissatisfied with Republican administration of affairs. They do not charge that the McKinley bill, or that the financial or any other Republican policy is responsible for hard times, nor is there any testimony which can be taken as evidence that the 'unbounded popularity' of Grover Cleveland or the (by the Democrats so called) broad financial and economic policy of that party, has brought about this sweeping victory. A talk with the independent voter shows, first, that there exists among the smaller tradesmen, among those whose votes turn the tide toward victory or toward defeat, dissatisfaction because, as they claim, they are unable to compete with combinations of capital; they want decentralization of capital, and trusts prohibited by law and the law enforced.

"A condition of affairs exists, the dissatisfied tradesman claims, in which he cannot earn a living. The Republican party was in power, and had been, with the exception of four years, for a quarter of a century, and while it possibly may not be responsible for trusts and for the centralization of wealth and capital, yet the tradesmen says, 'I cast my vote for Cleveland and Democracy to make an experiment, the result of which I am willing to take the consequences of.'

"The workingman was influenced to vote for Democracy more because he had been repeatedly told that all rich men and manufacturers are Republicans than for anything else. Capital, of late years, has been denounced so severely, and strikes, the cause of many of which are hard to determine, have of late been so frequent (fortunately for the Democratic party, because by these strikes Democratic speakers were able falsely to claim that they were caused by the attempt of the rich Republicans to crush the workingman, and because by the shortness of the campaign the Republicans were unable effectively to disprove these Democratic statements) that the Republican party, although its policy of protection was approved by the labor union leaders, has been in a measure handicapped.

"The independent farmer voted the Democratic ticket because the prices of farm products are not up to the figure he thinks they should be, and because the Democrats have told him that their financial and economic policies, if carried out, will enhance the value of his farm products, give him the markets of the world, and greatly decrease the cost of the necessities of life, although he cannot disprove that this state of affairs does not exist to-day, almost wholly because of a protective tariff.

GREAT NUMBERS OF NEW CITIZENS.

"But there is another element, and one which always has and always will contribute to Democratic success. Naturalization was unusually large this year; the citizen of foreign birth is a power in the land and the Democratic party was felicitously named. There is something in the word 'Democracy' which appeals strongly to the citizen of foreign birth. In this country 'Democracy,' as applied to the Democratic party, signifies to them that have left their homes in Europe, a party of the people in contradistinction to plutocracy and to aristocracy, the party of wealth and the party of people of noble birth. That this has weight with a certain foreign element is conclusively shown in the statement made by several foreign laborers in Washington County. Their knowledge of things American is not sufficient for them to grasp the import of the policies advocated by either party, and hence it is that they vote for the party whose name means the most to them. From a talk with many of them I am convinced that it is a natural antagonism toward the party in power, a love for the word 'Democracy' that caused not a few newly made citizens to vote for Mr. Cleveland. One of them told me that the Republican party was made up of bankers, of great manufacturers, of men who had formed combinations for the purpose of advancing the cost of necessities of life—the party, in fact, to which every one who has money belongs. In other words, that to be a Republican is to be a capitalist, and to be a Democrat is to be a man of the people: that by voting the Democratic ticket the power could be taken from the capitalist and put into the hands of the people, and that the people ruling the people would mean legislation which would give the greatest good to the greatest number.

"A talk with the people shows further that the Republican party is still very much in existence; that its defeat in this election does not mean a rebuke for anything that it has ever done, nor for any policy which it advocates, but it means that unless the Democratic party makes good the promise which it has given to bring about better times, it will meet with a defeat more overwhelming than that which overturned and shattered Republican hopes in 1892, and that the Democrats will not only lose the States which have gone from the Republican ranks this year, but that West Virginia, South Carolina, Alabama, and Louisiana will turn from their allegiance to Democracy, cast their vote either for a third party, for fusion, or for the Republicans, and for future years make what is now known as the Solid South nothing but a mournful Democratic memory.''

Through the whole of these interviews, when attention is directed to the subject, it becomes perfectly apparent that the thread of the story is the people's objection to the prevalence of social distinction among them. It is half expressed in nearly every one of these interviews, while they hesitate to put it in words; possibly because they highly appreciate that as the motive that so powerfully moved them on November the 8th. And then again, because of their hesitancy in expressing their recognition, even, of the attempt on the part of those possessed of greater wealth, to assume social superiority of those less fortunate.

CHAPTER III.

NOVEMBER 8, 1892.

NOVEMBER the 8th, 1892, will be noted, by the historian of the future, as a date constituting a milestone to mark the road and journey of struggling humanity. What July the 14th is to the French, July the 4th is, and November the 8th will be, to the American people.

The surface of the waters of public opinion presented a peaceful appearance at the dawning of that autumn day, but beneath the tranquil surface there raged subterranean and powerful forces, moving the deep waters of public sentiment. The much-discussed "general apathy" was the silent, sullen wrath, dangerous in individuals as it is in the masses. The silent fighter is tireless and terrible. The people had ceased to be moved by oratorical effort, brass bands, and torchlight processions. They had become surfeited with argument upon the subject of Protection. The changes had been rung upon the effect of the passage of a Force Bill, until the people had become as accustomed to the beating of the flanges of the newspapers upon the rails of this somewhat attenuated subject, as a slumbering passenger on a railway train. In fact, the cessation of the clangor would have attracted more attention than the continuation of the monotonous drumming.

The leading journal in the Force Bill camp had been that preëminently vigorous newspaper, the New York *Sun*. Under the guidance of the genius of the Hon. Charles A. Dana, the New York *Sun* had seized the most attractive, because the most novel, instrument of noise presented in this campaign of education. It had blown such vigorous blasts, that a large portion of newspaperdom, who regarded the opinions expressed by Mr. Dana as apt to be eminently reasonable, had joined in the chorus of the Force Bill farce, and created discordance and noise enough to have nauseated the masses with weariness of the subject. The pot-house politician, as well as his more exalted brother of the Fifth Avenue palatial political headquarters, was abashed and confused, by the fact that his efforts to arouse enthusiasm among the masses were utterly fruitless. They neither agreed with him nor disagreed with him. There was no room for argument. It was like the professional pugilist descanting on the beauties of the bruiser's art to a Whittier, Holmes, or Longfellow; the subjects, upon which the politicians of all degrees and kinds had exhausted themselves, were not interesting.

The issue before the people was sentimental. The detestation of the prevalence and growth of a pretended and sham aristocracy, became the important and all-absorbing theme within their hearts. They heard the talk; they read the dissertations of learned editors, and while it was all, doubtless, the product of powerful brains, it was not the most important matter in the struggle to be decided that November morning, between the masses and an assumption of "caste" in free America. Mr. Thomas Dolan, at the Clover Club, in Philadelphia, in referring to the result of the election, had at least the candor to admit the cause of the Republican party's defeat. Had he, and gentlemen of his doubtless aristocratic tendencies, realized the impression that their course of conduct was making upon the minds of the mass of the Common People prior to that eventful day, November the 8th, and had they taken warning by the signs of the times, had they believed less in the Burchard theory of Blaine's defeat in '84, and more in the efficacy of the impression, prejudicing the minds of the people against Mr. Blaine and his party by that banquet,— which has been dubbed in political parlance, "the Belshazzar feast,"—they might have been forewarned. But those who have been, for the last thirty years, attempting to create an artificial order to govern society, "caste," have become so puffed up by wealth, and blinded by the ever-narrowing view they are able to obtain from their assumed exalted position, that they have lost sight of every other consideration ; becoming absorbed in their own one overmastering emotion—love of money. Before this god of Mammon they had performed such obsequious service, that they imagined the only appeal necessary to make to the people, was the one so much paraded by the Republican press, *i. e.*, the advantage of Protection to the pocket of the poor man. Upon this day, November 8th, which was to decide, in no doubtful manner, the destiny of the nation with regard to its social life, in the silence, communing only with their outraged sense of the rights of man and the equality of all mankind, the voters sought the confessional-like closets in the booths, established by the introduction of the Australian system of voting. There was no hurrah, no noise, no violence, but a tremendous outpouring of men, filling every voting precinct in the land, creating a larger percentage of voters who exercise their right of franchise than on any former election ever held in America.

As the hours of the day passed, some of the keen observers and astute party leaders began to realize that the existence of a general "feeling of apathy " had been more apparent than real ; else what was the meaning of this outpouring of voters, who, silently and with determined, fixed certainty of purpose, sought to exercise their right as citizens? Even in those sections of the large cities where the wealthy reside, and in the back country, where it is difficult for the voter, often, to find the time, opportunity, and the means of getting to the polls on election day, it was the same story. The nation had been aroused in some magical and mysterious manner, which was beyond the expectation and prognostication of the politicians and party leaders. The people had taken the matter out of their hands. They had simply taken the ship of State into their own keeping, and the professional politician had to cling to the life-line in the wake thereof.

Wonderment seized these gentlemen of supposed miraculous political perspicacity. They asked one another, by their silent and inquiring glances: "What does this mean? Is our occupation, like Othello's, gone?"

The people, regardless of their mistaken mouthing, like some massive Percheron horse, had taken the bit; and, regardless of all attempts at guidance, were exerting the strength which, when aroused, they possess, contrary to the expectations of the learned gentlemen of the political profession. When the sun went down, November 8, 1892, none were less able to predict the result of this tremendous uprising of the people than those who by their diplomacy had arrived at that position, so enviable in the minds of petty politicians, Chairmen of various Campaign Committees. Chairman Carter might have exclaimed, with the drowning people at Johnstown, as he sank beneath the flood of indignant "Common People," "Whence comes this water?" Chairman Harrity might well have been drunk and delirious, as the result of his own good fortune, for as surprising to him as to Chairman Carter was the existence of this slumbering volcano of indignation which had brought about the overwhelming success of the candidate who represented, in the minds of the people, the opposition to the growing aristocracy which had become engrafted upon the Republican party. Chairman Harrity might well have been dazed by the remarkable results of his own endeavors, had he not realized that his efforts had been incidental to, and not the cause of, the success of Cleveland.

It is not presumed to criticise the conduct of the campaign as managed by the campaign committees of both sides. Their duties, without doubt, were performed in a most masterly manner. The organizations with which both committees worked with tireless energy to achieve success for their respective sides, cannot fail to impress even a very tyro in politics. It was, however, like two learned physicians, disputing over the disease of a patient, and both being in error; each applying established remedies that experience had taught him were efficacious in the disease he had imagined it to be ; both equally in error because they had mistaken the complaint of the patient. To the average politician of the present day, Tariff Reform and Protection constitute the sum of all evils and diseases of the body politic. Like Dr. Sangrado's instruction to Gil Blas, they have only two remedies: phlebotomy and plenty of hot water. And the astonishment expressed by them at the possible existence of some other disease and some other remedy, was productive of as much consternation as that in the breast of Gil Blas, at the result of the treatment of his patients at Valladolid. As the returns from the different States began to arrive at the headquarters of the different committees ; as the result of the opinion of the people upon this momentous occasion (so fraught with disappointment to the aristocratic believers in "caste") became apparent, surprise and astonishment were depicted upon every countenance ; while, mingled with unalloyed delight in the breasts of the Democrats, and with mortification in the hearts of the Republicans, the same surprise and astonishment existed. That Illinois, a State that had sent over 200,000 men to fight under the Federal flag, and in which such large sums of pension money had been annually distributed to the disabled veterans for many years, should have been so unmindful and heedless of the display of the time-honored and ensanguined garment, the "Bloody Shirt," and the howling of the Republican press about Cleveland's vetoes of pension bills, was simply outrageous to the minds of the stupefied Republican leaders.

Could it be possible that their so often victorious shout of sectionalism, and constant address to the pocketbook of the veteran, had been relegated to the shadowy shelf of "innocuous desuetude"?

They looked aghast at the result of the counting of votes in Indiana. That much-talked-of, recently-discovered Gas belt, in which had sprung up innumerable manufactories, whose workshops were filled with "Common People," had failed to find an all-obscuring attraction in the glittering gold that the magnates of wealth had held out to them as an inducement to perpetuate the power of the rich and to increase those privileges and class distinctions that they fondly hoped would be accorded to them by the American people. Verily, like DeFarge, in Dickens' "Tale of Two Cities," the workman of the manufacturers in Indiana had presumed to hurl the magical Louis piece back into the carriages of the wealthy, rejecting with indignation the attempt to bribe their honor, and their sense of the equality of man.

The negro of Alabama, Georgia, and Virginia, upon whom these bondholders thought they had a mortgage, by their claimed procurement of his emancipation, had, even in spite of his color, previous condition, and gratitude, joined with his fellow-citizens, the "Common People," taking as the representative of those who had most benefited him and his race, the immortal Abraham Lincoln, a man of the "Common People"; and, by the negro's vote, was added strength to the blow, struck by the white Democracy of the Union, at this arrogant assumption of that thing which the negro, along with the white man, had learned to hate and resent—the assumption of "caste" upon the part of any set of citizens in the United States of America.

The wool-grower of Ohio, the home of the popular McKinley, added sorrow to the cup held to the lips of the would-be aristocrats. He no longer felt bound to bow his head before the advantages held out by the party of wealth. He preferred to take a little less for his wool, and a little more respect for himself, his wife, and children in the social world, where every landmark of equality was being washed away by the tide of aristocratic tendencies. The bewildered Republican leaders gazed with terror upon the transmogrified weapons with which they had waged war. The sword of steel, when held by the hand clad in a golden gauntlet, had become a weapon of straw. They murmured to one another: "If these weapons have failed us, in what shall we seek safety?"

Consternation was in the council of the great of that party who, for more than a quarter of a century, had controlled the legislation of the Republic, and by whom was created, in the minds of the people, the errors of social distinction and "caste" that have crept into the country. The Republicans, assembled at their headquarters, became more bewildered at each new piece of evidence of the disapprobation and rejection of those doctrines, the understanding of which they deemed such conclusive argument to the minds of the people. The oncoming storm had no centre. It was blowing in all directions of the Union. Illinois, Indiana, Ohio, even manufacturing Pennsylvania, were sending a horrible howling of destructive wind, which would sweep away all their carefully-prepared barriers. At the Democratic headquarters, no less was the degree of wonder stamped, though with joyous imprint, upon the faces of the party leaders. Could it be possible that Illinois had cast the majority of its vote for the leaders of the Democratic party, those standard-bearers against whom so much had been said to prejudice the mind of that great Soldier State, the home of Lincoln, the birthplace of the Republican party and of the Grand Army of the Republic?

It was hard for the most hopeful to realize. Had the vaunted undoing of the Democratic party in the State of Indiana, the increase of the manufactures, and the personal popularity of a President, one of Indiana's chosen sons, been proved false and groundless? Had the negroes in Virginia, North Carolina, and Georgia joined the Democratic "Common People," in spite of the promised covenant of their salvation, The Force Bill, and added to the majorities in those Southern States? Connecticut—much-protected Connecticut; could it be possible that she would increase the few hundred majority accorded to the Democratic candidate four years ago?

All seemed so utterly out of keeping with the fondest hopes and expectations of the sagacious chieftains of Democracy, that incredulity was stamped upon every countenance. It seemed to be utterly beyond the comprehension of the wisest of the political world of both parties, that, possibly, they had been treating an unknown and unappreciated disease, the nature whereof they had failed to recognize. The result was not compatible with any established theory of either party. The people had evinced such utter disregard for all the old arguments and well-tried remedies, that it dumbfounded the physicians who pretend to minister to the wants of the nation. From such unsuspected quarters, and in such ridiculous proportions, had come the disapproval of the people, that all were at sea; some wrapping themselves in their own glory, proclaiming, like Cock

Robin, "I did it, with my little bow and arrow;" others, seeking to shield themselves behind the transparent, fragile shield of another's fault: "He did it, his unpopularity;" "Protection did it; it was his policy;" each trying to escape the general stampede, occasioned by the long-suppressed indignation of the people who objected, not so much to the economic doctrines of the Republican party (not that they had become converted to the tenets of the Democratic faith), but to that crime of "caste" which, with its many ramifications in the whole mass of society, was causing them unhappiness.

It is not well for the Democratic party to lay the flattering unction to its soul, that the mass of the people had become converted to the principles enunciated by that party in Chicago, at the Convention where Mr. Cleveland was nominated. It would be as delusive and disappointing to them, in some future election, as it has proved to the Republican party upon the occasion of their late discomfiture. On the other hand, the Republican party should be well convinced, by its downfall, that the people will not endure the wrapping up, in silken garments, of the progeny of the deformed and diseased state of European society, palming the enshrouded babe off as an offspring of that land that lit the torch of freedom for the world.

CHAPTER IV.

SOCIETY AS THE PEOPLE FOUND IT, NOVEMBER 8, 1892.

SOCIETY, as the people found it, on last election day, was certainly not as attractive as that autocratic gentleman, the distinguished Ward McAllister found it, and has helped to make it, as related by him in a book which has been published with much flourish of trumpets, entitled "Society as *I* Have Found It."

While the volume itself hardly rises to the dignity of a dime novel, it still, doubtless, is a true statement and record of the doings and pretensions of the very class of people who, by their presumption, have aroused the silent and sullen indignation of America. The book referred to, and its writer, Ward McAllister, of course, received a large share of criticism and ridicule. The absurdities of the book impressed the critics of the newspapers all over the land. It was made a butt for the squibs, sarcasm, and ridicule of some man on every newspaper throughout the country. Passages were selected from the book wherein Mr. McAllister poses himself in the position of a first-class cook, and where he recounts how he has been playing the millinery maid for some lady of fashion. Of course, it struck every one as ridiculous that any manly man who claimed to be an American should be impressed by the criticism made upon the "cut of the tails of his dress-coat," or to pay any attention to the advice of "a well-dressed Englishman, well up in all matters pertaining to society," as to the peculiar fashion to be adopted concerning a man's hat; how he should wear his watch-chain, etc. All such things were so extremely amusing and so utterly farcical to the brainworkers attached to the newspapers, that they held up the book and McAllister as objects to create merriment. That was the only possible view that could be taken by them of anything so absurdly funny as a man's highest ambition, his idea of dignity, his aim in life being so small as that evidenced in McAllister's autobiography.

There was another side to that question. A creature like McAllister is not a spontaneous or instantaneous creation of our great Republic. There must have existed a congenial atmosphere in his "smart set" to produce an exotic of such rare and unattractive perfume. Had it not been perfectly apparent that Ward McAllister was not the only person who imitated and aped foreign manners, and desired to create a social distinction in America, the book would have been a roaring farce. Had the people at large supposed that he was the single individual in America who approved of and earnestly desired to create a collection of idiots who should claim that "caste" could exist in our country, then the people would have regarded him much in the manner they would a buffoon on the stage of a theatre, or some idiot who, from a desire to attract attention, paints his face sky-blue. But the very advertising that this blooming flower of sham aristocracy received at the hands of the newspapers—which was done by the newspaper men in a spirit of levity, possessing, as they do, sufficient brains to find McAllister and his subject utterly absurd, in conjunction with many other well-advertised and extravagantly absurd assumptions on the part of the wealthy, made a much deeper impression upon the minds of the "Common People" than it was supposed that it would or could do. McAllister's "smart set" in this country—and his "smart set" is not confined to New York City, but exists in some form or manner in every city, town, village, and county in the Union—this McAllister-like "smart set" in each little community, as well as in the large cities, has managed by its arrogance and assumed superiority to arouse a spirit of resentment among the "Common People" of the Abraham Lincoln and Andrew Jackson stamp, because the masses have seen an attempt to establish something which would create an inequality between the citizens of the Republic.

It was a monstrous joke that the Knights of the Pencil saw in McAllister and his "Society as I Have Found It," and, like the keen-witted men that they are, they proceeded to hurl the javelins of their wit and sarcasm at this balloon of idiocy and impudence; but in piercing the balloon, the nauseating odor arising from its explosion pervaded the nostrils of the "Common People" with more than ordinary unsavoriness.

In every little village and town, and even through the farming sections, there is some would-be Ward McAllister and "smart set;" some little circle who from some imagined cause or reason, in their own conceit are a little better than the typical old settlers of our country, who brought the Republic into existence. They try to impress, and sometimes most insultingly, this supposed superiority upon the minds of the "Common People." In one little village it will be, for example, the owner of some protected little factory, which, in the wisdom of the legislators, has been protected to encourage and increase the industries of our country. In the solicitude of the legislators for the welfare of the people (acting honestly and in the best interests of the country), they have created the possibility for this man, this small manufacturer in the little village referred to, to accumulate a few thousand dollars more than his fellow citizens of the little village. The money has not been earned either by his sagacity, business ability, superior education, nor his intrinsic merit as a commercial genius. It is the result of accidents and the necessity that the legislators honestly felt existed, to create manufactories in our own country, to furnish the articles consumed by the people, rather than to buy the same from England and other foreign countries, sending our gold abroad out of the country in payment therefor.

The honesty of purpose and the wisdom of the action of the legislative part of the Government, it is not the province of this book to question. It is to record the result of the action upon the social relations of the different members of that little community, or village, in which the small factory was established, and the attendant unhappiness arising from the accumulation of a disproportioned amount of money in the hands of one of the citizens of the community. The manufacturer, becoming prosperous, began to assume an air of social superiority. He was enabled to take a trip every now and again to some near-by city. He there saw his model McAllister. He returned to his village with un-American affectations, aping the manner of his model—the McAllister of his near-by city. He began to draw around him (in much the same manner as McAllister describes the creation of the " Patriarchs " of New York) those whom he deemed suitable for that superior social position which he, modelling the machinery after the manner of the city McAllister, deemed so desirable.

Before proceeding to describe the birth of this superior social class, and the method of its organization, for which information we are indebted to this Prince of Cooks and Coats—McAllister—it is desirable to regard in a political way this local would-be aristocrat, the manufacturer. He imagines that Protection, the tariff, by which he has been enabled to amass the wealth, as the foundation upon which he bases his claim to a more exalted position, socially, than his fellow citizens, is entirely due to the doctrines of the Republican party. He loses sight of the fact that the Republican party did not owe its origin to Protection. The Abraham Lincoln Republican party did not owe its victory and popularity in the hearts of the people to Protection. There were other causes which operated powerfully in producing the result of the election in 1860 ; but the manufacturer of that little village, before mentioned, absorbed by the one idea that Protection has been the one cause of his success, and that it was due to the Republican party, becomes oblivious to the fact that the necessities of the Government, during a war to preserve the Federal Union, became so great that revenue had to be derived from some source, and that many of the duties imposed upon foreign importations by the Republican party had for their cause the stern necessity of the soldiers in the field, fighting to preserve the Union; that the war was not a battle for Protection. It had for its origin other and very different causes.

The war, which had been the outgrowth of the election of the candidate of the Republican party, created expenses which the Republican administration had to meet, and as a means to that end it became necessary to increase the existing duty and to place new duties upon imported manufactured articles. And by so doing they carried to a successful termination the great struggle for the preservation of the Union, to which the Republican party had pledged itself; which, together with the inclination and desire of some of the prominent members of the Republican party to increase the manufacturing industries of the country, has brought about that Protection and tariff by which he, the village manufacturer, has profited. He never stops to consider whether the tariff was a means to the end so profoundly desired, the preservation of the Union, a means of furnishing sinews of war by which the stars were retained upon our flag. He regards the tariff and Protection only in its personal aspect. The Republican party, to him, means his benefactor, to whom he owes an eternal debt of gratitude for enabling him to acquire that which, without Protection and tariff, he never could have obtained in the open field of the commercial battle wherein the world at large may contend. The position held by great thinkers of the Abraham Lincoln period is utterly unappreciated by him. That this tariff and Protection, which has been such a boon to him, was not created for his especial benefit, never suggests itself to his mind; that men of the Lincoln day and stamp should have had in view only the preservation of the Union and creating a fund to pay the expenses of those engaged to accomplish that end, does not occur to the village manufacturer.

In fact, many of the Republican politicians have made too much of the Protection doctrine and not enough of the cause that created it. This village, protected, small manufacturer, communing with himself, concludes that without Protection he could never have amassed that wealth which he is endeavoring to make elevate him above the social status of his fellow citizens. He acknowledges, possibly, to himself, that without Protection he might still be struggling for existence upon an equal plane with the "Common People," above whose heads he hopes to elevate himself socially. He regards only the Republican party of to-day, utterly oblivious to the fact that he and men of the McAllister and the "smart set" type have no just appreciation and no great admiration for the father of the Republican party, Abraham Lincoln, and his doctrines, which are the doctrines and sentiments of the "Common People." He merely knows that Protection helped *him*, and he cares nothing for what it was that brought about Protection and compelled the Republican party to advocate a high tariff during the Civil War.

Hence, this village manufacturer, this would-be social leader, the imitator of the city Ward McAllister, is a most ardent Republican. The little set of satellites which he gathers round him, glad to imitate the examples and opinions of one who has attained success and who is a recognized leader of this social movement to create "Caste" in our communities, become also ardent Republicans. In other words, it becomes almost a mark of respectability (so called) in the little community wherein resides the small protected manufacturer, to be a Republican.

The very word "Democrat" smacks so much of the "Common People." A man of intelligence, education, or wealth, who is a Democrat, becomes a social anomaly in that little community. A few prominent men through the land, who have become associated with the Democratic party, are spoken of merely as the result of inherited opinions through a long line of ancestry, similar to an inherited religion, or a motto on a coat-of-arms. A man who believes in Democracy, in its broad sense, is regarded in these little communities, when he is possessed of education, intelligence, and money, as a kind of firebrand. His every action is viewed with suspicion. So firmly has it become fixed in the minds of this little set of satellites, who surround the local manufacturing magnate, that "Republicanism" and "respectability" are synonymous, that they find it utterly incompatible with reason and refinement for a man to be respectable, according to their definition of the term, and not at the same time be a Republican.

The "Common People" in these little communities, many of whom have been Republicans with Abraham Lincoln, many of whom were veteran soldiers of the Union, became more incensed by the impression created by this local "smart set," than convinced by argument, during the campaign of 1892.

Before proceeding to more fully dissect the sentiment created by this kind of nonsense, and by its almost invariable association with the Republican party throughout the land, we will return to the admirable, unabashed Ward McAllister, and quote something from his text-book of snobbery, as to the methods adopted in the creation of the "smart set" in New York, which has furnished a model for similar creations through the length and breadth of the land.

"As a child," writes this scion of a race of nobles (?), "I had often listened with great interest to my father's account of his visit to London, with Dominick Lynch, the greatest swell and beau that New York had ever known. He would describe his going with this friend to Almack's, finding themselves in a brilliant assemblage of people, knowing no one and no one deigning to notice them; Lynch, turning to my father, exclaimed: 'Well, my friend, geese, indeed, were we, to thrust ourselves in here, where we are evidently not wanted.' He had hardly finished the sentence when the Duke of Wellington (to whom they had brought letters, and who had sent them tickets to Almack's) entered, looked around, and seeing them, at once approached them, took each by the arm and walked them twice up and down the room; then, pleading an engagement, said 'Good-night' and left. Their countenances fell as he rapidly left the room, but the door had barely closed on him when all crowded around them, and in a few minutes they were presented to everyone of note, and had a charming evening. He described to us how Almack's originated—all by the banding together of powerful women of influence for the purpose of getting up these balls, and in this way making them the greatest social events of London society.

"Remembering all this, I resolved, in 1872, to establish in New York an American Almack's, taking men instead of women, being careful to select only the leading representative men of the city, who had the right to create and lead society. I knew all would depend upon our making a proper selection. I made up an Executive Committee of three gentlemen, who daily met at my house, and we went to work in earnest to make a list of those we should ask to join in the undertaking. One of this committee, a very bright, clever man, hit upon the name of 'Patriarchs' for the Association, which was at once adopted, and then, after some discussion, we limited the number of Patriarchs to twenty-five, and that each Patriarch, for his subscription, should have the right of inviting to each ball four ladies and five gentlemen, including himself and family ; that all distinguished strangers, up to fifty, should be asked ; and then established the rules governing the giving of these balls—all of which, with some slight modifications, have been carried out to the letter to this day. The following gentlemen were then asked to become 'Patriarchs,' and 'at once joined the little band:

John Jacob Astor,	Royal Phelps,
William Astor,	Edwin A. Post,
De Lancey Kane,	A. Gracie King,
Ward McAllister,	Lewis M. Rutherford,
George Henry Warren,	Robert G. Remsen,
Eugene A. Livingston,	Wm. C. Schermerhorn,
William Butler Duncan,	Francis R. Rives,
E. Templeton Snelling,	Maturin Livingston,
Lewis Colford Jones,	Alex. Van Rensselaer,
John W. Hamersley,	Walter Langdon,
Benjamin S. Welles,	F. G. D'Hauteville,
Frederick Sheldon,	C. C. Goodhue,

William R. Travers."

These proud patriots, constituting a tribunal upon whose decision a man's claim to social equality with any other citizen in New York must rest, could find much in the conduct of their descendants to question with regard to their title to social superiority. The ventilation given to the Drayton-Borrowe-Millbank affair reflected no great credit upon the great name Astor—the first on the list of the "Patriarchs." The asinine utterances of a descendant of another of the "Patriarchs," which is here given, gives little evidence of inherited wisdom or common sense.

In the curious case recently tried in New York relative to the right of a women's association to erect a statue to a lady who, though counted among the metropolitan "Four Hundred," was possessed of much public spirit and philanthropic energy, one of the witnesses—a member of the same family—testified that her grandfather "never invited such people as Horace Greeley" to his house. A correspondent of the New York *World* enquires:

"Is it possible that we have an aristocratic society in this republican country of ours to which the great founder of the *Tribune* could not be admitted? Horace Greeley was born in New Hampshire, the native State of Gen. John Stark, Levi Woodbury, Daniel Webster, and a long line of soldiers, statesmen, and men famous in literature. If it is a title to aristocracy to belong to a family who were original settlers of the country, the Hamiltons are comparatively a new people, the great founder of the family being an emigrant from the West Indian island of Nevis about the year 1770. The Schuylers derive their distinction from Major-General Philip Schuyler, who was a distinguished officer of the Revolution, but whose services could not compare with those of that sterling old hero of Bennington—John Stark.

SOCIETY AS THE PEOPLE FOUND IT. 105

JOHN D. ROCKEFELLER,
A MAGNATE OF THE STANDARD OIL COMPANY.

"Why, Mr. Editor, there are thousands of good Democratic citizens who can trace back their descent to the Pilgrim Fathers, more than a hundred years before Alexander Hamilton landed from the West Indies. Is it not a relic of feudal times and barbarism to claim distinction above our fellows and superiority of birth on account of the deeds of an ancestor a hundred or more years ago?

"'Honor and fame from no condition rise.
Act well your part; there all the honor lies.'"

Shades of the great dead of journalism, the Bennetts, Raymonds, and others who have left the stamp of their genius upon newspaperdom in America, look down and pity the inane idiot who gives utterance to sentiments concerning Horace Greeley like those of the descendant of one of the "Patriarchs!" And men who occupy positions in the world of journalism, like Halstead, Cockerill, Clark Howell, how like you such utterances?

Really, had Horace Greeley been alive and known of such an utterly meaningless assertion, doubtless the old genius would have smiled ; but here is the query: Would it not have made a Democrat of every female member of his family, who regarded him as the epitome of worth, virtue, and merit? That a man like Horace Greeley, who had arrived at a position so pre-eminent as to disregard the snarls of puppies, should be amused at such a statement, would not be astonishing; but it would be none the less disagreeable for the women of his family. A woman's life is essentially social.

This illustration, and it would be impossible to find a better, of this nauseating attempt to establish "caste" in our country, will demonstrate the assertion that attempted class distinction has not been confined to the laboring man, the workman, or the poor man, but has been attempted, and made obnoxious, in every degree of wealth, learning, and position. The little country or village manufacturing magnate, whose Republicanism is not the Republicanism of *principles* nor the Republicanism advocated by Abraham Lincoln, has adopted the scheme set forth by Ward McAllister as a successful one, to be imitated in his little community, in establishing his own little "smart set"—his own local "Patriarchs." Proceeding upon that basis, he and his little band of innovators have attempted an improvement upon the social system of each little community, which has become associated in the minds of the "Common People" of these little communities with Republicanism; and, therefore, the Republican party, in November last, was forced to bear the opprobrium that attached itself, in the minds of the "Common People," to the "smart set" in their little communities.

Never was a greater mistake made than in supposing that the influence of this attempted social distinction shall only influence the laborers and working classes of a community. In proportion as a man, by increase of wealth and reputation, acquires in the work-a-day world a higher position with regard to the influence that he wields in the business or professional world, just so much more bitterly does he resent the arrogance of the few, who, like the Patriarchs, would establish a tribunal to try their fellow citizens concerning their social positions, at which those outside of the charmed circle have no opportunity to appear and offer proofs and evidence of their worth and merit. The banker who finds that his wife has been neglected when the invitations to the Patriarchs' ball are distributed, feels as keenly and resentfully the insult as does the longshoreman upon finding that his wife has not been invited to the butchers' ball.

Be honest with yourselves, and you will find, down in your hearts, a very ocean of bitterness occasioned by some slight or insult inflicted upon your family; and these are the things to which men do not give words, but which are silently felt, and to change which men silently voted.

American men bestow upon the women of their families a degree of devotion and admiration greater than that given by foreigners generally to their families. The Americans have exalted the women of our land, irrespective of wealth or condition, to a position of so much pre-eminence in our social affairs, that in that department of our lives our women are permitted to have absolute sway and control.

A man who dawdles around society, permitting it to absorb his time and attention, loses in a certain degree the respect of the large mass of American men. He is considered rather effeminate. Our social lives are controlled by the woman.

Our opinions are moulded by her; hence, we feel that, on subjects of a social nature, her judgment, opinions, and thoughts are entitled to the greatest respect—in fact, controlling largely our own. Hence the mighty influence of the women who had become resentfully Democratic because of social snubs. One woman had not been invited to the Patriarch's ball; another to the railroad magnate's ball; another to the Standard Oil Company king's entertainment; and, so on, it runs all down through the different stages created by this attempted crime of "caste," leaving behind it a sting in the hearts of each home as it passes, until it reaches the laborer and strikes him and his with telling force and effect. The Fricks, Carnegies, Goulds, Vanderbilts, Astors, become names as hateful to him as Tarquin's ever was to the Roman "Common People."

WARD MacALLISTER.
Self-Appointed Leader of the "Four Hundred"
of New York.
"A Prince of Cooks and Coats."

CHAPTER V.

SOME REASONS FOR WRATH.

HAD the spurious article, "American aristocracy," confined its vaporings and exhibitions to secluded spots, it would have been tolerated by the American people, exactly like many other "isms," shams, frauds, and delusions. Had the worshipers at the shrine of "caste," and supposed social superiority, reserved their devotions to some secluded chapel, they might have worshiped in peace at the feet of the tinseled god whom they adore—"caste." The American people tolerate almost any kind of "ism" for a time, provided the "ism" be not paraded before them, and flaunted in their faces in an insulting manner; but a determined people are the citizens of this nation, and when once aroused to a sense of outrage, they throw to the winds all consideration of law, danger, and consequence. The people of Chicago heard the howling of the anarchists with patience and amusement, Sunday after Sunday, along the lake front, but when the anarchists at Haymarket hurled one bomb among the citizens of the Republic, the day of anarchism was ended in Chicago. Innocent or guilty, the leaders of the movement must be punished. And they were!

Had the sham aristocrats of America been contented to reserve their exhibition of arrogance and presumption to those dervishes who worshiped at their own shrine—" caste"—and not to the general public, it is possible that their absurd "ism" might have been tolerated in a good-natured way for some time longer. It had certainly the advantage of anarchism, inasmuch as, when reserved to a few dervishes, it was excessively amusing. But, unfortunately for the champions of "caste," their followers, possessing neither a great amount of brains nor courage (and in these particulars, even the anarchists have an advantage over the sham aristocrats), have absolutely delighted in trifling with and imposing upon the good-nature of the public. In little, mean, spiteful ways, they have exhibited a smallness of soul, and an attempt, in a cowardly manner, to impose upon those who, poor in pocket, or dependent in some way, were unable to resent it. Take the evidence of the clerks, employés, servants, of the sham imitators of English aristocracy, and, almost without an exception, you will find their bosoms filled with resentment and hatred for that class; born, not with any desire to possess the property of their employers, nor from any socialistic tendency, but entirely the result of mean, spiteful, scornful snubbing. They have been wounded in pride, for, God knows! they are entitled, as free American citizens, to the possession of self-respect and pride.

Do you ask, Madame, why it is so hard for you to secure and retain servants? The reason is given above.

An explanation of the cause for the dearth of good domestic servants was sought by a great New York daily newspaper. It opened its columns and asked for communications explaining why a young woman preferred to work in a shop ten or twelve hours a day, and receive therefor three dollars a week, rather than accept a position as a domestic servant, in your house, Madame, where she would have greater comfort in the way of food and lodging, and receive more dollars.

Read the answers received by the *Recorder*, of New York. In almost every instance, the writer of the communication would say that it was not a matter of food, lodging, and dollars, but a matter of self-respect. They were snubbed and sat upon when engaged in serving the rich.

Go to any fashionable restaurant, or saloon, where the would-be swells swill champagne. Ask the attendants their opinion of those who, with a supercilious air, throw them a dollar to fee them for their services. You will hear expressed, in reply to your question, opinions like this: "I feel like knocking their heads off. I am ready to work,

I don't want their money for nothing; but I am a *man*, and as good as they are."

The workman was content, nor did it interest him if the rich should drive their Tally-hos. He had no desire to divide the money of the purse-proud devotee of "caste"; but when, weary from his day of labor, trudging along the road to his humble home, with tooting horn and flourish of whip the Tally-ho sweeps by him, and he has to scurry out of the road, he long remembers the derisive smile of the insolent, purse-proud occupants of the coach, and he objects—not to the coach—but to the manner and the smile of the occupants.

The heart of the shop-girl or the seamstress is not filled with envy because the fine lady (?) of fashion possesses garments of silk and laces; but the insolence and supercilious manner, when the fine lady (?) brought in contact with her, fills her soul with a sense of injured dignity. She knows she's quite as good as a lady of fashion. Possibly her father is not a protected, petty manufacturer; and she goes to her home, resenting the assumed superiority in the manner of the fine lady, and preaches to father, brother, and lover equality and broad democracy. The fine ladies (?) of fashion have ever been most potential causes for victories by the people. No orator so eloquent as the wife, daughter, sister, or sweetheart; and her wrongs were resented November 8th.

The New York *World*, of November 20th, 1892, publishes an article in connection with New York society, that, having received a place in that great Democratic journal, because of its undoubted truth, is worthy of a place in this volume. In speaking of the death of Mrs. Belmont, the *World* makes use of the occasion to express some remarkably forcible facts with regard to New York society. It says :—

"In the social history of New York it will be a lasting distinction to Mrs. Belmont that she was a conspicuous figure in good society before good society had been vulgarized. I have no quarrel with the society of to-day, which has merely followed the law of its evolution. I merely insist that the New York society of thirty years ago had all the good features of to-day, and was conspicuously free from certain faults which are now conspicuously prominent. The society which accepted the leadership of Mrs. Belmont had birth, and breeding, and culture, ample means and true refinement, and it had also that last test of a genuine aristocracy, that it held its rank by unquestioned title. It had so little fear of the security of its position that it freely admitted strangers of equal social rank.

"*It was possible for a rich merchant to permit a clerk to visit at his house*, and even scholars and educated people were not considered detrimental. While it had the respect of ingenuous youth for the older aristocracies of Europe, it did not abase itself in comparison with them, and was incapable of servility before them or before anything human. *It was singularly free from scandals."*

Then, thirty years ago,—that is, at the time of Abraham Lincoln's great popularity, succeeding by two years the great uprising of the Common People, the "mudsills," of the North and West,—a wealthy merchant of the North would receive his clerk, as a social equal, in his house. Then times have changed, and manners with them, within the last thirty years! The rich merchant of to-day has forgotten the force of the argument which resulted in the election of Abraham Lincoln, — "Americans enforce Equality." Two years was not enough, thirty years ago, to enable the rich merchant to forget that the first man of the nation, the President of the Union, had been a laborer, rail-splitter, clerk in a grocery store, and was, while chief of the nation, still a man of the "Common People." No, two years was not enough to bring about forgetfulness of these facts ; but *thirty-two* years was.

Hence, the overturning of the aristocratic party (or that party to which the aristocrats belong) cost what it might in dollars to the "Common People." It is not a new economic doctrine that they demand ; it is a new social system. While the assumed aristocracy of thirty years ago may have had respect for the older aristocracies of Europe, it most certainly did not abase itself, and was not as servile to them, as is the sham aristocracy of to-day.

Quoting from the Koran of that high priest of the "smart set," McAllister, who utters the sentiments of the most exalted in the holy of holies in swelldom :—

"It is well to be in with the nobs who are born to their position, but the support of the swells is more advantageous—for society is sustained and carried on by the swells, the nobs looking quietly on and accepting the position, feeling that they are there by divine right; but they do not make fashionable society, nor carry it on."

The "nobs," then, of this temple of "caste," feel that they occupy the high places by "divine right." The phrase, "divine right," sounds queer to Anglo-Saxon ears, to us, the descendants of a race who elevated Charles Stuart to the scaffold as a result of a "divine right." It sounds strangely in the ears of a nation that furnished the example of Liberty and Equality to the world, and which, when followed by the Frenchmen, caused Louis XVI. to kiss the guillotine by reason of his "divine right."

The meaningless, senseless sentences in "Society as I Have Found It," would be entitled to not the slightest attention, were it not for the fact that they give words to the sentiments of the "smart set," who have allied themselves—or rather stuck themselves on, as a piece of mud on a marble column—to the Republican party, and, hence, in the minds of equality-loving Americans, the Republican party became besmirched by that mud.

Quoting further from the New York *World*, and believing that the writer of the article knew whereof he wrote, the following is inserted :—

"I am writing about a period now thirty years gone by, and, consequently, beyond the personal knowledge of the great majority of my readers. But New York society of to-day is known to all readers of Sunday papers. They know it as an institution in which the prevalence of gigantic fortunes has made its atmosphere uncongenial for all who are not conspicuously rich. And while the valid claims of birth and breeding and culture have thus been crowded out at one gate of the social arena, the influences which have forced an entry at the other end in company with the mere millions, have all been vulgarizing influences. Society is no longer certain that it is the genuine article. If it were, it would not swagger so much, nor give so much thought to the effect it produces on the outer world. It is insolent, but not courageous; ostentatious, but not brilliant; it splurges, but does not shine; no glimmer of intelligence relieves the dullness of its boredom. It abases itself before the peerage of Great Britain, and the taint of corrupt living is unpleasantly frequent on its gilded exterior. Measured by the tests of a true aristocracy, it is below the standard of thirty years ago."

The readers of the papers, who are the people, know that society is an institution, as organized to-day, created by gigantic fortunes, which have been accumulated within the last thirty years, and, in many instances, by men of low and vulgar instincts, of mean origin, poor ability, who have become rich as the result of accident, and the result of the necessities of the nation while engaged in the war for the preservation of the Union. These very men, who had not the courage nor patriotism of the commonest soldier who shouldered his musket at Abraham Lincoln's call, and vindicated on the field of battle the right of the people, in a republic, to equality, and to the control of the government by the majority, who are beneficiaries of Protection and the exigencies of the nation, would assume a superiority over that common soldier whose courage and patriotism led him to risk his life in preserving the Union—for the fighting soldiers of "'61" were of the "Common People."

Society is not only no longer uncertain that it is a genuine article, but it *knows* it is a sham and a fraud, and seeks to make up by impertinence, insolence, and arrogance what it lacks of the genuine article. It *does* swagger; it does produce an effect upon the outer world, and that effect was evident by the overwhelming vote of the people, who said to it and to its successors in office, November 8th, last: "Thus far and no farther thou shalt go." It abases itself in such a disgusting manner before that peerage of Great Britain, as to cause feelings of indignation and contempt to arise in the bosoms of the descendants of those old Continental soldiers, who, more than a hundred years ago, said to Great Britain and her aristocracy: "We have had enough of you. This shall be a land of freedom, equality, and liberty; though it should cost the last drop of blood in our veins." And how effectively they demonstrated their determination to produce such a result, many a lord and lordling now mouldering in his grave, who sought these shores to impose the yoke of "caste" upon the colonies, could attest.

The tuft-hunting, and absolute courting of English titled adventurers, by the inheritors of the wealth taken from the people, has filled with disgust the breast of every manly and womanly citizen of this country. The people are not Socialists. Mrs. Hammersley is entitled to all that she inherited. Her right to it would be protected and defended by every good citizen of the Union, and there are few, very few, who are not good citizens, among the people. She may marry whomsoever she will. It was her privilege to select (or be selected by) the Duke of Marlborough, descendant of—not the over-honest, but original—soldier of fortune. She had a perfect right to prefer the position as wife of a divorced duke. She could take the money amassed in America and refurnish Blenheim, for the benefit (after the death of her divorced duke) of his first wife, who was still living, and will now be enabled to enjoy the fruits produced by the waters of American dollars poured upon the somewhat decayed and degenerate house of Churchill.

Mrs. Hammersley has the right to utilize the fortune of her deceased American husband under the wise provisions of his will (clever American he must have been!) as she chooses; but when she and her acquired (by purchase or otherwise) title is flaunted in the faces of American men and women, as something which entitles her to a more eminent position than she possessed as an American woman, the "Common People" object. Every time that the lady was spoken of, or written of, as "the American Duchess," as "Our Duchess," it aroused resentment. We have no American Duchess.

As an American wife, Mrs. Hammersley was a queen; as a duchess, by the exertion of great pressure and influence, she gained the privilege of kissing the hand of another, *called* Queen, because of the accident of birth.

Doubtless, Mrs. Hammersley was not responsible for being dubbed "the American Duchess" by the newspapers; but men of the Ward McAllister stamp, and the "smart set," indicated so plainly the kind of desire that seems to pervade the members of the sham aristocracy, to acquire by some method, and at any price, a title, that it was pardonable that the newspaper men assigned the peculiarly objectionable title of "the American Duchess" to one of America's daughters. The columns of our papers, day by day mirroring, as they do, the prevalence of this servile abasement of the dignity of the American woman in the "smart set" seeking alliances with a degenerate and unworthy offspring of a decayed and odoriferous aristocracy existing in Europe, have brought the subject to the atttention of the people all over the land.

What a relief it is to manly Americans to turn from a picture like that presented by the coroneted "Duchess," whose title and coronet have been purchased by the wealth of a common American citizen, an account of which is here printed, taken from the New York *World* of November the 13th :—

"A fine old illustration of the Duke's financial ability was shown in the way he obtained a *dot* of $500,000 with his wife. He made the Duchess borrow this sum in England and, to secure it, insure her life to that amount. She then returned with him to this country and here confessed judgment to her London creditors for the amount mentioned. They took the matter into tne court, which directed that the trustees set aside annually from the Duchess' income $50,000 a year to pay the interest on the debt she had incurred in England and the principal. This money the Duchess gave to her husband. She also bought and gave him a house in London."

And then to gaze with admiring glances upon that model of the American wife and mother, the late Mrs. Benjamin Harrison. To read of her, in the columns of a paper like the New York *Herald*, politically opposed to the party represented by President Harrison, that this good woman, Mrs. Harrison, representing that which is most queenly to the minds of the "Common People" of America, "was a model wife and mother;" that "during her husband's early struggles she helped him in many ways, and her wise counsel was often a great service to him." "She reared and educated her children thoroughly and sensibly, and made their home always attractive to them. * * * * She was also a skillful housekeeper, and few women were more adept in the art of domestic economy. * * * To do good works was her delight, and she was for many years one of the managers of the Indianapolis Orphan Asylum. * * * * At no time a woman of fashion. * * * In all the honors that came to her husband, she remained just the same consistent, helpful woman that she was the first day they were married. * * * * The domestic life at the White House has been something that all the world might be better for knowing of. Mrs. Harrison was the queen and centre of it all."

Of this good wife and mother, endeared to the hearts of the " Common People," by the possession of those same qualities and virtues that make the helpmates of the poor and lowly so dear to them, was said, in the editorial columns of the New York *Herald*, October 25th, the following:—

" In this hour of his affliction, the sympathy of the entire nation will go out to President Harrison and his household.

" The people of the country had only to learn of her worth to recognize and appreciate in Mrs. Harrison the virtues and graces of a noble womanhood. As mistress of the White House, she won the affection of all, as she endeared herself to her home circle by her qualities as wife and mother.

"Her brave and serene spirit through long suffering, and the President's tender devotion, have touched the heart of the country. Her death will be mourned as the loss of a good, lovable woman."

The sorrow occasioned by her death inspired even poets to place a wreath woven by their art, upon her tomb. It is well for the country that the President's wife should have been one

MRS. BENJAMIN HARRISON.

furnishing such a noble example to the women of America, that of her could be written what James Whitcomb Riley wrote of Mrs. Harrison :—

> Now utter calm and rest,
> Hands folded o'er the breast,
> In peace the placidest,
>   All trials past,
> All fever soothed; all pain
> Annulled in heart and brain,
> Never to vex again,
>   She sleeps at last.
>
> She sleeps, but, oh, most dear
> And best beloved of her,
> Ye sleep not, nay, nor stir,
>   Save but to bow
> The closer each to each,
> With sobs and broken speech
> That all in vain beseech
>   Her answer now.
>
> And lo, we weep with you,
> Our grief the wide world through,
> Yet, with the faith she knew,
>   We see her still,
> Even as here she stood,
> All that was pure and good
> And sweet in womanhood,
>   God's will her will.

The sympathy of the whole nation went out to President Harrison when he sustained the loss of that example of virtue and womanly excellence in the death of his wife. It was so deep and strong, that had the "Common People" not seen the party he represented through a glass clouded by the smoke and soot of sham aristocracy, he would have been re-elected.

By that bedside, the people saw the chief of their nation with bowed head, shedding tears for that lost love who had shared with him his joys and sorrows, his hopes and disappointments, ambitions, and his failures. No tenderer sympathy or kindlier feeling ever filled and moved the hearts of the American people than that felt for that good husband, good patriot, good citizen, Benjamin Harrison. He was bereft of a helpmate who by his side had fought the battle of life, the early struggles in Indianapolis when he was a young lawyer, hewing his way through the forest of difficulties, which, like the forests of Africa that surrounded Stanley, in American life present themselves before the struggling, ambitious men of our land. And when, at last, bursting through the maze and underbrush of obstacles, like Stanley, he came upon the open plain of success, her voice had been first to join his in a prayer of thanksgiving. The bowed head of the aged chieftain of the nation, upon whom the heavy hand of sorrow had been laid, was an object to occasion even the most partisan political opponent to pause and shed one sympathetic tear. How full must his mind have been of the recollection of the hours anxiously spent by this loving American wife and mother, while he was exposed to hourly danger

BENJAMIN HARRISON.
President of the United States, 1889-93.

in defence of the American Union. How each sad hour must have been recalled to him, and how slight had been the reccmpense, accorded in the harvest of time to the faithful heart that had beat in rhythmic accord with his.

The sympathy of the nation was deep, broad, and strong ; and had Benjamin Harrison represented anything else but what the people knew was the aristocratic party, on the flood-tide of that sympathy he would have been carried into office by an overwhelming majority. Let those who would excuse their own errors and the errors of their *class*, let the would-be astute politician and the abashed assumed barons ascribe the defeat of the Republican party to the lack of personal magnetism of their candidate, but the great heart of the people will feel that that charge was as false as the claim of the " Four Hundred" to social superiority.

Benjamin Harrison will long be remembered as an exemplary President, if patriotism and the performance of those pledges made to the people who elected him, entitle a President to remembrance. Great as we all recognize the personal magnetism of that magnificent statesman, James G. Blaine, to be, it could not have exerted the influence over the minds of the masses that the death of Mrs. Harrison in the White House did. Death robbed the President of the position of the First

Man in the Nation. He became at once the husband, the father, and the man ; and had the issue been alone to be decided by personal magnetism, sympathy of the people, the outburst of approval and approbation would have been in favor of Benjamin Harrison. But he and the party whom he represents, justly or unjustly, had become accursed with the crime of " caste " in our country. He was defeated by those who, to a man, bowed their heads in sorrow with him, and shed tears of sympathy at his great loss as a fellow-man and citizen, but could not give him their votes as representing what to them became the party of sham, affected, foreign aristocracy.

Another picture that rises simultaneously before the eyes of the masses as representing those queens in America, to whom more ready homage is paid than was ever accorded to a coronet or crown, is our Frances Cleveland. Ours, because the "Common People" claim her, as only an ordinary, sweet, lovely, modest American woman.

That picture made more votes for Grover Cleveland than any political chicanery could have accomplished. With her baby in her arms, she represents American womanhood, motherhood, and simplicity ; that which is best, purest, and dearest to the hearts of all of us, the " Common People." No higher place is it possible for woman to attain than that she occupies with her babe on her bosom.

THE AMERICAN QUEEN.

THE AMERICAN DUCHESS.

She had gone into the White House a young, guileless, average, common American girl; she had represented, in the high position accorded to her by the hearts of the people, the first lady of the land, with a simplicity and dignity pleasing to every American woman from Maine to Texas. She had welcomed the friends of her girlhood, before, as wife of the President, she became the most prominent female figure in the land, with the same cordiality that as Miss Frances Folsom she had exhibited towards them. The unassuming air with which she occupied her high position as sharer of the honors of the Chieftain of a free people, endeared her to the hearts of the mass of us, " Common People." The farmer's wife in Illinois, the mechanic's wife at Homestead, Pa., the banker's wife at Philadelphia, the railroad president's wife in New York, felt a ray of sunshine warming that spot in woman's heart, which is the Holy of Holies with them, young wifehood; and when Time, the great scene-shifter, had rearranged the setting of the stage, and presented to us the picture of the young mother, she became as interesting an object as the President himself. She had given to America another American. She had set an example for the women of our land which it would be well, my lady in your palace on Fifth avenue, to follow. Do not leave the future generations, who will rule the destinies of this nation, to be the offspring of foreigners ; forego your balls, receptions, entertainments, and your trips to Europe; endure the inconvenience and annoyance of the nursery. Let us have some American children born. The prattle of the baby's tongue will be sweeter music to your ear than the lisping flattery of some foreign duke. You may have the honor of being a mother of some future Jefferson, Jackson, Webster, Clay, Calhoun, Lincoln, Garfield, Cleveland.

God bless you, Frances Cleveland, for the example you have set ! Thoughts of you and sweet memories of the past, as dear even to the poorest woman as to the Queen of Great Britain and Empress of India, make Democrats of the hard-worked, poor old wife and mother in the little farmhouse of Illinois and Indiana. There is no scene in Grover Cleveland's career to-day so embalmed in the hearts of the people as that wherein he is described as refusing to talk politics with one of the political satellites that ever hover round planets of the political firmament, putting them aside that he might watch the tottering footsteps of baby Ruth. It was just like any other man of the people, and the people recognized, as they did in the life and acts of Abraham Lincoln, that Grover Cleveland is one of us.

When some member of the "smart set," who allies herself with the effete nobility of Europe, gives to the world a sample of what a man should be, as did the humble American wife, Nancy Lincoln, then the "Common People" will forget their wrath at the absurd assumption of the worshipers of the British peerage. Women like Martha Washington, Nancy Lincoln, Carrie Harrison, and Frances Cleveland, will ever be contrasted with those samples of the "smart set" who seek the society of the snobs and swells of foreign nations. The wrath of the people will ever be aroused at the arrogant assumption of snobbery and sham aristocracy upon the part of the successful searchers after titles.

The saying, by the "smart set," that the "Comon People" have nothing to do with them or their actions, or with how they dispose of their wealth, is quite true; but the unwise exhibition of an attempt to create class distinctions, can arouse such gusts of anger that that wealth, which is held only by paying such taxes as the "Common People" may decree (being, as they are, the majority), that much-prized wealth may be swept away, as a handful of dust, before the storm of the people's anger.

The correspondent of the New York *World* hastens to vindicate the just censure written, from any suspicion of prejudice concerning New York's "Four Hundred"; but, in the attempt to vindicate, gives evidence enough of the thought of the people with regard to the morals of any "smart set" possessed of unlimited millions, totally idle, selfish, and luxurious :—

"To vindicate my censures from any suspicion of prejudice, let me hasten to add that the tone of New York's 'Four Hundred' is better than that of any corresponding set in the world. Comparisons are not satisfactory, because the society of Paris is the society of all France, and the society of London is the society of the whole British Empire. Compared with these, the social aristocracy of New York is merely a little clique. It is only just to say that it has not yet reached the coarseness of that fast set in London, which it aspires to imitate, and, if it lacks the refinement which centuries of courtly teaching have given to even the most unruly elements of French aristocracy, it also falls short of that cynicism which ignores all moral influences. Perhaps the present lowered tone of society may be only a passing malady. Perhaps things may get better before they get worse. Who knows? We can only say that unlimited millions, total idleness, and selfish luxury, are conditions not usually conducive to the elevation of morals."

What the people meant by the exhibition of their wrath last November, in the vote that they cast against what they deemed the party of the "smart set," was the creation only of pictures in future, so sweetly pure as that with which the *World* correspondent winds up the article :—

"What a different social vista is presented to us when we turn to look back on the long and peaceful life of *Emerson's widow*, who died last week at the ripe age of *ninety*. Although she made no claim on the world's regard, we catch pleasant glimpses of her personality along the path of the great philosopher's life, like the sunshine showing through the leaves of the Concord elms. Beside the simple dignity of a life like hers, how unsatisfactory appears the career of an over-dressed, over-fed, over-rich woman of fashion, worn out in the scramble and struggle to keep up with the procession."

The people desire, and have so expressed themselves, by the mighty voice of the majority, a return to the simple, natural condition of social life in America, wherein "caste" has no place, from which social distinctions disappear; the simple, homely, every-day, virtuous life of the mothers, wives, and daughters of those who made the Republic.

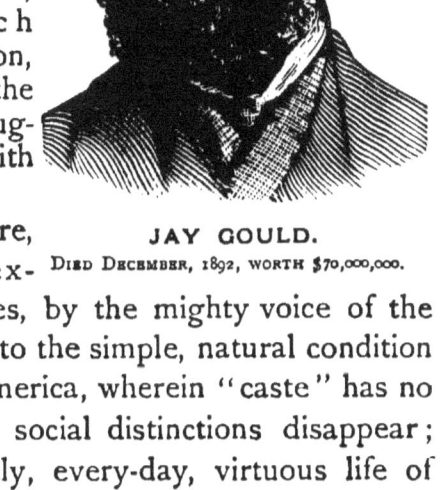

JAY GOULD.
DIED DECEMBER, 1892, WORTH $70,000,000.

The "Common People" have recorded their protest against snobbery, sham aristocracy, "smart sets," Ward McAllister, and multi-millionaires, who assume to be better, either by "divine right" or otherwise, than the ordinary American citizen. They have taught, by the lesson preached in the tremendous majorities for that party whom they deemed least tainted with this repugnant crime, that wealth, arrogance, assumption, and snobbery may have obtained an undue amount of influence, disproportioned to its merit, but that, thank God, on election day, every citizen of the Republic enjoys an equal right to the franchise, and that, by the voice of the majority, he will create such laws as to eradicate the insidious disease of "caste" from the wholesome body of the nation.

CHAPTER VI.

THE ARISTOCRATIC "CHAPPIE" *vs.* ABRAHAM
LINCOLN.

As that satellite of McAllister, that scion of the line of "Patriarchs," parades Fifth Avenue, creating by his presence an aristocratic atmosphere for the poor, Common People to enjoy, what a picture he presents! How admirable and worthy of emulation!

How the mind naturally recalls specimens of the *genus* Chappie when the subject of the young male aristocrat recurs to us! This descendant of a half-dozen fur traders, ferrymen, or land speculators, has become elongated and attenuated by the non-exercise of the muscles of his feet and legs in the long tramps that his forefathers used to take to barter for the peltries of the untutored Indian, exchanging rum and bad muskets therefor.

We will begin with Chappie's lower extremities, because of the greater importance of that part of his anatomy. The pimple which surmounts his structure is hardly worthy to be called a head, and is the least important part of his makeup. Around the thin shanks of his lower limbs are imported striped trousers, in imitation of his English model; these are turned up when it rains in London. His narrow, chicken-like bosom is covered by a hand's breadth of imported material. (There's no heart in his bosom, nor other organs worthy of naming within his whole body; hence, a little cloth will cover his trunk.) From sloping shoulders that would have done credit to a belle of the First Empire of France, hangs, in badly wrinkled folds, the latest thing "from Poole's, of London, y' know!" Rising from the apex formed by the slopes of his shoulders is a thing through which he breathes, and which he calls a neck; around which, to fence it from the cold blasts of heaven, he has had built a structure which he calls a collar, modelled absolutely after that of "our late lamented Prince Clarence." Above that thing he calls a neck is nothing; for that which in a human being would represent a face, in this creature is but a simpering mask of idiocy, arrogance, sensuality, intemperance, and licentiousness.

That thing he calls a face, with assured presumption and insulting attitude, he thrusts before the gaze and upon the attention of the daughters of the poor but honest workmen, whose children, not having a fur trader for a grandfather, have to labor. This *thing*—this "Chappie"—would assume the same privileges as one of the new nobility, the creation of men like McAllister and the "Patriarchs," as those assumed by the curled and perfumed darlings of the court which surrounded the licentious Louis XV. That which from fear he would not dare to do or say among the "smart set," he feels at liberty to do or say when thrown among the children of the poor and defenceless on a public street. It is nothing to him to insult the poor shop girl; he would say, "That is one of the evidences that I am of the upper class. It should be an honor to be spoken to by me."

It was ever one of the idiosyncrasies of the upper classes, wherever people have allowed them to exist, to insult innocence and outrage honor. History teems with it, and "Chappie," by tradition, thinks that necessarily he must act it, to be of the "Prince's set." "Chappie" thinks that the scandal of Cavendish Square was but a little episode—nothing, in fact, because the children of the poor were the only ones contaminated; for the brutes who led to these orgies in Cavendish Square had already become decayed and rotten morally.

"Chappie" in his exalted position sees in every unprotected woman (and he'll make sure she's unprotected) a victim upon whom to exercise his wiles, and if, God help her! through weakness, love of dress, finery, or pleasure, she allows herself to be led to lean upon his honor, she'll fall! For "Chappie's" honor exists only as aristocracy in America, that being a sham and a fraud, as is Chappie's honor.

This outgrowth of accumulated wealth, this polluting toad in the pure water of public life, never has and never will, nor can he, give one atom of return to the Republic for the honor of living in it. He whose life is spent in idleness, debauchery, and sensuality regards his valet, coachman, cook, clerk, tailor, hatter, merchant, banker, as his social inferior. And he is always attached, like a barnacle, to the good Republican Ship built by Abraham Lincoln.

Is it a wonder that the people said, in November last: "We'll burn the ship rather than endure such barnacles?"

This thing, so amusingly written of by that most excellent comic paper, *Life*, so ridiculed by *Puck* and *Judge*, held up for derision by the whole newspaper fraternity, is responsible for the loss of thousands of votes to the Republican party. Indignant wives, sisters, and daughters have returned with flaming cheeks to humble yet honest homes, and told the story of the insults offered them on the streets of this and other good cities in the Union by "Chappie" and those creatures of his kind ; and in their telling of the story have made more votes, more Common People's votes, than have been made by all the newspapers ever printed in the interests of the Democratic party. Each tear that was shed upon the bosom of the poor man by an honest working daughter became a nail in the coffin of the Republican party. Justly or unjustly, such is the case. The Grand Old Party had descended, in the People's opinion, to the level of enduring representation of it by such as "Chappie." "How have the mighty fallen !"

"Chappie," with his vacant semblance of a head, with his trousers carefully rolled up, with his insidious smile, insinuating manner, his suggestive gestures, and ogling glances, has proven himself a valuable assistant to Mr. Harrity, Chairman of the Democratic National Committee. Steadily he has increased the waters of wrath in the reservoir of the poor man's heart, until, bursting all barriers, it swept away "Chappie," his "smart set," and all, November 8, 1892.

"Chappie," after his late and dainty breakfast and stroll down Fifth Avenue (every city has its Fifth Avenue or something like it), enabling the daughters of the poor to gaze upon his charming proportions ; delighting their fancy with the possibility in the shape of finery that might be theirs would he only condescend to beckon to them; with a few chosen spirits similar to himself—all all of the "smart set," y' know!—seeks that most discriminating and select of saloons, Delmonico's. (And every city has its Delmonico.) There, after tickling his palate and tempting his satiated appetite with delicacies so rare and difficult of procurement that the cost of each one of such dainties would feed some poor man's family for a fortnight; forgetting that early grandfather, the fur trader, who considered pork a feast, leans back in his chair and lisps in affected imitation of the English, "Where shall we g-o, deah boys?"

Now let us draw the veil over where "Chappie" spends his evenings. "Chappie's" pleasures and "Chappie's" unnatural amusements would cause a blush of shame to redden the face of the humblest horny-handed son of toil. "Chappie's" exhausted nature has ceased to realize sensations natural to *men* and sons of God. "Chappie" is much poorer than his progenitor, the old fur trader; for the old fur trader was rich in all the natural inclinations and appetites created by a natural and vigorous manhood. The old fur trader had no coat-of-arms; but, "Chappie," that old fur trader would blush at the decadence of his own descendant! When the historian, "Chappie," shall make up the records of this great nation, that old fur trader, though he swindled the Indians and debauched them with rum, had that which you, "Chappie," lack—manliness, courage, and character, even though the character was of a peculiar kind.

You have no character, "Chappie." The Common People have found you a tumor, an excrescence upon the body politic. They have taken their knife to amputate, from wholesome Americanism, a foreign infliction. Be careful, "Chappie," that the amputation does not include the severance of that semblance of a head that you carry on your sloping shoulders. Be warned in time; you and yours have wealth, luxury, influence, and obedience upon the part of those you dominate. You have all that wealth will buy—villas at Newport, yachts, palaces. You revel in banquets, balls, and glittering assemblages. The poor man's home is illuminated alone by the light shed by honor. He who would steal or deprive him of that one light, takes all from him that makes his life worth the living. The poor man's honor is the honor of his wife and children. Your immoralities have increased, like appetite, by what they fed upon. It is not after you, the deluge, but it is around you, the deluge. It is in the air, because it is in the hearts of the Common People.

It is no exaggeration to say that the assumed license which young men of the "Chappie" class exhibit in their lives, morals, and manners, has done much to disgust the large mass of the people. The oft-repeated expression, that "virtue and honesty in England is confined to the great middle classes," is reiterated by those of the "Chappie" class in America as an excuse for their own misdemeanors. The flagrantly sinful lives, filled with debauchery, which they lead, is an evidence, to their poor intellects, of their being members of the sham aristocracy with which America is cursed. The society of the kind composed of "Chappies" is so objectionable to the decency and intelligence of the Common People that its exclusiveness would be almost a virtue.

The Common People of respectability would never seek "Chappie's" society, and their hearts are filled with resentment at his supercilious manner and ignoble intentions when seeking the society of the Common People.

To some it will appear ridiculous to have devoted so much space in this volume to such a nonentity. If we could confine the "nonentity," like an ape, in the Zoological Garden in Central Park, it is true so much space would be wasted as he occupies in this volume. But, the fact is, he is allowed to run at large, and in his peregrinations

ABE, THE RAIL-SPLITTER.—The "Common People" Made Him President.

"Chappie" on Fifth Avenue.—The Worthless Product of "Caste" and Sham Aristocracy.

around the country he creates a feeling of disgust among the Common People for that political party to which he proudly asserts he belongs ; claiming it to be the "only respectable party." Were he not, as a "sandwich man," a walking advertisement of the worst element that has become attached, like an octopus, to the Republican party, "Chappie" would be unworthy of the attentions he has here received.

But, in seeking for the true cause of the decisive and overwhelming overthrow of Lincoln's "Grand Old Party," it is necessary to mix even this worthless ingredient into the porridge of defeat with which the leaders of the Republican party have been fed.

It is a relief to turn from the despicable object of "Chappie," and regard and compare in our minds with him the men who have "left footprints on the sands of time" in the history of our nation.

What a contrast is presented when we shift "Chappie" from the scene of our mental vision and bring forth the loved "Harry" Clay, the miller's boy. That barefoot boy, on a bony, illbred horse, with shaggy mane and tail; holding a bag of corn in front of him, on his journey to the mill for his widowed mother, is a more inspiring picture, decidedly, than "Chappie" on his wellbred English cob whose coat is soft as fur from constant currying, whose tail is cropped off *a la* the fashion for riding-horses in London. As "Chappie" sits on his little imported English saddle, and daintily holds an imported English riding whip, prepared for a ride, to give the "Common People" an exhibition of the beauty, gallantry and horsemanship of the scion of sham aristocracy; with all his glory, backed with all of his millions, "Chappie" does not warm the hearts of the "Common People" like the picture of that miller's boy, Henry Clay, the great Commoner of Kentucky.

Daniel Webster, struggling as district school teacher in New England, clothed in ill-fitting garments, would somehow furnish a better model for the sculptor or painter who would make a statue or picture or a head of him who was, indeed, a mighty man.

The music of the voice of grand old Daniel Webster, even though he did not drawl in delightful imitation of the English, would give greater delight to the "Common People," plebeian as they are and unrefined, than "Chappie's" lispings.

There remains another figure, called to mind by the Common People when they view "Chappie," by reason of the vast difference between the figure of "Chappie" and the "rail-splitter" of Illinois. The long, uncouth, gangling, ungainly figure of a boy sprawled on his back, lying on the floor of a humble log-cabin, seeking knowledge in a well-thumbed book, by the light of a flickering fire, presents something that speaks more eloquently to the hearts of the Common People than "Chappie's" gorgeous appearance and apparel; for they know that' the name of the lad before that fire was ABRAHAM LINCOLN, and that from that uncouth figure, and by the aid of that difficultly-acquired knowledge, resulted the production of that man who, as representative of the Common People as their President, stood as the Rock of Gibraltar when the fierce waves of fratricidal war swept over our land; immovable, firm and unchangeable as that rock itself in the determination that the Union should be preserved, and that the Stars and Stripes should float over every inch of ground of the United States of America. While others lost hope and many were downcast, groping for support in the hour of gloom and peril to the national existence of our country, that man, who was the outcome of the ungainly figure by the fire, led the people of the nation as the pillar of fire of old led the hosts of Israel.

While men like Jefferson, Jackson, Clay, Webster and Lincoln present types which, to the minds of the Common People of America, are best and greatest, the picture of "Chappie," in all of his

ANDREW CARNEGIE.
A "Self-Made" Man. A Multi-Millionaire.
Made $20,000,000 in America;
Lives in Scotland.

splendid apparel, peculiar pronunciation, abnormal immoralities, will sink into insignificance beneath the flood of the people's contempt and disapproval; just as the party to which "Chappie" had allied himself were swept away and submerged, November 8, 1892.

CHAPTER VII.

HON. JOHN BRISBEN WALKER, ON HOMESTEAD.

IT is the good fortune of only a few to be possessed of the remarkable genius and imbued with the spirit of prophecy to predict coming events with the certainty and accuracy of the Hon. J. Brisben Walker, who, in an article published in the *Cosmopolitan* for September, 1892, foretold, with wonderful force, the rock upon which the Republican bark was drifting. It was not until the manuscript of this volume was almost completed that attention was called to Mr. Walker's article. To the credit of journalists, and writers generally, be it said that no class or profession are as willing to recognize the ability of their brothers as are the members of that profession whose aim it is to foretell the future, to weigh the evidence of public opinion, prognosticate as to the result thereof, and record the events that transpire, either in accordance with their prophecies or contrary thereto. To Mr. Walker be accorded the honor of justly appreciating the suppressed indignation of the people, and of sounding the warning note to the wealthy, prior to November 8, 1892. To the writer of this volume little credit is due for merely recording that which, since the result of the election is known, is perfectly apparent. Had Mr. Walker looked into the future and been blessed with prophetic vision, he could not have told, more clearly than he has, the forces that were operating in September, and which produced the results so surprising to many in November.

While Mr. Walker has taken Homestead for his text, the application of his article to the condition of the people of the Union generally is so apparent that each man for himself may shift the scene and make it applicable to his own little community. In every village, town, city, or county in the Union, is some one man, or some set of men, who arrogate to themselves a certain superiority resulting from the accumulation of wealth in their hands; this accumulation, having arisen from the inequality in the distribution of the increased wealth of the nation, being in many cases purely

HENRY C. FRICK,
MANAGER CARNEGIE WORKS, HOMESTEAD, PA.

accidental, and in others the result of the phenomenal development of the resources of this country, coupled with the wonderful spirit of invention shown in the land in the last thirty years. Mr. Walker takes Carnegie and Frick as types of the class to which the people object so strenuously. The building of a church, or the founding of a library, is but a small price to pay, in the opinion of the American people, for the right to assume privileges detrimental to the growth and continuance of that doctrine so dear to the hearts of the masses—the equality of man. Mr. Walker entitles his article, "The Homestead Object Lesson," and begins by saying:—

"An affair like that at Homestead educates the public mind rapidly ; more rapidly in a month than ten years of books and pamphlets. In the face of death, men stop to think. What led to this ? What does it mean ? What is the remedy ? And when the daily journal gives in one column the picture of Cluny Castle, or the magnificent pile from which the Lyttons have gone out to admit partner Phipps from the Homestead mills, and in another sketches showing the dead and dying upon the banks of the Monongahela, the contrast is so sharp that one draws a quick breath of discomfort, and even the most conservative, whose manhood is stronger than his love of dollars, admits that something is wrong."

If a man in the walk of life of Mr. Walker shall "draw a quick breath of discomfort" at the scene he pictures, because his "manhood is stronger than his love of dollars," how utterly obvious it ought to have appeared, and should now appear, to those possessed of wealth, that an appeal for the support of that class who, as American citizens, not only possess an abundance of manhood, but, in addition thereto, are sufferers by the wrongs or conditions written of by Mr. Walker, was and is useless.

"Lovers of the Republic may well tremble at this exhibition, so closely resembling the evil days when rich Romans surrounded themselves by hired bands of fighting bullies. True, our modern rich man does not parade the streets, surrounded by his gladiators. He sits in a secret office, removed from danger, and, in communication with the telegraph wires, orders his army concentrated from many States by rapid transit, and moves it unexpectedly upon his private foes. There is lacking that personal courage which gave a half-way excuse to the Roman who, sword in hand, shared the dangers of the fight. But the risk to the Republic is all the greater from these modern methods. For, if a man may hire 300 poor devils ready to shoot down their brothers in misery, there is no reason why he may not hire 10,000."

There are not a few of us who will recall the natural indignation aroused in our bosoms while witnessing that noble impersonator of *Virginius*, John B. McCullough; the idea of the degradation to which we were drifting, by the possibility of the existence of an aristocracy, whose hired bullies and parasitical clients acted as panders to the worst passions of man. If it be possible to adopt the old Roman method of hiring bullies and assassins, and maintaining paid private armies, how very possible to come to a condition similar to that so powerfully portrayed in *Virginius!* Lovers of the Republic, of honor, and virtue, may well tremble, at the bare possibility, vaguely imagined, but evidently more vivid to the minds of the masses, than was contemplated by those autocratic gentlemen who ordered their mercenaries to Homestead.

"There is another side to this matter. Raised up under the system which declares that any man has a right to control, without limit, the earth's surface and its productions, or the labor of his fellow-men, Mr. Frick, doubtless, feels that he is performing a sacred duty in protecting his property at Homestead, by any means that the law permits. Thousands of good men held the same thought regarding their slaves, before and during the war. It really seemed to them a divine right of property, and all classes of the community to-day—learned ministers and professors, intelligent merchants, and high-minded men of all professions—hold that our system of distribution is not only legal, but fair, and authorized by the teachings of the Gospel."

In the most lucid manner, Mr. Walker continues to give the causes of the existence of conditions conducive to the results which have been produced by the accumulation of wealth, and, in consequence, assumption of a superior social position by the possessors thereof:—

"Less than half a century ago the people of the United States were comparatively poor and the wealth of the country distributed with a near approach to equality, less than a dozen individuals having fortunes approaching the million mark. The laws had been made for the existing conditions of labor, and were, as a whole, of a satisfactory character. No one had yet dreamed of the marvelous inventions and discoveries of natural wealth which were to upset all the conditions of production, and make the succeeding fifty years a wealth-giving period, unprecedented in the history of the world. Anthracite and bituminous coals, petroleum, the cotton gin, the reaper, steam and electricity, with their thousand marvels, were suddenly emptied upon a community whose laws had been made for conditions the very opposite of those now existing.

"It is not to be wondered at that the American mind should seize upon the possibilities which old laws gave to individuals for grabbing these new-found treasures. They would have been more than human if they could have resisted the temptation, and besides, it must be recollected that the Christianity practised was of a perfunctory character, formal and nominal rather than real, and civilization just beyond the period of wild beast skin wearing. In fifty years the creation of wealth has become prodigious; the distribution of wealth has become frightful in its inequalities. The laws, which were beneficent for an agricultural and pastoral people, worked degradation and infamy in a manufacturing community. They permitted the few to grab the greater part of this new wealth. With great fortunes are coming upon the scene an unparalleled luxury upon the one hand, and a poverty upon the other, scarcely surpassed in the days when production did not equal one-tenth the present output. In the strife for wealth the law-making power was found to be a useful auxiliary. Judges were bought, senatorships were sold in the interests of railways and the great corporations ; and within the last ten years we find wealth—not contented with the advantages which the laws, confessedly in its favor, give it— hiring private armies to give force to edicts allotting to the laborer a lesser share of the product."

Experience and observation force the conviction upon our minds, that Mr. Walker is correct in his assumption that even the ministers believe that the distribution of wealth among the masses is not only legal, but fair, and authorized by the teachings of the Gospel. A little strange, however, is it for the teachers of the doctrine of Christianity to maintain principles so utterly at variance with those expressed by their divine Master: "If thou wilt be perfect, go and sell that thou hast, and give to the poor."

"There is only one class to dispute this proposition. They are the toilers, whose labor is the immediate cause of the production of our wealth. We may say that there must be intelligence to direct, and that to the intelligence which takes advantage should come the gains. But Mr. Carnegie and Mr. Frick are proofs that in the ranks of labor itself there is intelligence to direct. Many Carnegies and many Fricks would spring up tomorrow if opportunity permitted. If one would study the justice of a system of political economy, let him surrender his vested rights of property and take his place among those whom the system crushes, whose labor it devours, and whose reward for labor is a bare, joyless existence. We who have the money can reason speciously regarding the justice of our laws, the excellence of our system of government. The laboring man can only groan in spirit. He has not hitherto had the power of his vote, notwithstanding our boasted representative government, because his brothers, in the agony which poverty brings, in their effort to relieve the hand-to-mouth miseries of their existence, have sold at each election this birthright for the merest taste of pottage."

Fortunately, under the Australian system of voting, it was impracticable to buy Esau's birthright with a delusive mess of pottage held out by the protected, wealth-accumulating, sham aristocrats.

"Everyone knows that this has been true, that the labor vote has never been a unit, that its purchasability has been one of the well-understood factors in ward politics, that there has been no combination, no united effort, no intelligent direction, no willingness to submit to leadership, and that there is to-day no probability of the vote of these people being cast at an early election for the objects in which they are so deeply concerned. The issues that are before the public in either of the great political parties for whose candidates the votes will be cast, are very largely those which concern the people of means and influence. Platforms are dictated with reference to Wall street, and the great corporations and the rich men who supply the sinews of political war."

Fortunately, Mr. Walker's prophecy has proved incorrect. There was a time in the very near future when the objects so sacred to them would outweigh any possible advantage that might accrue to their pocketbooks by voting with those who would impose the yoke of a class distinction upon our country. It was nearer the day of retribution than even Mr. Walker, farseeing as he has demonstrated himself to be, supposed. The 8th of November was to witness the vindication upon the part of the workman of his inherent right to exercise his prerogative as an American citizen, uninfluenced by mercenary motives. Almost without an error has Mr. Walker gauged the public feeling. It is pardonable, in one who is so much nearer right than the majority, to make one single error. None of us appreciated how full were the hearts of the workingmen, the poor, and those oppressed by wealth and stung by an attempted exhibition of the privileges accorded to "caste."

"Nevertheless, there is a ground-current steadily moving across the continent. Workmen, who were wholly ignorant thirty years ago, are partly educated to-day. Within fifteen years, a highly-intelligent class has sprung up among the workmen themselves, and there are a few really able men who have been making efforts for their advancement. That man Powderly, for instance, is a statesman of a high order. He has capacity for organization, he has singleness of purpose, he has determination, and he has courage. And he is only one of a number. They have been educating their followers, and teaching them to unite upon certain simple propositions. It is like the fencing-master, who puts in the hands of his pupil the single-stick, before he confides to him the glittering rapier. There is talent enough among them to organize a movement more formidable than that of Spartacus. Thank God, they are men who love the Republic, and who hope for the elevation of their people through the evolution of the law."

Mr. Walker could have gone on and called the attention of the wealthy to the fact that, while these men loved the Republic, they did not love the foreign spirit that pervaded the would-be upper classes. It is well that a man of Mr. Walker's position should feel it incumbent upon him to compliment, or, more properly speaking, to duly appreciate, a man like Powderly. Mr. Powderly, were he not a statesman and a patriot, is possessed of dangerous powers; were it not for the great amount of virtue, honesty, and common-sense that resides in the bosoms of the masses, some dangerous, daring, and magnetic leader might spring into prominence and cause the overturning which Mr. Walker so ably depicts later in his article. Mr. Powderly, and men of his kind, have ever acted as the governing-power on this tremendous engine, called Labor, in this country. They have exhibited a degree of conservatism and consideration for the rights of the wealthy, as well as the rights of the laborer, which entitles them to the respect of all sound-minded Americans.

"Two things must always be borne in mind: First, that the laboring men have the majority, if they choose to exercise it, not only of votes, but of physical strength. Intelligence and cunning were, once upon a time, factors upon which the few rich could count to keep in subjection the many poor. The time is rapidly approaching when these will no longer avail. There is a prevailing thought that this must be a Republic, indeed, where all men shall be equal before the law; where the law will carefully guard the industrious man against the greedy man; where cunning will not place labor at the greatest of disadvantages; where labor will become honorable, and idleness contemptible; where effort will be expected from every citizen in the direction of his best talent, and where the needs of the unfortunate, through disease or inheritance, will be respected; in a word, the model government in which a near approach to the ideal Republic will be attained, an example set which the countries of Europe may well imitate. We have the opportunities here, with our rich territory, our great natural resources, and our population yet uncrowded, to do this. If we fail, the idea of a Republic may well be abandoned for the next 2,000 years."

Forcefully is it called to the minds of the fortunate possessors of wealth, by Mr. Walker, that the poor are in possession of a superior physical force. It would be well for those who enjoy the protection accorded to them and their property by this vast population, made up largely of the laboring classes, to consider what a small percentage the "wealthy" represent in the mass of 65,000,000 people. Their pronounced minority becomes apparent whenever they oppose the will of that great majority, the "Common People." Should it ever be necessary to arbitrate any question of difference by physical force, how absolutely unequal are the contending elements! Men like Mr. Powderly have ever sought to cast oil upon the turbulent waters occasioned by too much arrogance upon the part of the wealthy. It is not only equality before the law which the poor man prizes, but that equality which is rather of a sentimental than a legal nature. He recognizes no inequality as existing between the woman whom he honors as his wife and the woman whom men like Messrs. Carnegie and Frick may clothe in seal-skins and laces, and bedeck with jewels. It is not only before the law that the poor man desires to be equal. The sentimental portion of his nature is moved to create a difference, socially, resting only upon those natural inherent qualities, worth, merit, and virtue, and not that which has its foundation in the possession of wealth alone.

"That was a curious interview between the commandant of the militia, the gentleman born and bred—with an inheritance of belief regarding the rights to accumulate property, even if in so doing one crowded one's fellow-mortal to the wall —and the iron-workers who constituted the Homestead committee. Gold-spectacled, practised in the art of snubbing and sure of the physical strength at his back, the officer was more than a match for the laborer, who in his turn was awed by his inherited respect for wealth and power. Chilled and overawed, the representatives of labor went down the hill from this unequal interview. The general in charge had neither the grace nor the will to recognize a labor association which embraced a membership large enough, if properly organized, to sweep out of existence the entire army of the United States. They must have reflected, as they went down the hill, these representatives of labor, that if a militia organization carried such weight, permitted such freezing dignity upon the part of a citizen towards other citizens, it might possibly be well for their interests to have a few thousand of their own men enrolled in this same militia. There is nothing to prevent a body of American citizens from organizing themselves as a militia organization with proper arms and equipments. There are enough workmen in Pittsburg and vicinity to give a hundred regiments of the full complement of ten companies of seventy men each, with as many more left over for onlookers at parades. Six months of hard drill such as the enthusiasm of these men would permit would leave them equal to the best of the Philadelphia troops. Does anyone believe for an instant that if there had been a hundred such regiments among the workingmen of Pittsburg, General Snowden would have declared that he could not recognize the existence of such a body of men as the Amalgamated Association?"

We will assume, with Mr. Walker, that the commandant of the troops sent to Pittsburg by the Governor of Pennsylvania, was a "gentleman bred." About a man being *born* a gentleman, we may hold opinions at variance with Mr. Walker. Horses may exhibit the fact that they are thoroughbred, when intelligence in the shape of a jockey is perched upon their backs; but born gentlemen in America have never, as a rule, by their scintillating genius and danger-defying patriotism, carved out names upon the eternal monuments of the nation to rival the names of Clay,

Webster, and Lincoln. We hope that the man put in command of the Pennsylvania militia was a "gentleman bred," but the exhibition that he made of himself, while clothed with that brief authority, would not be conducive to the formation of such an opinion.

In his meeting with the citizens of the Commonwealth of Pennsylvania, who were contributing towards the payment of the taxes from which the expenses incurred by the State were to be defrayed, he did not conduct himself in a manner such as to make a shining example for those who shall command, in the future, the citizen-soldiery of the Republic. He seemed utterly oblivious to the fact that he came, not as a conquering hero, but as a private citizen, invested with a brief and circumscribed authority exercised for the greatest good to the greatest number in the prevention of lawlessness and violence and the peaceful solution of a local difficulty with which the Sheriff of the county appeared to be unable to contend. The arrogance assumed by this "gentleman bred" was not calculated to create any great amount of good feeling in the breasts of his fellow-citizens, to pacify whom he was sent by the Governor of his State. There would have been but slight loss of dignity upon his part to have allayed their anxiety by a little exercise of that "good breeding," patience, and consideration for the feelings of others, which are supposed to be characteristics of the gentleman the world over. General Ulysses S. Grant, commander of the armies of the nation, as victor in a contest of four years' duration, has set a magnificent example in the treatment of his vanquished but great opponent, Lee, by his courteous, kindly, and magnanimous behavior toward Lee and his vanquished legions whom Grant had so long faced and at last vanquished.

"I choose to ask this question as a *reductio ad absurdum*, in the hope that it will cause my own class, who have power and authority, to stop and reflect that perhaps it will be best to concede something in the way of law, to regulate this one-sided distribution of wealth, lest it should be regulated through bloodshed, or, what is more horrible still, should throw into power, through sheer brute force, elements which will bring our Republic to anarchy. If there could have been pointed out to the nobles of Louis XVI. the things which were liable to follow their arrogance, the children of these French rich would have cause for congratulation to-day."

Mr. Walker says that he chooses to ask this of men of his class. He hardly means that. Men of his class, like himself, would have brains enough not to require the question. Mr. Walker doubtless refers, in speaking of men of his own class, to the wealthy, and to them it is well addressed and worthy of their careful attention. France had its 14th of July, which should have taught Louis XVI. and his nobles the lesson which it is hoped has been learned thoroughly by the rich of this country, as taught in the result of the election of November 8, 1892. These are but the premonitory symptoms of a terrible scourge that might sweep over our country. The poor may be robbed with impunity; the "Common People" will good-naturedly submit to a lot of snubbing; but it would be well for men accustomed to exhibit their impudence and assumption, to forego the snubbing process when brought in contact with the people, as General Snowden was, while commanding the military power of the State, as he did at Homestead. General Snowden might well be taken as a type of the "smart set" of Philadelphia, imitating the manners of the McAllister "smart set" of New York.

" The fact is, we have two separate worlds in this country. The man who lives in what is known as the world of society has no conception of what the world of labor is thinking. Their worlds are almost as distinct and as completely cut off from each other as if one had its capital at Kamtchatka, and the other at Terra del Fuego. The poor do injustice to the kindly-hearted people whose minds have been warped by the teachings of inheritance and by their environment of wealth; and the rich do not dream of the thoughts which fill the minds of the poor. It is a dangerous ignorance. These two factors are like the nitre and charcoal of gunpowder. Any stray spark may produce disastrous results. The laborer believes now that the law is gradually being altered to suit what he considers the equities of his position. Let him become fairly convinced that the government is for the few, that the military is but a means of carrying out schemes of aggrandizement by the rich, and that votes are bought or majorities counted out in the same interest, and the crucial hour of the Republic will at once have arrived.

"Can science do nothing towards the solution of these difficulties? Statistics show us that if we were all to labor, no one would want for anything, neither the necessities of life, nor reasonable pleasures, nor enjoyments. Again, is there any intelligent rich man, who would not wish his sons to labor? Who does not believe that labor, in moderation, brings happiness, if only that it gives a keener zest for recreation? Who does not believe that idleness brings mental and physical injury? Who, then, would wish for his children existence in a community where idleness is to be their lot? Is there any thinking man who can feel reasonably comfortable, when only a few blocks distant, thousands are eking out a dark existence by labor that extends, in many cases, over double the allotted number of hours, who have few pleasures, and fewer still of what we call the comforts of life?"

It is not simply that those not possessed of wealth may live within a few blocks of those who are possessed of wealth; it is not that their lives may be eked out in darkness; it is the crushing shame to them that their miserable existence is made still more hard to bear by the flaunted superiority, socially, of the possessors of wealth, who live a few blocks away. Poverty, when accompanied by none of the other and more objectionable features, is not so hard to bear. The poor man believes in the dignity of labor. He does not feel degraded by the fact that he may toil with his hands. He only feels a sense of shame, and his bosom only swells with wrath, when the disdainful dames of the wealthy class presume to snub or insult his wife, the sharer of his toil and privations. She is to him the light and life of even his miserable hovel, only a few blocks away from the wealthy; hence, the keener pang that he experiences when the one bright spot in his life, sacred to him, is invaded by snobbery and pretended class distinction.

"Yet wise laws could regulate much of this in the brief period of one generation. Lighten the burdens of taxation upon the poor, by letting those whose wealth is protected by the State chiefly furnish the means of subsistence for the State, at the same time offering a discouragement to the amassing of great wealth. The well-known expedient of income-tax would be a step in this direction. Take out of the control of private individuals the power to amass great fortunes, at the expense of the public, through the management of functions like railway, express, and telegraph, which are purely of a public character. Establish a system of currency, self-regulated, by means of postal savings banks; tax highly the unimproved properties which are held for purposes of speculation. Finally, let it be a recognized principle that when men employ many laborers, their business ceases to be purely a private affair, but concerns the State, and that disputes between proprietor and workmen must be submitted, not to the brute-force of so many Pinkerton mercenaries, but to arbitration."

The espousal, by Mr. Walker, of a doctrine which, to most of the wealthy, is rank heresy,— an income tax,—is a step in the right direction. A graduated tax, to be regulated by the amount of income received and enjoyed by the taxpayer, would furnish a speedy, practicable, and just means, not only of preventing these vast accumulations in the hands of individuals, by accretions resulting from that part of their income which they are unable to spend, but it would also furnish a means whereby the Federal Government might be supported without the imposition of even the existing internal revenue tax, and only such protective tariff tax as would prove absolutely necessary to sustain our manufactures. It was a great step in the right direction, for the owner of such a prosperous magazine as the

Cosmopolitan, the possessor of much of the world's goods, to propose such an expedient for the relief of the people ; especially when coupled with the suggestion that corporations, like those of the railroads, telegraph, *et al.*, should not be controlled and managed for the profit of individuals. We should have fewer strikes, and much less labor trouble, if the Government controlled the great corporations who employ large numbers of laboring men.

This article is given prominence and so liberally quoted from—not alone from the intrinsic merit of the article and discernment of the writer in predicting the overthrow of plutocracy, and warning the rich against their insolence to those less-favored brothers, as far as worldly wealth is concerned,—but also, because of the position of the writer of the article ; a man of brains, enterprise, energy, and wealth.

THE MISTAKE AT HOMESTEAD, PA.—JULY, 1892.

CHAPTER VIII.

SURRENDER AT HOMESTEAD.—ORGANIZED LABOR DEFEATED.

IT is fitting to follow the chapter composed so largely of what Mr. Walker has written concerning the condition of affairs at Homestead, with an account of the surrender. Carnegie, the owner of castles and coaches in Scotland, the many times millionaire, and Frick, his representative, living in luxury and attempted social superiority, have vanquished the forces of organized labor. They have won the battle.

Some victories are more disastrous than defeats, and this victory, at Homestead, of capital, wealth, sham aristocracy, against the people, will teach the people to seek other methods by which their wrongs may be righted. It will show them, coming as it does just after the exhibition of the great power of the people, November 8, 1892, that their plan of action must be changed; that the effective missile to be used against the autocratic aristocrat is not the bullet, but the missive called the "ballot."

The plan of campaign of the poor "Common People" must be changed. Their defeat at

Homestead will be the precursor of a long line of victories yet to be recorded. Organizations of *voters* will spring into existence, instead of Knights of Labor. The nation will give birth (as it ever has, when necessity has demanded) to men of organizing abilities. The Carnegies and Fricks will find the ballot of organized voters more effective in preventing encroachment on the rights of the people than the bullets of the strikers at Homestead hurled at the hirelings of Pinkerton. As Mr. Walker so ably says, in a conflict of physical force, the people—that is, the poor—are superior ; when, according to law, they deposit their ballots, they will enforce the election of the chosen of the majority in spite of all the private armies of the Carnegies and Fricks. And, should that occasion arise, the militia and General Snowden will be found acting *with* the people in defending the rights of the people. There will be no insolence and arrogance then upon the part of the commander of the militia ; for, after an election wherein the people have legally chosen their representatives and legislators, not one militiaman would obey the orders of the " well-bred " gentleman of Philadelphia, if such orders were contrary to the will of the majority as expressed at a legal election.

The representatives of the first grade of "caste" have won at Homestead ! In their "well-bred" bosoms, exultation may be the feeling of the hour. Enjoy the brief respite in the fullness of selfishness; but the hour is at hand when, according to the laws as enacted by legally-elected representatives, the people of the Union shall fill your "well-bred" bosoms with a sorrow and disappointment occasioned by your arrogance, selfishness, and disregard of their claim for respectful treatment upon your part of their representatives of organized labor. When their representatives, as *organized voters*, issue their mandates, no supercilious commander of militia, blessed with a little brief authority, will dare resist them.

Organized labor is defeated at Homestead. Organized labor, organized in heart and spirit, if not by an expressed Association, won a great battle November last. The victory of the sham aristocracy at Homestead was but a skirmish. The victory at the polls in November was a Waterloo and Gettysburg rolled into one. The commander-in-chief of the victorious army is Grover Cleveland. In his hands the people place the power of their support—the great majority. He represents the choice of the "Common People"— not because he's a Democrat—not because the people have become Democratic, in the narrow sense of the word, but because Cleveland represents to their minds the opposition to sham aristocracy, "caste."

Grover Cleveland is an exponent of that sentiment that made Abraham Lincoln President in '61 ; Jackson, President in '28 ; Jefferson, President in 1800. Call the party by whom he was nominated any name that best suits the fancy of the speaker. It's the same grand old, broad party of the people ; triumphant now as it ever will be, God grant, in this Republic! We want no Republic in America like that of Venice. The people have entrusted Grover Cleveland with the executive power of the nation. At his hands they will expect the righting of those wrongs which these petty tyrants, sham aristocrats, believers in social distinction and "caste," have inflicted upon the people. They have chosen representatives in Congress who control both branches of the legislature, through whom the people shall express their will and pleasure ; and the people will expect of Grover Cleveland, as they did of Abraham Lincoln, Jackson, and Jefferson, the execution of their wishes. The people have never been disappointed by the actions of their former chieftains in this matter. When made ohief magistrate of the nation, every former leader of the people has executed the will of the masses, according to the laws as enacted. No former chief magistrate has ever presumed to use his power of veto contrary to the will of the people as expressed by a majority of their representatives.

The eyes of the nation are upon Grover Cleveland. In return for the defeat in their skirmish at Homestead, the people will expect to reap the fruits of their victory in the great battle of ballots last November. Long have they suffered, and now that the golden opportunity has arrived, the people are not to be thwarted. With kindly but scrutinizing gaze, the people regard their new leader, Grover Cleveland.

The New York *Sun*, of November 20th, in an account of the defeat of the Amalgamated Association, prints the following :—

"A prominent member of the Association was seen at his house this afternoon. His grate was piled high with burning pamphlets. Pointing to them, he said :

"'I have no more use for them. They contain the laws and rules of the Amalgamated Association, and I have taken this means to be rid of them. I hardly think the Amalgamated lodges will be continued here, as nothing can be derived from membership in it. A potent fact in losing the strike was that too many of our men returned to work, and this helped the company to get its mills into working order. It was not the company, but our own men, that lost the strike.'"

This prominent member of the Association, who was engaged in burning the laws and rules of the Amalgamated Association, was inadvertently acting in accordance with the unexpressed thought that the people had found a surer means of righting their wrongs than that furnished by associated labor. They had learned that their power, when opposed to the rich and aristocratic, was better utilized in the exercise of the ballot than when expressed through associated labor and associations of crafts and certain kinds of labor. If the Carnegies and Fricks were wise, they would view with fear and trembling the disruption of this thing called organized labor, which has been a toy by which the people have been amused and entertained and diverted from the use of their most effective weapon, the ballot.

Organized labor and association have proved a pretty tin toy sword, which was attractive to gaze at upon a holiday parade, but utterly valueless in actual warfare. Its absolute inefficiency was never more clearly demonstrated, because it had never been so thoroughly tested in any previous contest of labor, as at Homestead.

Here is given concisely—as that most excellent journal, the New York *Sun*, always presents all matters of public interest—an account of the cost of the strike to the laborers, to the capitalist, and to the State of Pennsylvania. Even the most careless reader and the most superficial inquirer after truth will read in this statement the evidence of the brave and valiant battle made by labor, which was defeated because the very sword it fought with was not of the kind of metal for actual warfare. The Ballot! the Ballot! the Ballot! is the weapon of the future :—

"It is almost impossible to give figures at this time on the cost of the strike, but conservative estimates place it at about $10,000,000. Of this, about $2,500,000 were in wages to the men. The firm's loss is thought to be two or three times that. The direct cost of the troops was nearly half a million. The indirect loss has been very large indeed.

"This contest was brought on by a demand for a reduction of wages of about $33\frac{1}{3}$ per cent. on certain classes of work in the open hearth departments, Nos. 1 and 2 mills, and in the 119-inch and 32-inch plate mills. This reduction directly affected only about 325 out of the 3,800 men in the works, but the others took up the matter as a common cause through sympathy, and agreed to stand by the men interested in case of a strike.

"The scale expired under which they were working on June 30th. The company wanted the Amalgamated Association, which controlled the workmen in the mills, to sign the scale at the reduction. The scale was to be renewed on January 1st, instead of July 1st. The Association refused, and the men threatened to strike should the request for the existing scale not be granted before July.

"On June 30th, the company locked out all men before they had the opportunity to strike.

The wages question was soon lost sight of, and the contest for the recognition of organized labor followed. On the dawn of July 6th, the famous battle took place between the workmen on the mill property and the Pinkerton force attempting to land and take possession of the mill.

"Then followed the trying times at Homestead, the reign of the Advisory Board, the scenes of lawlessness, the calling out of the troops, their long and trying stay, the shooting of Mr. Frick by Berkman, the departure of the troops, the arrest of the Homesteaders, the beginning of their trials, and now the ending of the strike.

"According to Superindent Wood, of the Homestead works, not more than 800 or 900 of the total number of old employés will be able to secure employment. Before the break of last Thursday, there were left in Homestead about 2,800 of the original 3,800 men who were locked out. Of these 2,800 men, 2,200 were mechanics and laborers and 600 Amalgamated Association men.

If Carnegie, Frick, son-in-law W. Seward Webb, of the New York Central Road, and men of that class can find any comfort in this evidence that the "Common People" have at last realized the utter lack of merit in their weapons, called "Organizations and Associations of Labor," then most heartily are they to be congratulated. Let them enjoy for a brief period their dreams of autocratic power ; for there will be a sad awakening as the result of the realization upon the part of the people that the ballot-box is the place for effective battle, and not the lodge rooms of Associations and Organizations.

Grover Cleveland is the Grand Master of the great Organization of the Associated People, who legally will now enforce the demands of the " Common People."

The defeated laborer, mechanic, and workman of Homestead has a prospect before him, so full of hope and promise, presenting a picture so pleasing to his oppressed soul, that the scene of his disastrous defeat becomes obliterated. Let him turn from those days of suffering, so vividly portrayed by the *Herald* of November 25th :—

" There were dozens of tables in Homestead to-day where the Thanksgiving Day bird was absent, and on many of these tables hunger was the only sauce in sight.

" To-day while plenty ruled in American homes, starvation and cold were closing their grip on the families of the Homestead strikers. While the horn of plenty unrolled its golden store into the hands of the nation, there were children in Homestead crying for bread, with weeping mothers and despairing fathers.

" While well-clothed citizens were going to highly respectable churches to return thanks, there were people in Homestead shivering over scant fires, wondering where the next meal would come from. There were men with shoes so full of holes and clothes so ragged as to barely cover them.

"The present sufferings of these men, women, and children were made all the keener by their forebodings of the future; of a winter without work, to be passed at the gates of starvation; with no work to be had at the Carnegie mills or any other mills on account of the terrible blacklist."

The question will arise in the mind of the poor man, when recalling HIS Thanksgiving dinner, With what did Andrew Carnegie and H. C. Frick feed their families that day? With what kind of conscience did they bow the knee and raise their voices in their costly churches and address the throne of the lowly Jesus, who left in the records of His life, utterances like these:—

"If thou wilt be perfect, go and sell that thou hast, and give to the poor." "Sell that ye have, and give alms."

The answer which will force itself upon the minds of the "Common People" will not be such as to lessen or moderate the demands which they will make for the fruits of their victory in November.

They have endured much; they have starved at Homestead; they have been cold and hungry; they have been led astray by false gods; but the Land of Canaan is now spread before them. The ballot-box has become their guiding star and hope. The bitter experience endured that Thanksgiving Day will prove a benefit to them in removing from them the danger of relying upon the tin sword in future. Every line of this article in the *Herald* is full of danger to the insolent power of the rich, arrogant, sham aristocrats. It is brimming over with a lesson that the blindest is bound to read by the light of the recently-achieved victory of the people :—

CANNOT LEAVE HOMESTEAD.

" Dozens there are who cannot leave Homestead or its vicinity. They are under heavy bonds to appear in the Allegheny County courts on charges of murder, treason, and riot. To stay means starvation, because here they will find little or no work. To go means to be sent to jail, because bondsmen are fearful and do not relish the idea of forfeiting thousands of dollars.

" Most of the storekeepers in Homestead have ceased to give the locked-out men credit. If they did, it would mean bankruptcy. All of them are already creditors for hundreds and in some cases thousands of dollars, with poor prospects of getting any of it back for months, possibly years.

" The last strike benefits that will be paid by the Amalgamated Association have been received by the idle men. Right here be it said that these benefits were by no means as reported during the strike. Not one-half of the men got $4 a week, and the majority received about $2 a week.

The Homestead steel-workers and their families are in need of almost everything that goes to make life comfortable. All need clothing more or less. One man I met to-day was trying to prevent the biting wind from sweeping a well-ventilated straw hat from his head.

"Then there is fuel. There is hardly a street or roadway in Homestead on which there did not stand a house or several of them in which the cold stoves made the temperature more frigid by contrast. Those families that did burn coal or wood did so through the kindness of the neighbors or the good-will of the fuel merchant.

PLAYING THANKSGIVING.

"In walking through Homestead to-day I passed a vacant lot on Fourth avenue, in which a fire was burning. The fuel consisted of logs dragged from the river. Surrounding the fire were ill-clad boys and girls. They were keeping warm and roasting potatoes. One of the boys told me that 'Maw hadn't much for dinner at home, and we are playing Thanksgiving.'

"This was their feast.; they were children of the strikers, who lived in a clump of shanties near by."

Playing Thanksgiving ! God of justice ! look down upon such a picture. Playing at praying ! Absolutely making a game and jest of thanking Thee ! So cynical has become the hearts of even these children, caused by the oppression and injustice of the oppressor, that they would make a game, a jest, of giving thanks to the Giver of all good things ! because the good things were on the tables of Carnegie, Frick, Webb, and others, while they, somebody's children—poor, "Common People's" children, perhaps—were cold, ragged, and hungry; making a feast of half-burned potatoes, veritably, in a spirit of irony. So hard and desolate has become the destiny of the poor of our land that the children cease to be natural, loving, gentle, and sincere, and have become ironical, sarcastic, holding so lightly the respect due to the God of all men, that they make a jest of the day consecrated to rendering thanks to the Giver of all good things of life!

A picture like this, for which the sham aristocrats are absolutely responsible, does more to arouse a feeling of socialism and anarchism in the breasts of even the best citizens, than all the ravings of crazed nihilistic leaders. Stop such scenes now! Socialism and anarchism have no foothold in America. Don't allow these dangerous "isms" to form an entering wedge. Such scenes as those poor children, playing Thanksgiving, are the greatest allies of the socialists and anarchists.

The gentleman (?) known as Ollie Teall should receive, at the hands of the disciples of anarchy and socialism, a medal for his valuable services in attempting to present a picture to the delectation of the assembled "Four Hundred," of the children of the poor feeding (as animals, poor creatures!) in Madison Square Garden, last

Christmas. This man, Teall, may have no qualities to recommend him other than this, that he is a superlative example of those who would create a state of anarchy in this country.

It was his proposition, so it appears from the newspapers, to make a kind of horse-show at Madison Square Garden, wherein the children of the poor should perform the part of the horses, the animals. It was proposed to sell boxes to the rich, that they might sit around and behold the exhibition of the animals ! To the originators of this novel exhibition is due the thanks and praises of the anarchists, who have sought a haven here, for they played into the hands held by the anarchists with wonderful precision.

We must all respect the courage and manliness of one man who, justly conceiving his duty as a teacher of the doctrine of his Master, arose and protested. Yes, and he was worth more than a brigade of soldiers in quieting the wrath of the people, the Rev. Dr. Rainsford, of St. George Episcopal church, in Brooklyn, and let his name be remembered for his courage in denouncing the most damnable exhibition of the tendency of the "Four Hundred" of New York. The name of the Rev. Dr. Rainsford, of the St. George Episcopal Church, will ever be remembered by the poor as that of a man, a Christian, an American, and a gentleman. Vigorous was his denunciation of the spectacular exhibition of the feeding of the poor like so many cattle.

Yes, fair "Four Hundred," as the nobles of France told the peasants to "eat grass" and were amused at their attempts of the performance, so you would feed a lot of poor children in Madison Square Garden, and take stalls and boxes to look on at the peculiar performances of the hungry eating ! You know that each child is but the coming American man or woman. You would make a Roman holiday to exhibit the necessities of the People, who are your rulers. Delightful entertainment for the exclusive " Four Hundred,"—to sit around with their many millions and gaze at the ravenous appetites exhibited by the children of the poor. It was a holiday like the holidays in Rome, when the nobles assembled to see the persecuted Christians torn and mangled by every form of beast that, by research, could be brought to the Roman arena. Dr. Rainsford, thou art "a man for a' that."

Do you wonder, millionaires, why the people whose children you would exhibit to create a carnival for you, did not vote with you November 8, 1892 ? Of the purchasers of the boxes at Madison Square Garden for this unique performance, ninety per cent. were Republicans. Shades of Abraham Lincoln, look down and see the strong oak of thy creation benumbed by this parasite entwined around it! Imagine the creator, the originator, the father of the Republican party, this high priest in the hearts of the "Common People," Abraham Lincoln, at such a scene. He would have been down with the children. In his loving arms he would have held the children of the poor. And these "Four Hundred," a little better than the "Common People," would look on at the feeding of the "common folks," and, from their assumed exalted position, view the performance gotten up by their money, and would have had a sensation of almost hunger aroused where abundance had produced satiety. The proposition to hold such an exhibition as the feeding of the poor children in Madison Square Garden was in itself an insult to every American citizen. Imagine, fair lady, as you loll in your carriage drawn by your high-priced bays on Fifth avenue, how pleasant it would be to have your little curled and perfumed darling, left at home under the watchful eye of some imported French *bonne*, exhibited as a freak in a dime museum. Think of the tears that should be shed on a mother's bosom, being paraded before the public as an object of amusement. A child's sorrows and its joys are as sacred as the law of God delivered to Moses on Sinai, for a child has more of God in it ; and you would make of the children of the poor, and their wants, and needs, and appetites, a spectacle that you may pay so much money and see?

The lisped prayer of the child of the poor ascends to the throne of God as surely, though it proceed from a hovel or the gutter, as that from the downy couch of the ease of luxury in the palace on Fifth avenue. Do not the poor love their children with the same earnestness and fervor as the rich? Have you to learn this lesson anew? Need you wonder, you people who seem astonished at the result of election, why the mighty voice of the people should be raised against you? You who wonder why the party of you," the respectable," should have been so overwhelmingly defeated, recall to mind the contemplated carnival you would have held in Madison Square Garden, feeding like pigs, the children of the poor, and thank God that the volcano upon which in seeming security you rested found a vent without tossing you heavenward. There would have been rivers of blood instead of lava; the ballot of 1892 was your salvation.

Slumbering wrath was in the breasts of the people. One Robespierre or Danton would have set aflame this feeling, and the "Common People" only need a leader, an organizer who will teach them under form of law that their mighty voice is paramount, and the sham aristocracy will be crushed and annihilated, as was a better aristocracy in France in the latter part of the eighteenth century. Don't let history repeat itself.

Can such pictures as depicted in these few lines of the *Herald* about those poor children's Thanksgiving dinner, the feast proposed by the " Four Hundred " at Madison Square Garden, be accurate and represent scenes in free America, the richest, freest, best country on earth? or are these some occurrences seen in poor, starving, Czar-ridden Russia ? A bow of promise was in the sky that Thanksgiving Day, however. The people had spoken a few days before. They had selected their representatives to make laws relieving them of the presence of such scenes as above described. They had selected an Executive of unquestioned honesty, who will execute such laws as will emanate from the representatives of the people.

The people had given no sign, but in silence had been thinking of scenes like that proposed at Madison Square Garden. They had voted November the 8th in silence.

Silence is often more dangerous than utterance. The deadly cobra gives no signal before he strikes. " General apathy" and the silence of the people was deadly earnest, and you know whether it was forceful or not. And if the party that the people have put in power will not do the will of the people, then the people will put some other party in power which *will* execute the desire of the masses. It is a quicksand that the rich tread upon. So accustomed have the rich become to the patience, long-enduring suffering of the poor, that they deem it impossible that any condition could exist other than the present. Only remember that Charles Stuart, Louis XVI., Tarquin, all thought it was impossible that aught could interfere with the set order of things; but righteous indignation, the wrath of the people, like a whirlwind may obliterate the little edifices of dust built upon the past.

The rest of the story, so vividly portrayed by the *Herald*, is worthy of consideration and attention:—

"I visited the house of J. W. Grimes, a striker, on the hillside, above the mill. He had a pair of rubbers on his feet. The rubbers were worn away and had been sewed together with twine. 'You see, my shoes are so bad,' said the millman, apologetically, 'that I have to wear these rubbers. Jim Sweeney threw them away, but I found them and sewed them up,' and he exhibited a shoe that would almost have fallen from his foot, but for the rubber which held it.

"Grimes was doing the family washing when I met him. His arms were covered with soapsuds. He told me his wife was very sick. He had been injured in the mill before the strike and had been able to save but little. Since the strike he has been able to get only a few days' work, and his wife took in washing and did scrubbing to keep the family in bread. Now she is near death's door, a mere apparition, while her husband has no work and there is little in the house.

"I went to the house of Bridget Coyle, who, during her testimony in the Critchlow case the other day, said she would not tell a lie for all the money Carnegie is worth. Two of her boys worked in the mill; one has secured work in another city, but is making barely enough to keep himself. Another son is at Homestead, and idle. 'We have enough in the house to keep us another week,' said Mrs. Coyle, ' but after that the Lord knows what we'll do. I just got a little coal on trust, and do wish I had a pair of shoes.

"'We own this little house; my son paid the last on it just before the strike.' She had rented out a couple of rooms to Joshua Bradshaw, a millman, with his wife and four children. 'They owe me six months' rent, but Lord, I know they can't pay it, so I don't ask them. They are poor people, and the missus is badly sick.'

"Patrick Sweeney, another ex-striker, who can't get work in the mill, and who lives on Sixteenth street, has been hunting for a pair of shoes for several days. Those he has were shoes once, now they are tatters. Sweeney, like dozens of the other men, has paid no rent for several months, and lives in daily dread that his family will be evicted. Being blacklisted, he cannot find work in Homestead or elsewhere.

"William Davis, of Fourteenth street, told me there wasn't a pound of coal in his house, and a little less in the house of his mother, who lives alongside of him."

AN APPEAL FOR AID.

"The instances mentioned are only an index to the suffering. Through personal pride most of the misery in Homestead is hidden as yet. When winter sets in, dozens of cases will come to light.

"On Saturday a meeting will be held to issue a call for aid. It has been called by Elmer Bales and John Wilson.

"Mr. Bales said to-day: 'There is positive suffering in Homestead from lack of food, fuel, and clothing. The sufferers will not speak of their distress to you or any other outsider, but we who live here know of it only too well. In a week or two it will be much worse.'

"Hugh O'Donnell did not eat any turkey in the Allegheny county jail. There was no observance of Thanksgiving in his case. He was compelled to put up with the regular prison fare, which is not fattening to those who have tried it."

Capital has vanquished labor at Homestead; but the skirmish left scars which will long remain unforgotten. Labor suffered, and learned that the power of the people resided in their presence at the polls on election day, when Carnegie, Frick, Webb, and others of the sham aristocrats and believers in "caste," became of no more importance than each poor laborer, workman, mechanic, clerk, shopkeeper, or farmer, to whom on other days they assumed an air of superiority. The learning of the lesson was worth all the suffering that it cost the "Common People," as represented by the workmen and strikers at Homestead, Pa.

CHAPTER IX.

POSSIBLE FRUITS OF VICTORY.

WE have considered, and we hope with charitable eyes, the scenes resulting from the victory in that skirmish at Homestead, between Carnegie, Frick, and the Common People; we have thought of the result of the picket fire at Buffalo between organized labor and the combination of capital represented by the New York Central Railroad; both of which engagements, while only out-post encounters of the on-marching army of the Common People, were decisive victories for the capitalists, the sham aristocrats, believers in "caste." In the name of law and order (so dear to the American heart) they had appealed to the power of the State to protect, with militia, their property, and that militia, ever loyal and truly American, had responded to the call of the Executives (both Democrats) of the two most powerful States in the Union. That militia, largely composed of poor men, and men of the people, absolutely abhorring anything like the disregard of established laws, had responded to the call of the Governor of each respective State, New York and Pennsylvania. Law and order were re-established by the people of which the militia is but part. Two Democratic Governors, like patriotic citizens that they are, had bowed their heads before enacted laws—no matter what their personal feeling may have been upon the subject—and granted protection to the property of the capitalists, who, as citizens of each State, were entitled thereto, no matter by what means the capitalists and sham aristocrats may have acquired that property. The result of the action of these two Governors, and the acquiescence by the people and the support of the militia, is incontestible evidence that Socialism and Anarchism have no home in America.

The people accepted the result, as did the people of Homestead starvation and distress, because its presence at every hearth became a matter of trifling consequence; each hearth of the poor "Common People" of America is illuminated and warmed by the patriotic fires lighted thereon by our forefathers in 1776. The law must be obeyed! As long as that law exists, unrepealed, unmodified, or unamended, it must be obeyed! And the might of the people, the "Common People," the Abraham Lincoln party, the Andrew Jackson party, the Thomas Jefferson party, and the Grover Cleveland party, all guarantee the enforcement of every law upon our statute-books. And the chiefest of these is the Constitution of the United States of America, wherein is guaranteed the franchise of every citizen ; wherein is declared that the "majority shall rule in America." The poor, the "Common People," have suffered defeat in their strikes and attempted resistance to the claim of social difference existing in our country. They have borne the arrogance, insults, and wrongs inflicted by a sham aristocracy. All attempts at correction of the evil have proved abortive.

On November 8, 1892, the "Common People" resorted to that most efficacious of remedies in this great Republic, the ballot-box ; and their victory was as great and pronounced as their suffering had been severe in the past. As the fruit of their victory, as in 1860, they will place in the Presidential chair at Washington a MAN OF THE PEOPLE—Grover Cleveland—whom they believe to be honest, as they believed that Abraham Lincoln was honest, in 1860. They have elected the men of their choice, men representing the "Common People," to both branches of the Legislature of the National Government. They have selected those who will express the sentiments of the "Common People" in the legislative halls of the nation. They, the "Common People," will be heard through their representatives in the Congress of the Union.

From the sad picture of unsuccessful strikes, starvation, and destitution, let us turn to the more pleasing picture of the possibilities offered by this exhibition of the POWER OF THE PEOPLE.

Carnegie, Frick, Webb, and others, have enjoyed a transient, delusive dream in which the delights of victory were enjoyed for the moment. Now comes the time of the people! They have learned that their power does not lie in associations, amalgamations, and organization. It lies in the selection by the majority, at the ballot-box, of representatives who will express the will of the people in making the laws of the land, such laws as will enforce and insure equality, the extinction of "caste," and the protection of the poor men, who constitute the larger portion of the population of our country, and are therefore greater, being the majority on election day, than the rich, sham aristocrats, who have insulted, jeered, and snubbed the poor during the past twenty-five years.

Now will come the crucial test of the honesty and fidelity reposed, by the people, in the administration and legislative bodies elected by them. Should they prove recreant and traitors to the trust reposed in them, it would be the first time in the history of the nation (with possibly the single exception of John Tyler, who became President by the death of William Henry Harrison). Then, should the will of the people become manifest through the agency of their representatives, in Congress assembled, whereby the present laws be repealed; if it become evident that it was the will of the people that the Constitution of the United States should be amended, so as to be in accordance with the laws the enactment of which the people demanded, the legislators would be obliged to so amend and change the Constitution of the United States to make it consistent with the will of the people. Rock and foundation of the edifice of the Federal Government, the Constitution as it is, that which is more powerful than even the Constitution is the will of the people, the majority of the citizens of the Union, irrespective of wealth or assumed social position. It has been demonstrated that by some peculiar kind of method the wealth of the nation is becoming centralized in the hands of a few families and persons who render possible the construction of an oligarchy similar to that existing in the Republic of Venice.

Suppose that the people should demand and insist upon the passage of an income tax for the support of the Federal Government, which would relieve them, the "Common People," from paying for the privileges enjoyed by the rich, of living in a Republic and the security which their property there enjoys.

And, suppose that the sham aristocracy should cry, "Inherent Rights," as they would; the people might respond that it is not a question as to the Inherent Right of Mr. Astor, Mr. Vanderbilt, Mr. Rockefeller, *et al.*, to possess, under the present system of laws, any amount of property. It is a mere question of the Will of the People. Many good, learned, and great Constitutional lawyers have argued, and with much apparent truth, that the federation of States prior to 1865 was but a mutual copartnership entered into by the sovereign States, springing from the original thirteen colonies, constituting but a copartnership, surrendering no right to the firm or copartnership except such rights as had been specifically named in the Federal Constitution.

Without entering into the legal aspects of the case, as to whether these claims be just or not; without assuming to know whether the nullification proposed by John C. Calhoun was legally sound; without discussing the question whether South Carolina and the other States of the South had a *right* to secede and disintegrate the Union; assuming that they had the right, inherently, and to draw a parallel to the assumed Inherent Right of the rich of America under the laws and the Constitution as they now exist, their attention might be attracted profitably to the lesson that was taught the minority in the South when they assumed to exercise Inherent Rights contrary to the wishes of the majority. 2,800,000 bayonets, with the flag of the Union floating over them, was conclusive argument that the Inherent Rights claimed by the Southern States were actually Wrongs in a Republic.

"Vox populi, vox Dei." The voice of the people, the majority, is the voice of God in a Republic, from which there is *no appeal.* Seek it, as the South did in 1861, and the result will be the same. THE MAJORITY WILL RULE.

Suppose that the Common People should demand a repeal of all the revenue laws, a repeal of all tariff duties and protection which did not result in direct benefit to them; suppose that they should insist that, except so far as protection benefited them (the " Common People ") by an increase of wages, which should be arrived at by a fair adjustment of the conflicting interests of capital and labor, adjusted by a board of arbitration selected by them, the Common People; suppose that the people should demand that these tremendous incomes enjoyed by the Vanderbilts, Astors, Goulds, Carnegies, Fricks, and others, should pay the pensions of the Federal soldiers who fought for the preservation of the Union ; suppose the people should demand that the expenses of the Federal Government, instead of being levied upon *them*, should be levied upon the incomes of those who remained at home in safety during the four years of the Civil War ; who, while far away from the field of battle, have speculated upon the necessities and needs of the nation, who have utilized that protection, born in a spirit of patriotic desire to furnish means for the support of the defenders of the Union, emanating from patriotic principles of the Abraham Lincoln Republican party ; suppose that the people should demand that they— not out of the accumulated mass, but out of the interest upon the amount accumulated under existing laws—which said laws the people, through their representatives, shall deem wise to change— requiring that in the future these masters of immense wealth shall contribute a share to the defraying of the expenses of the Government commensurate with the advantages they have derived, from the load of debt, in the shape of pensions and otherwise, occasioned by the Civil War, wherein the Union was preserved.

Let us imagine a scale of income tax for the people of America : $5000 and under, untaxed ; $5000 and over, to be taxed. If the chosen representatives of the people, selected by them last November and to be selected by the various State Legislatures elected by the people within the near future, refuse to make such an enactment as an income tax upon all incomes of more than $5000; suppose the people organize themselves, and call upon the country in a general election; gentlemen of aristocratic proclivities, where will you be? Of the mass of freeborn American citizens (quite asgood as the sham aristocrats) not five per cent. enjoy an income as great as $5000. Would you resort to physical force? The Hon. J. Brisben Walker, in his article in the *Cosmopolitan*, indicates the true position that you would occupy. Consider the possibility. Yell " Unconstitutional." Proclaim that it is illegal. The people would change the Constitution. By the voice of the majority, they would change the laws.

What have you to offer to stem this tide of indignation that you have provoked? Do you say, "Capital would leave the country?" Well, you can't carry the railroads, the factories, the soil, the buildings from America. You may have your castles in Scotland, but we have your plants of machinery, your buildings, and that upon which your security depends and is founded is in our power in America. Would you secede, as the Plebeians proposed to do from the Patricians at

Rome, and found a city on the Sacred Hills of your sham aristocracy? The Plebeians, the Common People, would never seek you with the olive branch of peace and promise offers of compromise, as did the Patricians of old seek the Plebeians, but they would recall to your attention in forceful manner the lesson taught to the Southerners in 1861, when the "Common People," the majority in America, by their might, overpowered and overturned the seceders who, when they found that the minority, even though blessed with an attempted social superiority, could not rule in the American Republic, sought to secede.

The Carnegies, Vanderbilts, Astors, Fricks, and others, would be as helpless in such a struggle, and never as brave and earnest, as was Lee's decimated army at Appomattox.

What the people *should* or *will* do, it does not interest us to discuss. What they *can* do is to require that the payment of the taxes for the support of the nation be derived from those sources which have become hateful and oppressive to the people; and, at a general election, the men who form the majority would be those whose incomes do not exceed $5000—no, not even $2000 per annum.

Then, let us establish for the fancy of our sham aristocrats a picture for those who believe in the crime of "Caste" in our country, to dwell upon. The victors at Homestead and at Buffalo would do well, while imbibing the sweet draughts of victory, to consider the bitter cup of hemlock that the people can require them to partake of. Anything is possible in a Republic, by the votes of the majority.

All incomes less than five thousand dollars to be entirely exempt from taxation; from five to ten thousand, a tax of five per cent.; from ten to twenty thousand, ten per cent.; from twenty to fifty, twenty per cent.; from fifty to a hundred, forty per cent.; from a hundred to two hundred, fifty per cent.; from two hundred thousand to half a million, seventy-five per cent.; from half a million and onward, ninety per cent.

There is no pretence in this scale to be equitable or just. That could be arrived at by the statistician and the legislators. It is merely an example of what the people CAN AND MAY DO. The fund thus derived would more than defray all the expense of the Federal Government, pensions included, and increase the pensions besides.

What is to prevent the enactment of such a law, if the majority should demand it?

You may say, Gentlemen of the Privileged Classes, "It is contrary to the spirit of the Republic. It will amount to confiscation." To men of the Carnegie, Frick, and Webb stamp the people might reply, "Was the hiring of armed bullies, outcasts, and residents of other States consistent with the spirit of the Republic? When you have formed those hirelings into a private army to do your bidding against the lives of your fellow citizens, is it not late in the day for you to call up 'the Spirit of the Republic'? You have gloated in triumph over your victories and the wants of the people. You have seen us surrounded by starvation and destitution. You, professing Christianity, have made us objects of your contempt and insult. Our daughters have not been safe from the contaminating gaze of your weak, puerile progeny. You have adopted crests, castes, social distinctions, sham aristocracy. You have bowed the knee before the degenerate British peerage. You have taken the money earned by our labor to purchase alliances with the decayed aristocracy of Europe. Is it not *late*, good my would-be lords and barons, to call up the Spirit of 1776?"

And, even should it come, like the spectres of the dream of Richard III., would it not make you quake and quiver, so contrary are your wishes to the spirit of the founders of the Union?

"Impracticable, the collection of these taxes," is one of the excuses for their non-imposition.

The people have trusted Grover Cleveland with the power of executing the laws of the nation. The people believe that, as Lincoln, Jackson, and Jefferson, he will not be recreant to the trust reposed in him. He will collect the taxes; he will seize the property of the corporations; he will imprison the perjurers. He will perform the duties imposed upon him, in the high office of the nation to which the will of the people has called him. He will see that the mandates of the people are obeyed. This tremendous accumulation of fortunes must cease! A Vanderbilt leaves a hundred million to one son! At five per cent. per annum, the income is five millions each year. It is impossible for him to spend it. The difference between his expenses and his income is added to this mighty mass of money, which is concentrating each year more and more, compounding the interest thereon, in the hands of a few citizens of the Republic. Mr. Gould dies and leaves a hundred millions. If evenly distributed between his children, it would be impossible for the income to be spent, and it would simply accumulate, generation after generation. The Astors have adopted a habit, like most of the rich men of the nation, in imitation of English entailment, of leaving the bulk of their property to the eldest son, while apportioning off the younger children with a million or two. The impossibility of that elder son spending the income is perfectly apparent. The object is to accumulate, in the hands of a few families, the wealth of the nation. The tendency is exactly in that direction.

Not only is it un-American, but especially obnoxious to the people generally, as it tends toward the accumulation of wealth, not only to an unwholesome but to an alarming degree, in the hands of the eldest sons of these families. It is practically the entailment of the estate, without so announcing it. Let us take, for example, the Goulds, Vanderbilts, or Astors, and let this peculiar kind of distribution of their property continue, apportioning out the younger members of the family with a comparatively small sum, but leaving the bulk to the first son. Is it not concentrating wealth in the hands of one man, the income of which it is impossible that he should spend? The accumulation still goes on from generation to generation until, practically, the money power of our land lies within the grasp of the representatives of a few families. Let us imagine the condition of affairs a few hundred years hence, if we allow the Vanderbilts, Goulds, Rockefellers and Astors to apportion off, from generation to generation, the younger sons and daughters of the family, concentrating the vast accumulation from the interests of their tremendous fortunes in the hands of one representative of the family. Some dozen men of this great Republic, by a combination, could then practically control at all times the financial situation of the nation. There is no possibility of an equalizing process and the scattering of the wealth and accumulations of these families. From generation to generation, under this peculiar method of distribution and disposal adopted by our would-be nobility, there would be created a condition exactly similar to that existing in the pre-eminently commercial Venice, from which thraldom the Common People were only relieved by a foreign conqueror, Napoleon, whom they welcomed with unpatriotic joy because he brought relief from the discriminations with which the masses were cursed.

No one will deny that, under the existing laws, Mr. W. H. Vanderbilt, the gentleman (?) who so forcefully and elegantly expressed himself in the utterance of his sentiments, "The public be damned," had a perfect right, under the laws as they now exist, to leave the bulk of his property to his eldest son. Nay, he might have called him the Duke of Vanderbilt, if he pleased. By the pleasure of the people, he had the right to dispose of his possessions as to him seemed best.

WM. H. VANDERBILT,
AUTHOR OF THE FAMOUS SPEECH, "THE PUBLIC BE D——D."

This is all perfectly within the bounds of and consistent with the laws that the people have made; but remember, that these people who made these laws can UNMAKE them; they can require that a man's property shall be equally divided among all of his children; they can tax it so that this infernal and ever-increasing income shall not create such an accumulation as to present a danger to the life and existence of the Republic. And this is not against the law. Good my lords, as the barons, the Common People will kill this "caste," not by the headsman's axe that decapitated the Stuart, not by the guillotine that drank the blood of a Bourbon; but they'll do it with legislation, more peaceful, more quiet, and with more "general apathy;" but the result will be just as efficacious.

Now that the nation, composed of the Common People of America, has suffered the assumption, upon the part of these few families, of a sham aristocracy and attempted "caste" in this country; suppose, when the people have felt the power that lies in them, that they should rise in their might and decree that the support of the Federal Government shall come from that surplus income, instead of permitting it to accumulate in the hands of each succeeding generation of a few families in America. What, again it may be asked, can the sham aristocrats do about it?—you people of the Carnegie, Astor, Vanderbilt class. The people decree it, and you must bow your heads to their will.

The people are not socialistic. They do not believe in the division of property. Men like Dolan, at the Clover Club in Philadelphia, and others of his kind, deliberately libel and traduce the Common People when they pretend to explain the defeat of the Republican party upon the ground of a socialistic tendency in the people of this nation. The lie is apparent by the action of the militia, composed of the Common People, both at Homestead and Buffalo. The people are for law and order.

The poor man's morals are quite as good or better than the morals of the rich. His home is as sacred, and the slimy serpent of Nihilism is as objectionable in his home as it would be to the millionaire in his palace of grandeur. The little holdings of the poor man, his farm, his tool chest, and his furniture, are his; and he holds the right to own them as dear as Astor holds his right to his property in many hundred houses. The poor man, the Common People, nowhere in this broad Union wants anarchy. He'll stamp it out, as he did in Chicago, and it is a libel upon him and the nation, for the rich and those who would impose the yoke of "caste," to attempt to wave the bloody shirt of Socialism by their speeches on this subject.

But this accumulation of property in the hands of the few, to the detriment of the nation, has become so pronounced and overwhelming in its productiveness of evil that, suppose the people should—for they could, by means of an income tax—decree that it should cease. Now, men of a sham and wealthy aristocracy, what would you do about it? You would be obliged to drink your cup of hemlock, as the striker at Homestead was obliged to partake of his draught of defeat.

Gentlemen, who assume to be better every other day in the year, but who realize on election day that your votes are no better, and count for no more, than the laborer's, mechanic's, and the poor man's all over our land, what are you going to do about it? It is a condition so pregnant with possibilities that it should occasion you to take thought. Do not arouse the resentment of your fellow-citizens; poor they may be, but rich in their rights as freemen. By the exercise of their franchise they can make legal that which would demand a division of some of your ill-gotten gains for the support of the Federal Government, thus lightening the taxes upon those who can least afford to pay them.

The poor have learned; the workman has been taught by sad experience; the laborer has had it forced down his throat, by the point of the bayonet in the hands of the militiamen, that he cannot hope to win in the battle against capital by strikes or organized labor. Homestead, and the wretched condition of the people there, is fraught with significance, to the laboring man, of the consequences of his ineffectual battle against capital. He knows that to resort to violence, mob law, dynamite, is against the spirit of the people of America. In his heart of hearts his home is as dear to the

POSSIBLE FRUITS OF VICTORY.   223

W. SEWARD WEBB,
VICE-PRESIDENT OF THE NEW YORK CENTRAL R. R.

workman as yours is to you, Mr. Carnegie. He
does not believe in anarchy, and the dissolution
of law, order, and the morals of the people any
more than you do. He doesn't believe, any more
than you do, Mr. Son-in-law Seward Webb, in the
destruction of property. He feels oppressed; he
feels that the burden has been laid too heavily
upon his shoulders; he is irritated at the load he
is carrying; no longer will he resort, as the acme
of his hopes, to a strike or a labor organization;
he has learned in the election of 1892 that the

power to correct these evils is his; that on election day, at the polls, he may right these wrongs. Be you warned, who count your millions, that the bandage which has blinded the eyes of the poor, making them fight at shadows, has been removed from their eyes, and that they will make such a vigorous and effectual onslaught upon your cherished bulwarks of bullion that the equalizing process may become so rapid and effectual as to demolish your cherished fortresses of wealth.

It is not to disorganize society; it is not to overturn religion, or resort to Nihilism, that the tendency of the workingman's mind leans. It is your presumption, arrogance, and overwhelming self-esteem that has offended him. A baby's finger may touch the spring holding the bar by which is caged the lion. The lion once uncaged, and a hundred men cannot restrain its freedom. A little stream of water, flowing over the top of a dam, might have been stopped by a handful of mud in the hands of a child; increasing, the stream weakens the barrier; the dam has gone, the flood has come.

There's a little stream of truth trickling over the dam that holds back the flood of the resentment of the people; silently, softly, with an appearance of "apathy," it began to move, until the rich received the first spray, notifying them of its approach, November the 8th, 1892.

CHAPTER X.

THE CAUSE OF BULLETS, '61; BALLOTS, '92.—ABRAHAM
LINCOLN, THE PEOPLE'S CHOICE IN '60.

OF political parties in America, De Tocqueville declared that "Aristocratic or democratic passions may easily be detected at the bottom of all parties, and although they escape a superficial observation, they are the main point and soul of every faction in the United States."

That greatest conflict of American history, the military and political struggle between the forces of slavery and the forces of human freedom, was no less a conflict between aristocracy and democracy. In the South, which President-elect Cleveland only the other day termed—with undoubted historical accuracy—the cradle of American liberty, there had been developed a social and political aristocracy as distinct and powerful as almost any the world has seen.

To this development, which did not become marked until after the early part of the present century, many causes contributed. The industry of the South had become centralized in the hands of large land owners who cultivated extensive plantations with slave labor. The tremendous growth of slavery exerted a depressing effect upon the manufacturing spirit; the artisan, the mechanic, and the trader came to be regarded as socially inferior. The planting of rice, sugar cane, and especially cotton, which was found to be the most profitable business, was also the most esteemed; and the South became an almost purely agricultural section.

Lorin Blodget lays it down as an accepted rule that "the country wholly devoted to agriculture necessarily tends to aristocratic despotism, or some form of enslavement of the masses;" and he quotes similar expressions from Adam Smith, Buckle, and other recognized authorities on political economy.

Nor are reasons hard to find. De Tocqueville points out that the great guarantees of popular liberty in America are universal education and the general division of landed property. Now, in a purely agricultural country the education of the people is certain to be defective. The population is necessarily dispersed, for where there are no manufactories there can be few towns; and where there are few towns there are fewer and less efficient schools, and libraries and lyceums are practically unknown. Harrison's

"History of Virginia" states that that State had, in 1848, 166,000 youths between seven and sixteen years old, of whom only 40,000 attended any school.

Landed property had naturally tended to fall more and more into a few hands. As John Stuart Mill said of ancient Rome : "When inequality of wealth once commences in a community not constantly engaged in repairing, by industry, the injuries of fortune, its advances are gigantic; the great masses swallow up the smaller. The Roman Empire ultimately became covered with the vast landed possessions of a comparatively few families, for whose luxury, and still more for whose ostentation, the most costly products were raised, while the cultivators of the soil were slaves or small tenants in a nearly servile condition." The description is closely applicable to the landed aristocracy of the South in the years immediately before the war.

It is a mistake—a not uncommon mistake—to suppose that the *ante-bellum* South was poor. It was rich—considerably richer than the North, in proportion to its population. In 1860 the South had much more than its share of the assessed wealth of the nation. The total value of property in the Union was $12,000,000,000, and of this the Southern States, with only one-third of the country's population (and less than one-fourth of the country's *white* population), had $5,000,000,-000, or more than forty per cent.

But in the agricultural South wealth was far more unevenly distributed than in the manufacturing and commercial North. In the latter great fortunes were made, but were almost sure to be distributed among several heirs, or lost in the fluctuations of trade, while the prevalence of the industrial and inventive spirit opened the path of advancement to those born at the bottom of the ladder. In the former, large landed properties were handed down from father to son, and tended to grow larger by accretion, as is the rule with great estates. The small land owner could not compete with them. The peasant, whose only calling was the tilling of the soil, had little prospect of bettering his condition.

"The Southern planter," says a member[1] of one of the old landed families, who is now well known as the self-appointed manager of New York society, "was a born aristocrat. He had literally as much power in his little sphere as any old feudal lord. His slaves were the creatures of his caprice and pleasure. The work of their hands supported him, gave him his position and

---

[1] Of course I mean Ward McAllister. This is not from his book, but from a recent article of his published in the New York *World*.

influence. I have lived on a plantation with twelve hundred slaves, all devotedly attached to their master, evidencing as much loyalty and fealty as an Englishman to his sovereign, and taking great pride in their master and mistress."

The planter's life was one of patriarchal magnificence. His entertainments, according to the same authority, "would be appreciated in the old Faubourg at Paris;" his wines were old and abundant; his songs were the ballads of his historical prototype, the mediæval baron of England:

> "Lord Thomas, he was a bold forester,
> The keeper of the King's deer;
> Lady Eleanor was a fine woman,
> Lord Thomas he loved her dear."

Political power within its own commonwealths was of course practically monopolized by this landowning caste. Of power in national politics it wielded a tremendous share. It had taken advantage of that feature of the Federal Constitution which, when it was first framed, Patrick Henry attacked when he prophesied that "an aristocracy of the rich and well born would spring up and trample upon the masses." Outnumbered in the House of Representatives, it had firmly intrenched itself in the United States Senate.

In that body, up to the time just before the war, when it was no longer possible to create a new

Southern State to offset each Northern State, it held half the seats and votes—a position that gave it complete control of all Presidential nominations to office. Through its possession of this unassailable veto power on appointments, it had come to pass that, as Mr. Blaine observes in his " Twenty Years of Congress," "the Courts of the United States, both Supreme and District, throughout the Union, were filled with men acceptable to the South. Cabinets were constituted in the same way. Representatives of the government in foreign countries were necessarily taken from the class approved by the same power. Mr. Webster, speaking in his most conservative tone in the famous speech of March 7, 1850, declared that from the formation of the Union to that hour the South had monopolized three-fourths of the places of honor and emolument under the Federal Government. It was an accepted fact that the class interest of slavery, by holding a tie in the Senate, could defeat any measure or any nomination to which its leaders might be opposed; and, thus banded together by an absolutely cohesive political force, they could and did dictate terms.

Such was the land-holding, slave-holding, office-holding aristocracy, against which the first directly and avowedly antagonistic movement was that of the Republican party. Young and weak in its first Presidential contest of 1856, the new organization gathered strength steadily; and when, on April 29, 1860, the Democratic Convention at Baltimore was rent asunder by the Secessionists, it became clear that the Republicans would have to face the threatened disruption of the Union.

The Republican Convention met at Chicago and chose, in preference to the able and experienced Seward, Abraham Lincoln, of Illinois, a man who, then comparatively unknown, was to take rank as perhaps the noblest and greatest of all America's sons.

Lincoln, when asked for an account of his boyhood, said that it might be summed up in Crabbe's famous line: "The short and simple annals of the poor." J. G. Holland thus reviews the career of the man who led the struggle that began in 1860: "Born in the humblest and remotest obscurity, subjected to the rudest toil in the meanest offices, achieving the development of his powers by means of his own institution, he had, with none of the tricks of the demagogue, with none of the aids of wealth and social influence, with none of the opportunities for exhibiting his powers which high official position bestows, against all the combinations of genius and eminence and interest, raised himself by force of manly excellence of heart and brain into national recognition, and had become the local center of the affectionate interest and curious inquisition of thirty millions of people."

To the end of his life, Lincoln was the very incarnation of democratic simplicity. He was never at home in a drawing-room ; he never could dispose gracefully his hands and feet— appendages whose size was proportionate to his huge stature. After his nomination for the Presidency, he used to answer his own bell at his little house in Springfield, Illinois.

The people's man of 1860, ABRAHAM LINCOLN! The pulse of patriotism quickens at the pronunciation of the name. The people's plain Abe Lincoln ; one of them, a commoner, of them, with them, like them. To foreign nations, he may have appeared as "President Abraham Lincoln, Chief Magistrate of the United States." He may have been "Commander-in-Chief of the Army and Navy," in the minds of his subordinates in those two important branches of his administration from '61 to '65. History may record him as the "wise, able, and philanthropical." But his memory will last enshrined in a temple more lasting than bronze or stone—the hearts of the people.

To them he was Abe Lincoln—one of them, feeling their sensations, a common bond between him and them. He was a democrat by birth, by experience, by sentiment, reason, and patriotism. He was a President of the masses, and how well and loyally did they love him! His homely ways and phrases, his unadorned and vigorous speeches, were the ways of the people, speeches of the people; loved by the people for the very enemies he had made, for his enemies were the enemies of the people. Every caricature of Lincoln was a caricature of the people; every attack upon his personality was an attack upon the personality of the "mudsills" of the people, and his call to arms was their call to arms, and they sprang forward, responsive to his appeal, recognizing in it their appeal, as no sham aristocrat or autocrat can ever hope to have a nation do.

His memory will not remain green in the minds of the masses by his martyrdom; but dear will the picture be, from generation to generation, of the boy studying by the light of a flickering fire, and splitting rails for daily bread; fighting his way onward and upward without wealth, or powerful friends, until at last, in the supreme hour of the people's need, he comes to bear their standard in the battle which they waged against "caste." He did not come to the contest as a hired soldier, but as a volunteer, feeling all that was felt by the common soldier. It was *his* battle, for he had felt the sting of class distinction, as did every private soldier of his army.

Loving, loyal, faithful Abe Lincoln! May your name never be belittled by any of your descendants adopting a crest or coat-of-arms. Your coat-of-arms is engraved in figures as lasting as the eternal hills of America upon the minds of the people. Should a degenerate descendant seek a coat-of-arms, let him make it an axe and rail, surrounded by the laurel wreath bestowed by the loving, trusting people; for Abe Lincoln was best and only loved by the very term by which the aristocrats attempted to disparage him—"the rail-splitter." After the election of Abraham Lincoln, while he remained at Springfield, the chosen representative of the people, he was the most approachable man in America; even though at that time he must have felt the heavy weight of responsibility thrust upon him, viewing as he could the mass which, like a snowball, was increasing as it progressed under the weak administration of his predecessor. Think of the anxious hours that this man spent, knowing what the people expected of him, and seeing the number of his difficulties being added to, day by day, while those who had the burden to bear were obliged, until the fourth of the succeeding March, to sit still and watch the accumulation. Yet in those anxious hours, while receiving counsel of the mighty of the political world, many of whom were strangers to him and to whom he was a stranger, yet, still, while watching thus, the pillar of the Union, stone by stone falling away ; while thus counselled, advised by those he knew not whether to trust or not; while his mind must necessarily have been weighed down with the thought of his own possible inability to meet the expectations of his friends, the people, in that great new sphere to which they had called him, Abe Lincoln still had time to grasp the hand and wish good cheer to an old friend, neighbor, or one of the people. From birth to death, his life will form a lesson that the new Chief of the people whom they have called to be President of the United States, Grover Cleveland, could well study, and Abe Lincoln's example emulate, if he would hold the love of those who, by their votes, put him into the Presidential chair.

This man, Abraham Lincoln, represented that class of people who had been dubbed "mudsills" by the orators who represented the believers in "caste" in the South. He stood as the very personification of "mudsillism," which, read in the light of recently written history, meant the Common People—that is, the majority ; and the majority ruled after his election in 1860, even though it required the use of bullets against the aristocratic class, just as the majority will rule in 1892, after the election of Grover Cleveland as representative of the Common People.

The South sought by secession to absolve itself from the domination of the masses. It was like the patricians of Rome seeking the Sacred Hill to build a new city. It failed, as will ever the minority, representing a false idea of American society and a false conception of the spirit with which every American is imbued, do in the future. But, be it said to the credit of the believers in aristocracy in 1860, that they had the courage of their convictions, and they fought a manly battle to establish that which is impossible in America. The history of the Southerners' sufferings and dangers, endured uncomplainingly, forms a bright and shining exception to the conduct of the typical believer in "caste." Sham aristocracy, which has disregarded the rights and wounded the feelings of the people for the past twenty-five years, that sham aristocracy which is a direct outgrowth resulting from the suppression of the Southern aristocracy, if tested as the Southern aristocracy has been, would be found deficient in those qualities of courage and determination which made even the Southerners' false ideas respected and respectable.

The sham aristocracy of to-day, unlike the false aristocracy of 1860, would hire bullies, outcasts, and vagrants to do their fighting, as did those magnificent illustrations of "caste" in our country, Carnegie and Frick, at Homestead, and Son-in-law Webb at Buffalo.

The advocates of "caste" in 1860, the Southerners, not alone possessed courage and determination, but, accepting the result of the conflict, have exhibited since the days of Reconstruction that wonderful degree of political acumen for which they have ever been famous. Early recognizing that in their struggle for an independent national existence, the Southern Confederacy, they had been defeated—not by the aristocracy of the North and West, but by the Common People; that is, the most powerful portion of the population of the Union—the Southerner, the secessionist, the aristocrat of 1860, submerged himself in the ocean of the Common People, the great majority, the democracy! The Secessionist, who opposed Abraham Lincoln's administration in 1860 and used bullets to express his opposition in 1861, had firm conviction carried to his hesitating heart by the events that transpired between 1861 and 1865, that the "Common People"—the majority—must rule; and that with the freeing of his slaves he had lost the only possible foundation upon which he could rest his claim of social superiority in this country. Therefore, as the wise man that he has demonstrated himself to be, the aristocrat of 1860 has become the most earnest and patriotic member of a broad democracy in 1892; realizing from experience that upon that rock alone he can build the edifice of prosperity in his section of the country; also realizing from a sad experience that the Common People, democracy (though it was called Abraham Lincoln's Republican party), was the crag upon which his bark of Secession was shivered in 1865.

ANDREW JACKSON.
The "People's" President, 1828.

CHAPTER XI.

ANDREW JACKSON, 1828.

JACKSON was in truth a popular idol. Hickory poles, the emblem of devotion to "Old Hickory," stood in every village throughout almost every State, and at the street corners of many a city. In his own Tennessee, less than three thousand votes were cast against him in the entire State, and in many precincts he received every ballot.

The story is told of a stranger who visited a Tennessee village on the afternoon of the election, and found its male population turning out with their guns, as if for a hunt, and in a state of great excitement. On inquiring what game they were after, he learned that they were starting in pursuit of two of their fellow-citizens who had had the audacity to vote against Jackson, thereby preventing the village from casting a solid vote for "Old Hickory." The miscreants had avoided a tarring and feathering only by taking to the woods.

The result of the campaign was a triumph for Jackson. New England was the stronghold of

Adams, who received all its electoral votes except one from Maine. The National Republicans also carried New Jersey and Delaware, and New York and Maryland were divided. Every other State declared solidly for Jackson, whose total vote was 178, to 83 for Adams.

During that campaign, the same question appeared on the surface as that presented in the campaign of '92. The Whig party represented apparently higher tariff, and the Democrats were opposing the increase of duty; but the fact remained that John Quincy Adams represented the aristocracy of New England, and the Whig Party had become encrusted with the same false stucco of "caste" that concealed the merits, worth, and virtue of Lincoln's Republican party in 1892. E'en the most wonderful orator that America has ever produced, the great and honored Daniel Webster, with all of his personal magnetism, magic of speech, and logic of argument, could not boost the aristocrats of the Whig party into power; even though the bill for a higher tariff had passed, the cry was kept up, and was made to appear as one of the issues of the campaign of 1892.

Andrew Jackson represented, in his person, the people, the masses. By birth, education, and mode of living, Andrew Jackson was identified with the Common People, and, as we are all common, with all of the people. Like Abraham Lincoln, the masses saw in Andrew Jackson a champion, ready and brave enough to resent the attempted differentiation sought to be foisted upon the people of America by the then Whig aristocracy—the claimed parent of the Republican party. However, Abraham Lincoln's Republican party was not a progeny of the aristocrats of the Whig party. Andrew Jackson, in his person, represented the purest type of the western pioneer, patriot, and soldier, and such men in America will only be found in the ranks of the people.

In 1828, John Quincy Adams, and his party of the would-be "Four Hundred," received at the hands of the people the same punishment and rebuke that was administered to Benjamin Harrison and the Republican party, which, just like the Whig party, had become hidden from the view of the people by the glamour of wealth and would-be aristocracy that was thrown over it. In Andrew Jackson, the people elected as their chief one possessed of great firmness and decision of character, one who was honest and true; not always correct in judgment, but when he erred the people were ready to forgive him, because the error was one of judgment and not of intention.

He was of them, and like them, as Abraham Lincoln was in 1860, and the people's love and trust in him erased from their memory mistakes that in another would have been judged with a critical eye. He was often rash in expression and action, but his very rashness was the rashness of a man untrained in duplicity. He was not a diplomat. The people are not diplomatic, and he, as one of them, could not be expected to possess characteristics other than those of the mass. His actions were as a mirror in which the people saw themselves. How the chord he struck, when he threatened to hang John C. Calhoun and the nullifiers, finds a responsive echo in many of the utterances of Abraham Lincoln! What two men so nearly resemble each other to the people?

The mere idle calling one a Democrat and the other a Republican is, as Hamlet says : "Words, words, words." There is no significance in the mere word Democrat and Republican. Both were men of the people, elected as the choice of the masses, in the constant battle that the masses wage against the crime of "caste." The similarity in the characters of Lincoln and Jackson is nowhere more forcibly illustrated than in that both were patriots of the purest stamp.

Andrew Jackson took up the administration of the government with fearless energy, feeling confident that he had the unalloyed loyalty of the people to support him. Let us hope that Grover Cleveland, with the same fearless courage, will wage war upon those things objectionable to the people who have placed in his hands the weapons with which to do battle.

The distinguishing act of Jackson's first term was his veto of the bill to re-charter the United States Bank—the boldest defiance that a President ever cast to the money power of the country. "When President Jackson attacked the Bank," De Tocqueville notes, "the country was excited and parties were formed. The well-informed classes rallied round the bank, the Common People round the President." It is a commonplace of history that, in such cases, the "Common People" are more often right than those who claim superior information. Jackson's veto is regarded by most observers as a remarkable popular victory over a great capitalistic monopoly.

In none of the six Presidential campaigns between the time of Jackson and that of Lincoln was the question of popular sovereignty *versus* class pretensions brought into the contest as an issue, although events were gradually shaping themselves for the great struggle in which the period ended. Yet, in 1840, the Democratic personality of General William Henry Harrison, the Whig candidate, contributed not a little to his success. The veteran soldier, statesman, and frontiersman had spent most of his life in a log house beside the Ohio River, at North Bend, Indiana. A log cabin was chosen by his political followers as the symbol of his plain and unpretentious way of life, and a barrel of cider as an emblem of his simple but generous hospitality. During the "log cabin and hard cider" campaign all over the country, in cities, villages, and hamlets, log cabins were erected as rallying places for Harrison's partisans, who met there to toast their champion in abundant glasses of cider.

THOMAS JEFFERSON.
The "People's" President, 1800.

CHAPTER XII.

THOMAS JEFFERSON, 1800.

IN 1800 Adams was a candidate for re-election, and fully expected to be successful. But the Democratic-Republican party, as the opposition was now called, defeated him, and elected to the Presidency its great leader, Thomas Jefferson.

At a glance, it will be seen that the Republican of 1800 was the father of the Democratic party, the canonized Thomas Jefferson. The people, even thus early in the history of our nation, had begun to give evidence of that discontent at the aristocratic tendencies that even "The Father of his Country," George Washington, and his successor, John Adams, displayed.

It would be considered almost sacrilege were we to republish here the many attacks that were made upon George Washington, when President of the United States, on account of the odor of aristocracy with which he had become so strongly impregnated before the Revolution, and which clung to him like the scent of the roses to the shattered vase. While there can be no doubt, of course, in the minds of us all, that Washington was pre-eminently a patriot, with a firm and steadfast faith in the doctrine of the rights of the people; still, he belonged to a section, to a State, that had been settled by Cavaliers who believed that they were somewhat better by birth than the Pilgrims of New England. And, having been born and educated in that atmosphere, it is small wonder that his character should have been somewhat attainted by his surroundings.

Upon Washington's elevation to the Presidential chair he surrounded the executive mansion with more of the air of ceremony and evidences of "caste" than were pleasant to the mass of the people. He was attacked, during his first and second terms, by pamphleteers, who, in most scurrilous articles, wrote of him as one designing to perpetuate aristocracy and "caste" in our country. The debt of gratitude which the new Republic and the people thereof owed Washington was too great for any effect to be produced similar to the revolution in 1892. However, an impression was made; reluctantly, John Adams, Washington's Vice-President, was elected as second President of the Union. This reluctance became apparent by his failure to be re-elected four years later.

A Minister from the United States to England always seems to become a suspicious object in the minds of the people of America. No man ever added to his popularity by being sent as Minister to the Court of St. James. John Adams, who was our first Minister, was but the beginning of a long list of unfortunates. In fact, the American people will heartily endorse the opinion of that great statesman, James G. Blaine, which is being so vigorously advocated by the New York *Herald*, that foreign Ministers are expensive and useless appendages of this Republic. The election of John Adams was occasioned more by the reflected glory of Washington and the gratitude of the people, which, like the rays of the declining sun, became diminished as it sunk behind the horizon of time. In Thomas Jefferson, the people, even thus early in the history of our nation, saw *their* friend. His simplicity of life, purity of character, and honesty of purpose, surrounded his name with the same halo, in the sight of the people, as that with which the names of Jackson, Lincoln, and Cleveland have since been made luminous. Though Jefferson was called a Republican, still, to the people, he was a Democrat in the sense that democracy means equality.

Never was there a statesman more thoroughly imbued with the principles of popular liberty than Jefferson. "Rebellion to tyrants is obedience to God"—Oliver Cromwell's saying—was the motto engraved on his seal. He had taken a leading part in the colonies' struggle for freedom. He was a member of the Continental Congress, Governor of Virginia during the war, and—a yet greater title to immortality—author of the Declaration of Independence. After the war he had been sent as American Minister to France, where he sympathized warmly with the revolution against Bourbon tyranny.

Jefferson's election to the Presidency was universally regarded as a great popular triumph. He was hailed everywhere as "the Man of the People," and the day that saw him inaugurated was celebrated with such rejoicings as had not been witnessed since the news of peace came, in 1783. No business, no labor was done on the 4th of March, 1801. It was a day of powder and parades, of church services, of bell-ringing, of speeches, and illuminations. The country's satisfaction seemed unanimous.

"The exit of aristocracy" was a toast drunk at one great banquet that evening; and when it had been duly honored, the band appropriately struck up the "Rogue's March."

The inauguration itself was a simple affair enough. It has, indeed, been asserted that Jefferson rode up Capitol Hill without a single attendant, tied his horse to a picket fence, and walked alone into the Senate chamber to take the oath of office. Professor McMaster offers evidence to prove this story inaccurate. Jefferson was not surrounded, on his induction into the Presidency, by such throngs as attended the inaugurations of Washington and Adams in New York and Philadelphia. But he went to the Capitol in the midst of a gathering of citizens, with the accompaniment of drums, flags, cannon, and a troop of militia. His dress was, as usual, that of a plain citizen, without any distinctive badge of office. On taking the oath of office he said, in a brief speech to the Senate: "I know that some honest men fear that a republican government cannot be strong—that this government is not strong enough. I believe this, on the contrary, to be the strongest government on earth."

Jefferson's administration—so economical, business-like, and democratic as to have made "Jeffersonian simplicity" a proverb—met with such approval that when he was re-elected in 1804 only fourteen votes were recorded against him. Only in one State—Massachusetts—was there any excitement in the campaign.

The supremacy of the Democratic-Republican party lasted practically unchallenged until John Quincy Adams was elected, under peculiar circumstances, in 1824. There were in that year three leading candidates for the Presidency—Adams, Clay, and Jackson. As neither of them commanded a majority of the Electoral College, the question was referred to the House of Representatives, which selected Adams as being, in a measure, a compromise candidate.

John Quincy Adams was at that time acting with the Democratic party, but he was, as James Parton points out in his "Life of Jackson," "a Federalist by birth, by disposition, by early association, by confirmed habit." And it soon became clear that Federalism, long supposed to be dead, was "living, rampant, and sitting in the seat of power." Federalists were appointed to office—notably Rufus King, the most conspicuous survivor of the original Federalists—who was sent as minister to England. Adams was for stretching the Constitution, as the old Federalists were. In his first message to Congress he advocated government roads and canals, a government university and observatory, government exploring expeditions, and the like.

His personality and manners revived the aristocratic traditions of his father. In the state he maintained at Washington he was said to go beyond the first President Adams. He refurnished the White House on a grand scale, and shocked the frugal taste of the day by placing a billiard table in it. The East Room, in which his excellent mother had hung clothes to dry, was now a luxuriously fitted apartment.

"John II." was the name that John Randolph of Roanoke bestowed upon the son and heir of the "Duke of Braintree." Randolph had hated the Adams family since an incident that occurred on the day of Washington's inauguration, which he recalled long afterwards in one of his speeches. "I remember," he said, "the manner in which my brother was spurned by the coachman of the Vice-President—John Adams—for coming too near the vice-regal carriage."

Even Mr. Blaine, who in his "Twenty Years of Congress" shows himself a kindly critic of the Federalist ideas and Federalist leaders, admits the "general unpopularity attached to the name of Adams."

During John Quincy Adams' administration the mutterings of a coming political upheaval began to be heard. It began to be said that the Presidency was growing too much like an hereditary monarchy. It was becoming too settled a practice for each incumbent, after eight years in office, to make his Secretary of State his political heir. It gave the President what was almost equivalent to the power of appointing his successor. John Quincy Adams, it was said, counted confidently on the usual double term, and upon seeing his friend Clay, to whom he had given the chief post in his Cabinet, elected to succeed him.

"The issue is fairly made out: Shall the government or the people rule?" asked Andrew Jackson, and on that issue he appealed to the country in his memorable electoral campaign against Adams, in 1828. That was the bitterest Presidential contest that had ever been fought. Jackson was attacked with unexampled ferocity. One day at his Tennessee home, the Hermitage, his wife found him in tears. "Myself I can defend," he said, pointing to a newspaper which he had been reading; "you I can defend; but now they have assailed even the memory of my mother." And it was, in great part, her distress at the invective that was heaped upon her husband that caused the death of Mrs. Jackson just after the election.

It was a pitched battle between the "classes" and the "masses." As James Parton says, in his biography of Jackson: "Nearly all the talent, nearly all the learning, nearly all the ancient wealth, nearly all the business activity, nearly all the book-nourished intelligence, nearly all the silver-forked civilization of the country, united in opposition to General Jackson, who represented the country's untutored instincts."

CHAPTER XIII.

THE REVOLUTION IN 1776.

REVOLT from aristocracy and detestation of "caste" in politics, in religion, and in society, have been the key-notes of the whole history of the Anglo-Saxon race in America. They were the incentives that first led men of that race to seek homes beyond the Atlantic, and have ever been the cardinal principles of the nation those pioneers founded.

The westward movement began with that era of English history marked by the intolerable pretensions, in matters both of Church and State, of the Stuart monarchs. The doctrine of the "divine right of kings," which cost Charles I. his head, was, with all that it meant, the grievance that drove from England the settlers of the American colonies.

When James I., soon after his accession, was petitioned to allow liberty of assembling and of discussion to all classes and sects of his subjects, he replied that such a privilege "agrees with monarchy as well as God and the devil. Then Jack and Tom and Will and Dick shall meet, and at their pleasure censure me and my council and all our proceedings. Then Will shall stand up and say: 'It must be thus;' then Dick shall reply and say: 'Nay, marry, but we will have it thus;' and, therefore, here I must say: 'The king forbids.'"

The king forbade, but the native spirit of English liberty did not acquiesce without a murmur. There were mutterings of the storm that was to burst upon his son and successor in the full fury of rebellion. The subservient Wentworth complained that "the very genius of this nation of people leads them always to oppose, both civilly and ecclesiastically, all that ever authority ordains for them."

Most outspoken in opposition to royal encroachment were the Puritans—those stern disciples of Calvin, who had furnished England her first Protestant martyrs, Hooper and Rogers, and who, in the early seventeenth century, were, as Hallam says, "the depositories of the sacred fire of liberty."

Many Puritans preferred to leave their native country rather than submit. In 1607, a company of them were about to take sail for Holland from the Humber, when they were arrested and forced to return to their homes. In the following spring, they again attempted to escape. They reached the Lincolnshire coast, and were embarking, when soldiers, who had been dispatched in pursuit, rode down to the shore, and seized some of the women and children. As the only fault of these prisoners was that they had followed their husbands and fathers, they were afterward released.

The fugitives, whose leaders were John Robinson, their minister, and William Brewster, their ruling elder, first tarried at Amsterdam, and the next year settled at Leyden. There they lived for eleven years—a body of exiles, who did not fraternize with their Dutch neighbors, and who gradually formed a plan of migrating to the new country beyond the Atlantic, where they might be under their old flag, and yet hope for civil and religious liberty.

In 1617, they sent two of their number to England, to secure for their project the consent of the London Company, to which James I. had granted proprietary rights over Virginia—then the general name of the North American coast. The two embassies received a permit, although they put no great trust in it. "If," said they, "there should afterward be a purpose to wrong us, though we had a seal as broad as the house floor, there would be means enough found to recall or reverse." They did not foresee their future strength against oppression.

Thus it was that in the August of 1620 the Pilgrims set sail from Delft Haven, and in November landed on the shores of Massachusetts—forty-one families, numbering in all a hundred and two souls. Before they landed, they signed a mutual agreement, covenanting "to enact, constitute, and frame such just and equal laws as shall be thought most convenient for the general good of the colony." The agreement was loyally kept in the face of hardship and danger from within and without. The colony they planted grew in the spirit of popular liberty as it grew from penury to prosperity.

Bancroft remarks that "in the early history of the United States, popular assemblies burst everywhere into life, with a consciousness of their importance and immediate efficiency." This development of freedom was attained in Virginia even earlier than in Massachusetts.

Virginia's first struggle against usurping pretension was in 1624, when James I. sent out royal commissioners with orders "to enquire into the state of the plantation." The colonists protested against the commissioners' proposal of absolute governors, and demanded the liberty of their Assembly; "for nothing," they said, "can conduce more to the public satisfaction and public utility." And the Assembly succeeded in retaining its rights.

Thirty years later, a domestic attempt at usurpation was met with equal firmness. Samuel Cotton, the elected governor of the colony, had a quarrel with the Assembly, and arbitrarily proclaimed it dissolved. The representative defied his authority, and speedily forced him 'to yield. For even in that colony in America, where existed more of the inclination to class distinction than in many other of the colonies, the same spirit of hatred to "caste," and the exercise of any assumed superiority was deep-rooted, and thus early gave evidence of its presence.

At the foundation of Virginia's sister colony of Maryland, the king expressly covenanted that neither he nor his successors would lay any imposition, custom, or tax upon the inhabitants of the province. The proprietors had the right to establish a colonial aristocracy, but it was never exercised. "Feudal institutions," says Bancroft, "could not be perpetuated in the lands of their origin, far less renew their youth in America. Sooner might the oldest oaks in Windsor forest be transplanted across the Atlantic, than antiquated social forms. The seeds of popular liberty, contained in the charter, would find in the New World the soil best suited to quicken them." One of the early acts of the Provincial Assembly of Maryland was the framing of a declaration of rights. And yet, it was in Baltimore, the metropolis of the State of Maryland, that the first resistance was offered to the soldiers of the people, who were going to enforce the will of the majority upon the minority. Maryland, while, from proximity to the Federal capital, was less inclined toward the secession movement, was still sufficiently influenced by the aristocratic slave-holding part of her population as to be the scene of the first actual resistance to the will of the people in 1861.

The same spirit animated the pioneers of Connecticut, where Hooker declared that "the foundation of authority is laid in the free consent of the people." When John Clark and William Coddington founded the settlement of Newport, it was "unanimously agreed upon" among their people that the body politic should be "a *Democracie* or popular government." The colonization of Pennsylvania—"the holy experiment," as Penn called it—was inaugurated by its great leader with a solemn pledge of "liberty of conscience and civil freedom." And similar incidents accompanied the birth of nearly every new colony.

As Massachusetts grew to be the most prosperous of the northern colonies, she "echoed the voice of Virginia like deep calling unto deep. The State was filled with the hum of village politicians; the freemen of every town on the Bay were busily inquiring into their liberties and privileges." [Bancroft.] The American spirit, which was to leaven the world with a new ideal of liberty, found its philosophers and statesmen in the farms and hamlets of the young and simple community. It found, of course, its critics and its doubters. Lechford, a Boston lawyer, prophesied that "elections cannot be safe long here," where manhood suffrage was the rule. John Cotton spoke against the accepted principle of rotation in office; but neither could stem the current of democratic doctrine, because the early settlers of America still retained the scars of their recent conflict with the aristocrats of Europe. Their arrival in the then wilderness of America had been too recent to obliterate the impression made on their minds by "caste" in Europe.

In 1635, there was a short-lived possibility that the aristocratic system of Britain might be transplanted to Massachusetts. Henry Vane, younger son of a titled English family, emigrated to the colony, where he was kindly received, and elected governor a few years after; and two noblemen, Lord Brooke and Lord Say-and-Seal, expressed their intention to follow him if the colonists would agree to establish a second chamber of their legislature and constitute them hereditary members of it. But the burgesses, easily perceiving the trend of such a proposal, declined it, courteously but decidedly.

Aristocracy never found a foothold in any of the colonies. The only approach to it was the privileges accorded in some of them to the "proprietors," and these were, while they lasted, regarded with some jealousy. For instance, when Pennsylvania, after Braddock's defeat at Fort

Duquesne, decided to raise £50,000 for self-defence by an estate tax, the proprietors—heirs of William Penn—claimed exemption from the levy; but, though Governor Morris approved the claim, the Assembly refused it.

Bancroft thus characterizes the elemental beginnings of the American nation : " Nothing came from Europe but a free people. The people, separating itself from all other elements of previous civilization ; the people, self-confident and industrious ; the people, wise by all traditions that favored its culture and happiness—alone broke away from European influence, and in the New World laid the foundations of our Republic." And periodically, as we see from the records of our nation, the might of the majority has been exercised to suppress anything like the attempted institution of "caste" in our country. This often-recurring crime begins to upraise its head, slowly at first, after each defeat, but eventually its growth becomes sufficiently great to attract the attention of the " Common People," and, as a result, receives its punishment, so justly due.

And the same historian adds : " Of the nations of Europe, the chief emigration was from that Germanic race most famed for the love of personal independence. The immense majority of American families were not of 'the high folk of Normandie,' but were of 'the low men,' who were Saxons. This is true of New England; it is true of the South."

It is true of the South, in spite of the fact—influential throughout the history of that section —that its population contained an element drawn from the wealthier classes of the mother country. It has indeed been said that Virginia was "a continuation of English society." The seeds of privilege may have existed in the Old Dominion, but, nevertheless, in no colony was the spirit of personal independence more signally evinced. "With consistent firmness of character," to quote again from Bancroft, "the Virginians welcomed representative assemblies; displaced an unpopular governor; rebelled against the politics of the Stuarts; and, uneasy at the royalist principles that prevailed in their forming aristocracy, soon manifested the tendency of the age at the polls."

With the aims of the English rebellion against Charles I., the American colonies were in full sympathy. Immediately after its outbreak, the general court of Massachusetts directed the governor to omit the oath of allegiance to the king, "seeing that he had violated the privileges of Parliament." But the civil war had no effect upon the colonial governments. In England, the monarchy, the peerage, and the prelacy were at swords' points with the people; in America, there was neither peerage nor prelacy, and monarchy was rendered remote by the Atlantic, so that there were no two parties to join battle.

The Restoration opened a new era in the history of the colonies—a period of conflict between royal usurpation and aristocratic oppression on the one hand, and popular liberties on the other ; a period that, after many years of difficulty and struggle, culminated in events that gave rationality and independence to the greatest democracy the world has ever seen.

It was a period marked in England by the political ascendency of the aristocracy. At the Restoration, the nobility resumed possession of the hereditary branch of the Parliament. Through their influence over elections, they, to a great extent, controlled the House of Commons—and through it the crown, over which the Commons had given recent and striking proofs of power. It was the aristocratic element that dictated the policy which goaded the colonies into secession from the mother country. It supplied the officeholders—"carpet-baggers" they might have been termed in modern political slang—whom the home government quartered upon the colonials by an official system tainted with nepotism and corruption. Its foe—Pitt, the great Commoner—was the friend of America, and one of her few champions in Parliament.

Equally the friend of America was the English democracy—politically far less powerful during the century after the Restoration than in the preceding and the subsequent periods. When the hated Stamp Act was repealed, the "Common People" of London lit bonfires and illuminated the streets, rang the historic Bow Bells, and decked the shipping in the Thames with flags.

But the House of Commons, before whom came the critical measures of legislation for the colonies, reflected the feeling of the aristocracy and not that of the populace. "The majority," said a member, during a debate on American affairs in 1770, "is no better than an ignorant multitude." Sir George Saville, a man of rare independence and integrity, replied in strong words. "The greatest evil that can befall this nation," he declared, "is the invasion of the people's rights by the authority of this house. I do not say that the members have sold the rights of their constituents; but I do say, I have said, and I shall always say, that they have betrayed them." But his protest was shouted down as treason, and Parliament blindly pursued its course of usurpation.

Long before that time, there had been in America thoughts of independence as a refuge from usurpation. The colonists cherished a genuine loyalty to the old flag, and a strong pride in the Saxon blood, whose latest and, indeed, most typical product they themselves were. Yet, as far back as 1638, when Charles I. tried to revoke the original patent of Massachusetts, the settlers threatened to "confederate themselves under a new government for their necessary safety and subsistence."

In 1698, Governor Nicholson, of Virginia, reported that "a great many in the plantations think that no law of England ought to be in force and binding upon them without their own consent." Three years later, a public document noted that "the independence the colonies thirst after is now notorious."

The sentiment grew gradually during the reigns of the Georges, slowly overcoming the strength of the old attachment to the mother country. Every encroachment attempted by royalty or officialism aroused a hostility that reinforced the spirit of liberty. For instance, when Samuel Shute, Governor of Massachusetts in 1719, tried to prevent the publication of the Assembly's answer to one of his speeches, claiming power over the press as his prerogative, he only succeeded in evoking a vigorous resistance, that finally disposed of his pretension, and gave the press untrammeled freedom.

And thus it was that a generation later the patriotic Otis, of Boston, the man "who dared to love his country and be poor," spoke so boldly in reply to Hutchinson, who summed up his aristocratic preferences in the odious Horatian maxim, *Odi profanum vulgus*, and who avowed his dissatisfaction that "liberty and property should be enjoyed by the vulgar."

"God made all men naturally equal," said Otis. "The ideas of earthly grandeur are acquired, not innate. No government has a right to make a slave of the subject." And again, "to bring the powers of all into the hands of one or some few, and to make them hereditary, is the interested work of the weak and wicked."

Such was the philosophy that was daily preached among the burghers of Boston. Such was the doctrine that Patrick Henry came from the Virginia backwoods to voice with his burning eloquence. Such was the spirit that was everywhere animating the colonies, while Parliament enacted one unjust and oppressive law after another. "The sun of American liberty has set," Ben Franklin wrote from Europe to a friend in America, when he heard of the enactment of the ill-fated Stamp Act; "now we must light the torches of industry and economy." "Be assured that we shall light torches of another sort," replied his friend.

The torches were lit; they blazed forth in the shots fired at Lexington, and on Bunker Hill, and in the Declaration of Independence, at Philadelphia ; and they were not put out until Parliamentary oppression had been forever ended, and a new nation—a plebeian democracy—took its place by the side of the proudest of earth's empires.

The war was fought and won by the " Common People," in the face of the armed force of the foreigner, and the treachery, active or passive, of not a few colonists, whose aristocratic connections or pretensions held them aloof from the movement for liberty. Even in the darkest days of the struggle, when Washington, driven from New York, was retreating before Howe's advance, and many men of prominence were giving up the patriotic cause as hopeless—Joseph Galloway and Andrew Allen, of Pennsylvania, Samuel Tucker, of New Jersey, John Dickinson, of Delaware, and others—even then the Commander's wonderful faith and courage was reflected in the fidelity of the populace. That alone made possible the final triumph.

"When the war of independence was terminated," remarks DeTocqueville, in his famous study of "Democracy in America," "and the foundations of the new government were to be laid down, the nation was divided between two opinions—two opinions which are as old as the world, 'and which are perpetually to be met with under different forms and various names, in all free communities—the one tending to limit, the other to extend, indefinitely, the power of the people. The conflict between these two opinions never assumed that degree of violence in America which it has frequently displayed elsewhere. Both parties were agreed on the most essential points, and neither of them had to destroy an old constitution, or to overthrow the structure of society, in order to triumph. In neither of them, consequently, were a great number of private interests affected by success or defeat ; but moral principles of a high order, such as the love of equality and of independence, were concerned in the struggle, and these sufficed to kindle violent passions."

The party that sought to limit the power of the people was that of the Federalists ; its opponents took the name of Republican, which afterwards became Democratic-Republican, and finally, under Andrew Jackson, Democratic. In view of the fixed bent of the American national character, it is not difficult to discern the inevitable result of the conflict between them. The Federalists were certain to be ultimately overcome. America is the land of democracy, and the anti-democratic partisans were always in a minority.

Thus for the brief period succeeding the Civil War, while the wounds of the conflict were still fresh upon the body politic, the party of the aristocracy—for such had the Republican party become—utilizing the soreness still existing as the result of the conflict, succeeded, by the clamor of sectionalism, in diverting the attention of the masses from the tendency towards social superiority and "caste," which the continuance of the Republican party in power was creating.

This brief ascendency during the first twelve years of the republic was due to several temporary causes. Most of the great leaders of the war for independence believed in a strong, centralized government, and therefore ranked themselves with the Federalists. The failure of the first attempt at federal control—the Continental Congress—and the local disorders that arose after the war, had inspired the people with a dread of anarchy. They were willing to accept, for a time, restrictive political theories, which it soon became safe to throw off.

The Federalist leaders were more than suspected of aristocratic tendencies. Elbridge Gerry, of Massachusetts, declared in the Constitutional Convention of 1787, that "the ills of the country come from an excess of democracy. The people do not want virtue," he added, as if in apology, "but are the dupes of pretended patriots."

Sherman, of Connecticut, said at the same time and place that "the people should have as little to do directly with the government as possible."

John Adams repeatedly advocated, in his writings "a liberal use of titles and ceremonials for those in office," and the establishment of an upper legislative chamber to be filled by "the rich, the well-born, and the able." The words, "well-born," gave intense offence. Their inconsistency with the grand democracy of the Declaration of Independence was bitterly commented on. The whole Federalist party was sarcastically called "the well-born"—a fatal appellation!

The expression "well-bred," as describing the commander of the Pennsylvania militia at Homestead, will be recalled by the mass of the people long after every vestige of the militia's visit to Homestead has departed. To the American mind such expressions as "well-born" and "well-bred" present an absurd attempt at class distinction.

Hamilton shared the same theories. He was openly accused by Jefferson, while both men were members of Washington's cabinet, of a desire to overthrow the republic. He was closely connected with the rising financial power of New York. The people, while they admired his able and amiable personality, never quite forgave him for the part he took in defending one Holt, a rich Tory of New York, in a suit for redress brought by a poor widow whose house he had seized during the British occupation.

George Washington himself, who was a Federalist so far as he belonged to any party, was a man of ceremony and *hauteur*. He never forgot that he had descended from a titled English family, and belonged to the wealthiest class of Southern landed proprietors. When he assumed the Presidency, he established an almost courtly etiquette. On Tuesdays and Fridays he gave stately receptions to visitors ; on Thursdays, Congressional dinners. While New York was the Capital of the Union, he had a Presidential box at the theatre (the only theatre the city then boasted), elaborately decorated, and whenever he occupied it, the orchestra played the " Presidential March " (now known as " Hail Columbia").

At his inauguration, the House of Representatives addressed him simply as " President." The Senate, probably cognizant of his personal wishes, sought a more high-sounding title. " His Excellency " was rejected as too plain, and after some debate the Senators decided upon " His Highness, the President of the United States, and Protector of their Liberties."

The Senate's suggestion was referred to the House, where it aroused no little opposition. Congressman Tucker, of South Carolina, inquired : " Will it not alarm our fellow-citizens ? Will they not say that they have been deceived by the Convention that framed the Constitution? One of its warmest advocates—nay, one of its framers—has recommended it by calling it a pure democracy. Does giving titles look like a pure democracy? Surely not. Some one has said that to give dignity to our government we must give a lofty title to our chief magistrate. If so, then to make our dignity complete, we must give first a high title, then an embroidered robe, then a princely equipage, and finally a crown and hereditary succession. This spirit of imitation, sir, this spirit of mimicry and apery, will be the ruin of our country. Instead of giving us dignity in the eyes of foreigners, it will expose us to be laughed at as apes."

So decided was the feeling of the House against the adoption of a sonorous title for the chief executive, that the Senate's proposal was dropped. Nevertheless, a more elaborate ceremonial was maintained at the Presidential mansion —at first in New York, then in Philadelphia, and finally at Washington—during the first twelve years of the government, than after Jefferson's accession in 1801.

Washington's two elections to the Presidency was the nation's tribute to the splendid personal character and military record of the man who, above all others, gave it nationality. When he refused a third election, the honor went to John Adams, as his political heir, although the Federalists, whose candidate Adams was, had only a bare majority of the electoral college—seventy-one votes against sixty-eight for Jefferson. It was at that time the almost invariable rule for the electors to be chosen by the State Legislatures, not, as now, by a popular vote. Had the conflict between Adams and Jefferson been waged before the people at large, it is probable that the latter, the champion of advanced democracy, would have been successful.

John Adams was a man of decided aristocratic tendencies. He was the first American minister to England, and had spent ten years at the courts of Europe. He did not conceal his admiration for English institutions. While in London he wrote a "Defence of the American Constitution," which proved to be a laudation of the British form of government rather than that of the United States. In his "Discourses on Davilla," he advocated a powerful centralized executive and a system of titles. He was frequently charged with favoring a monarchy and a hereditary legislature like the House of Lords. His political opponents nicknamed him "the Duke of Braintree"—Braintree being the Massachusetts town where he lived.

Thus early in the existence of the nation was evident the detestation on the part of the people at any attempted introduction of "caste" in the country. The Stamp Act, and taxes, and unjust discrimination while truly expressed caused the revolution in 1776, were only supplemental causes. In the record of every colony will be found traces of the opposition to " caste," and the strong objection that existed among the people to the introduction of class distinctions among them. While the immediate cause of the rebellion on the part of the colonies, the revolution, and consequent creation of a nation, may appear to be the resistance to the imposition of taxes and therefore a matter of pocketbook ; still, beneath it all, the foundation upon which the strength and duration of the resistance to the British power rested, was the strong sentiment in the hearts of the early patriots, demanding *equality*, social as well as " equality before the law." Our forefathers endured suffering at Valley Forge, not for the sake of the pocketbook, but because they had in their bosoms that ever-present sentiment of the Anglo-Saxon people, that all must be equal in every respect. It is rather a petty cause to assign for the revolution and the exhibition of heroism upon the part of the forefathers of the Americans —a matter of taxes.

CHAPTER XIV.

THE FRENCH REVOLUTION.

FEUDALISM, introduced in France a tnousand years ago, reconstructed society on the only basis then possible. It was a bridge from barbarism to monarchy. The invasion of the Northmen, though apparently a calamity, was a blessing. They brought fresh, lusty life. Their courage and vigor gave the country a new and needed impulse in progress and civilization.

William, Duke of Normandy, conquered England in 1066, and proved an able and stern ruler.

While many of her nobles were engaged in the Crusades in the East, a social revolution was going on in France, full of significance. This was the rise of free cities. The feudal bishops became so intolerably oppressive that the people succeeded in buying the privilege of electing their own magistrates ; then the king, for a goodly sum of money, confirmed it. Appeal was thus secured from the bishop to the king. He encouraged the practice, for it freed him, to a degree, from dependence on his nobles, and gave him greater control over the cities. The process went on during the eleventh, twelfth, and the first part of the thirteenth century.

The result was shown at the battle of Bouvines (A.D. 1214). King John of England, in the hope of recovering Normandy and other provinces which he had ignominiously lost, attacked France. He formed an alliance with the German emperor and with the Court of Flanders.

The army of Philip, the French king, made up of barons, bishops, and knights, clad in steel, and a large body of foot-soldiers sent by sixteen free cities and towns, gained a complete victory. It was one of the most memorable contests of the Middle Ages, for on that hard-fought field three great branches of the Teutonic race—German, Flemish, and English—went down before the furious onset of "hostile blood and speech." Lords, clergy, and Common People fought side by side against a foreign foe, and henceforth were united by a common bond of pride. It was the hardy yeomanry of Edward, the Black Prince, who won the battle of Crecy (1346), at the beginning of the Hundred Years' War, against three times as many Frenchmen.

It was in 1598 that Henry IV. issued the Edict of Nantes, which secured to the long and bitterly persecuted Huguenots the rights they demanded.

It marked a new era in history. It was the first formal recognition of toleration in religion made by any leading power of Europe, and anticipated a similar act in England by nearly a century.

The king saw what all have since come to see, that freedom of conscience is one of the surest guarantees of national strength.

Henry IV. of France was essentially the people's king. He was popular with the masses to the same extent that Louis XV. was unpopular. To the Common People in France, Henry IV. represented as much democracy in that age of tyranny as Abraham Lincoln and Grover Cleveland do in a better age and country. Henry was murdered on the streets of Paris by the fanatic Ravaillac, whose dagger inflicted an almost mortal wound upon France herself.

With the aid of Richelieu, the absolute power of the crown was built up; then followed the despotisms of Louis XIV. and Louis XV.; the revocation of the Edict of Nantes; the disastrous failure of the Mississippi Scheme; the struggle between England and France for mastery in the New World, and the complete triumph of the former, and the preparation for the awful revolution of 1789.

France had materially and powerfully assisted the American colonies in their struggle with Great

Britain for independence. Many illustrious sons of France, like Lafayette and Rochambeau, had joined and fought side by side with those sons of liberty who were then creating the great republic of America. America was a storehouse of freedom, liberty, and concentrated hate of "caste" and class distinction, from whence Frenchmen like Lafayette carried to France the spirit of freedom. It may fairly be said that the struggle on this continent lighted the torch of liberty which has illuminated the world since, torn Spain's oppressed colonies in America from her grasp, and made possible the existence of the French Republic, which has now taken its place among the most powerful nations of the earth.

The dormant desire had long been present in the breasts of the poor of the French nation for equality and liberty. The quickening influences and light radiating from the new Republic of the West, among whose children the sons of France had served in the struggle for independence, soon ignited the fires in the heart of the impetuous Frenchman.

Louis XVI. had been more condescending than any of his predecessors; he occupied, possibly, a higher position in the hearts of the people than any king the French had had since Henry IV. But the time had come when, inspired by the example of the Americans, the crime of "caste" in France had become unendurable. Louis XVI. was, of all the Bourbon kings, probably the least objectionable.

His character, while weak and influenced by the stronger will of Marie Antoinette, did not represent the worst phases of the character of Louis XV. or Louis XIV. Gradually, but irresistibly by attrition, the will of the people had been making marks upon the royalty of France. The tyranny, insolence, and arrogance of Louis XIV., in whose presence one dared not speak, had been lessened in Louis XV. to the extent that one could speak in a whisper; but in the presence of Louis XVI. one might speak aloud. With tireless, resistless, sullen determination the billows of the sea of humanity, wherein all is equality and fraternity, had beaten upon this rock of adamant until these divine Bourbon kings had become impressed by its constant, ceaseless energy.

Weak, amiable, and pliable as Louis XVI. was, poor Jacques had been so long deprived of one heart-beat of feeling that his bosom could no longer restrain the emotions of liberty and equality. The nobles of France, more than Louis XVI., retained the impress of the reign of Louis XIV., "the Glorious" (?), who had proclaimed that he was a Sun ; and while the ruling monarch, as the bulwark of royalty, "caste," and social inequality, had received the first shock of the wave and been marked thereby; still the nobility, sheltered behind the bulwark of the personality of the king, continued to indulge the wild license of their privileges and "caste" distinction, gamboling like lambs upon the greensward of their delusion, becoming fattened for the knife of that butcher that was sure to follow, the guillotine. A more powerful, touching, and realistic picture was never drawn of the arrogance and presumption of the nobles, privileged classes, "higher caste," than that made by the people's author, the man who of all others has nearer touched the hearts of the Common People, who will be loved and revered when others more learned may be forgotten, because he wrote of scenes of sensation, emotion, and relations of the Common People—Charles Dickens—in the "Tale of Two Cities," and for our purpose it would be impossible to find words more fitting than those used by this master delineator of the feelings, thoughts, heart-throbs, and wrongs of the Common People:

"What has gone wrong?" said Monsieur, calmly looking out. A tall man in a night-cap had caught up a bundle from among the feet of the horses and had laid it on the base of the fountain, and was down in the mud and wet, howling over it like a wild animal.

"Pardon, Monsieur the Marquis!" said a ragged and submissive man, "it is a child."

"Why does he make that abominable noise— is it his child?"

"Excuse me, Monsieur the Marquis, it is a pity—yes."

The fountain was a little removed, for the street opened where it was, into a space some ten or twelve yards square. As the tall man suddenly got up from the ground and came running at the carriage, Monsieur the Marquis clapped his hand for an instant on his sword-hilt.

"Killed!" shrieked the man in wild desperation, extending both arms at their lengths above his head and staring at him. "Dead!"

The people closed round and looked at Monsieur the Marquis. There was nothing revealed by the many eyes that looked at him but watchfulness and eagerness; there was no visible menacing of anger. Neither did the people say anything; after the first cry, they had been silent, and remained so. The voice of the submissive man who had spoken was flat and tame in its extreme submission. Monsieur the Marquis ran his eyes over them all as though they had been mere rats come out of their holes. He took out his purse.

"It is extraordinary to me," said he, "that you people cannot take care of yourselves and your children. One or the other of you is forever in the way. How do I know what injury you have done to my horses. See! give him that."

He threw out a gold coin for the valet to pick up, and all the heads craned forward that all the eyes might look down as it fell. The tall man called out again, with a most unearthly cry, "Dead!"

He was arrested by the quick arrival of another man, for whom the rest made way. On seeing him, the miserable creature fell upon his shoulder, sobbing and crying and pointing to the fountain, where some women were stooping over the motionless bundle, and moving gently about it. They were silent, however, as the men.

"I know all, I know all," said the last comer. "Be a brave man, my Gaspard. It is better for the poor little plaything to die so, than to live. It has died in a moment without pain. Could it have lived an hour as happily?"

"You are a philosopher, you there," said the Marquis, smiling.

"How do they call you?"

"They call me Defarge."

"Of what trade?"

"Monsieur the Marquis, the vender of wine."

"Pick up that, philosopher and vender of wine," said the Marquis, throwing him another gold coin, "and spend it as you will. The horses there; are they all right?"

Without deigning to look at the assemblage a second time, Monsieur the Marquis leaned back in his seat, and was just being driven away with the air of a gentleman who had accidentally broken some common thing, and had paid for it and could afford to pay for it, when his ease was suddenly disturbed by a coin flying into the carriage, and ringing on its floor.

"Hold!" said Monsieur the Marquis. "Hold the horses! who threw that?"

He looked to the spot where Defarge, the vender of wine, had stood a moment before; but the wretched father was groveling on his face on the pavement in that spot, and the figure that stood beside him was the figure of a dark, stout woman, knitting.

"You dogs!" said the Marquis, but smoothly, and with an unchanged front, except as to the spots on his nose; "I would ride over any of you very willingly, and exterminate you from the earth. If I knew which rascal threw at the carriage, and if that brigand were sufficiently near it, he should be crushed under the wheels."

So cowed was their condition, and so long and hard their experience of what such a man could do to them, within the law and beyond it, that not a voice or a hand, or even an eye was raised. Among the men not one. But the woman who was knitting looked up steadily, and looked the Marquis in the face. It was not for his dignity to notice it; his contemptuous eyes passed over her and over all the other rats; and he leaned back in his seat again, and gave the word, "Go on!"

In vain would we seek for words describing better the horrible condition of the Common People, and the tremendous extent of the assumption of a superiority upon the part of the nobles, than in the foregoing picture so ably portrayed by Charles Dickens. Such a condition of the social life in France could produce but one result. The harvest was ripe for the sickle. The people had witnessed an illustration of the might of the Common People of America when opposed to the representatives of "caste" in the British army. That the storm should have burst that so long had been hovering over the heads of the French nobles is not a matter of surprise, in view of the fact that Dickens is historically correct in his picture of the oppressed condition of the poor in France. The only wonder to us Anglo-Saxons is that brave men, as the Frenchmen are, should have borne so long the cruel, heartless oppression of the rich nobility.

Duruy says: "The French Revolution was the establishment of a new order of society, founded on justice, not privileges. Such changes never take place without causing terrible suffering. It is the law of humanity that all new life shall be born in pain."

When Louis XVI. ascended the throne, in 1774, revolution was in the air. The outward splendor of Versailles, as Carlyle intimates, was the rainbow above Niagara : beneath was destruction.

There was a general feeling that a crisis was at hand. The spirit of free inquiry aroused by the leading writers and thinkers was ominous. Government, religion, social institutions, were all burned in the crucible, and a new order of things was inevitable. The country was hopelessly deep in the mire of debt;. the tax agents were brutal, and the peasants ground to the lowest depths of misery and suffering.

The power of the nobles over the peasants living on their estates was absolute. Large tracts of land were declared game-preserves, where wild boars and deer roamed at pleasure. To preserve the game with its flavor unimpaired, the starving peasants were not allowed to weed their little plots of ground. The nobility and clergy, who owned two-thirds of the land, were nearly exempt from taxation.

The peasant must grind his corn at the lord's mill ; bake his bread in the lord's oven, and press his grapes at the lord's wine-press, paying whatever the lord chose to charge. If the wife of the seigneur fell ill, the peasants must beat the neighboring marshes all night to prevent the frogs from croaking, and so disturbing the lady's rest.

French agriculture had not advanced beyond the tenth century, and the plow in use was the same as that used before the Christian era. The picture of rural wretchedness is completed by the purchase and sale of 150,000 serfs with the land on which they were born.

Louis desired to redress the wrongs of his country, but did not know how. Ministers came and went in a continuous procession, Turgot, Necker, Colonne, Brienne, and Necker again, tried to solve the problem, and gave up in despair.

As a last resort, the States-General, which had not met for one hundred and seventy-five years, assembled May 5, 1789, and that day marked the opening of the Revolution.

The National Assembly, proving to be the most powerful body of the States-General, invited the nobles and clergy to join it, and declared itself the National Assembly. Louis closed the hall. The members repaired to a tennis-court near by, and swore not to separate until they had given France a constitution. The weak king soon yielded, and, at his request, the coronets and mitres met with the commons. The court decided to overawe the refractory Assembly, and collected 30,000 soldiers about Versailles.

Four members of that assembly were Lafayette,

Count Mirabeau, Robespierre, and Guillotine, inventor of the fearful instrument of punishment bearing his name.

The Paris populace were infuriated by the menace from the soldiers. They stormed the old Bastile and razed its dungeons to the ground. The insurrection spread like a prairie-fire. Chateaux were burned, and tax-payers tortured to death. Soon a maddened mob surged toward Versailles, screeching "Bread! bread!" The palace was sacked and the royal family brought to Paris.

Political clubs sprang up like mushrooms, chief among which were the Jacobins and the Cordelies, whose leaders, Robespierre, Marat, and Danton, advocated sedition and organized the revolution.

The Assembly, in its burst of patriotism, extinguished feudal privileges, abolished serfdom, and equalized taxes. The estates of the clergy were confiscated, and upon this security notes were issued to meet the expenses of the government.

Austria and Prussia took up arms in behalf of Louis, and invaded France (1791). This step doomed the monarch and the monarchy. The approach of the "foreigners" kindled to unrestrainable fury the wrath of the masses. The "Marseillaise" was heard for the first time on the streets of Paris; the palace of the Tuileries was sacked; the faithful Swiss guards were slain, and Louis sent to prison. The Jacobins were triumphant. They arrested all who spoke against their revolutionary projects; assassins were hired to go through the crowded prisons and murder the inmates. For four days during September the terrible carnival of blood raged.

The Prussian army was checked at Valmy, and soon recrossed the frontier. Then the Austrians were defeated at Jemmapes, and Belgium was proclaimed a republic. The leaders of the French revolution were electrified, and the next Assembly established a republic in France. The king was arraigned and guillotined. As the bleeding head tumbled into the basket the furious crowds shouted "*Vive la République!*" Europe was horrified, and a league, with England as its moving spirit, was formed to avenge the death of Louis. The royalists held Marseilles, Bordeaux, Lyons and Toulon.

The Convention appointed a Committee of Safety, which knew neither mercy nor pity. Revolutionary tribunals were set up, and the work of slaughter began and raged with a ferocity beyond the power of imagination to conceive. To charge a person with being in sympathy with the aristocrats was his death warrant. Men saved themselves by denouncing their neighbors before their neighbors could denounce them. Intimate friends suspected each other, and members of the same family became mortal enemies.

Marie Antoinette, her head silvered by the awful woe and desolation and horror, perished on the same scaffold where her husband had died. At Lyons, the guillotine was too slow, and the victims were mowed down with grape-shot; at Nantes, boat-loads were rowed out and sunk in the Loire. The people were made frantic by their thirst for blood.

Marat rubbed his hands and chuckled with glee at the carnival of murder. He showed his admiring friends his reception room, papered with death warrants.

But his turn speedily came. Charlotte Corday, a young girl from Normandy, gained access to him, and, while he was jotting down the names of fresh victims, stabbed him to death, and then walked proudly to the guillotine.

Danton expressed a suspicion that the massacre had continued long enough, for which he was promptly guillotined, and then for nearly four months the appalling Robespierre reigned supreme. His aim was to destroy all the other leaders; the axe worked faster and faster, but not fast enough to suit the clamoring tigers; the accused were forbidden defence, and were tried *en masse*.

Finally, when common safety demanded it, friends and foes united for the overthrow of the colossal monster. He was arrested and beheaded July 28, 1794. The reign of terror ended with his life. It had lasted little more than a year. But what a year of woe, massacre, murder, and blood! From the first outbreak of the revolution to its close, it has been estimated that 1,000,000 lives were sacrificed.

From this appalling furnace of fire and death emerged the true life of France. The revolutionary clubs were abolished; the prison doors flung wide; the churches opened, and the emigrant priests and nobles invited to return.

But, though the Convention had organized the government of the Directory in name, it had yet to fight for its existence. The Royalists hoped they might restore the monarchy. The National Guard was persuaded to join the monarchical party. In October, 1795, the combined forces, 40,000 strong, marched on the Tuileries to expel the Convention or prevent the establishment of the Directory.

The Convention called on General Barras to defend them. Barras asked a Corsican artillery officer of twenty-six, who had distinguished himself at Toulon, to act as his lieutenant. He speedily converted the palace into an intrenched camp. He had 7000 troops, but he planted his batteries with such admirable skill, and used his grape-shot with such effect that the advancing hosts were defeated and scattered, and the Convention, with its defender, Napoleon Bonaparte, was master of the situation.

Thankfulness should fill the hearts of all the citizens of the American Republic that the history of our own country will not present a duplicate picture of the scenes portrayed in this chapter. It certainly is not the fault of the good management of the sham aristocrats that these scenes of such monstrous horror, exhibiting the birth of liberty in France and the erasure of the word "caste" with its most objectionable features from French life, were not reproduced in America. Fortunately for the would-be aristocrats, the volcano, upon which they slept, had a crater known as the BALLOT-BOX, where the pent-up steam of the indignation of the people found a vent-hole. November 8, 1892, the safety-valve was opened by the people, and the believers in "caste" should be thankful that there existed some means of relief; had such not been the case, the pent-up energies and the indignation of the people would have caused another explosion, which would have rivalled in force, if not in the howling scenes of blood, the French Revolution.

CHAPTER XV.

ENGLAND, 1645.

THE American regards England with more than kindly eyes. Her history has been the history of our race. The sterling valor of the Englishman early made itself felt in the demands made by him upon the reluctant kings who ruled him. At no time in the history of Great Britain, from the Norman Conquest, had the peasantry and "Common People" been submerged as completely by the power of the privileged classes as has been the case in France, and, in fact, as in all of continental Europe. When John, known as "Lackland," the younger brother of Richard Cœur de Lion, came to the throne of England (1109–1216), he ruled weakly and lost nearly all the English possessions in France. The peasants rose against the imbecile monarch and, joined by the barons and feudal lords, compelled him to sign the Magna-Charta or Great Charter, at Runnymede (1215).

By this immortal instrument the king gave up the right to demand money when he pleased, to imprison or punish when he pleased. He was to take money only when the barons granted the privilege, for public purposes, and no freeman was to be punished except when his countrymen judged him guilty of crime. The courts were to be open to all, and justice was not to be sold, refused, or withheld. The serf villein was to have his plow free from seizure. The church was secured against the interference of the king. No class was neglected, but each obtained some cherished right.

Thus, early in the history of England, we find the " Common People " of that nation from whom we derive our blood and many of our laws—the foundation, in fact of all of them—and much of our domestic and social conditions and manners, asserting rights for which Americans afterwards contended with the parent country, England. The Magna-Charta was wrested from King John not by the lords and barons alone—but by a union between the nobles and the "Common People."

Thus early the "Common People" of England learned to appreciate their might and strength. And the Americans, as inheritors along with their blood of so many of the traditions and characteristics of the English, have not failed to possess themselves of that quality which is inherent in the Anglo-Saxon heart—the fearless demanding of the right to equality.

Pronouncedly did the American people, November 8, 1892, reiterate in an unmistakable manner the sentiment of the race who, in 1214, had forced from King John of England the Magna-Charta which has been, ever since, the foundation of English liberty.

English kings have continually tried to break the Magna-Charta, but have ever failed in the attempt. They have been compelled, during reigns succeeding that of King John, to confirm its provisions thirty-six times. The early assertion of the right to representation by the people is interesting as a step onward in the march of the Anglo-Saxon toward equality and liberty.

Henry II.'s foolish favoritism to foreigners caused a revolt, under the leadership of Simon de Montfort, Earl of Leicester, who defeated the king at Lewes. Earl Simon thereupon called together the Parliament, summoning, besides the barons, two knights from each county and two citizens from each city or borough to represent free-holders (1265). From this beginning, the English Parliament soon took on the form it has since retained of two assemblies—the House of Lords and the House of Commons. Thus, the thirteenth century became ever memorable in the history of the English-speaking people of the world, for the granting of the Magna-Charta and the forming of the House of Commons—that House of Commons, which, as its name indicates, was and is made up of the representatives of the

"Common People," and which has ever been the bulwark of the liberty of the "Common People" of England, resisting every attack of autocratic monarchs upon the rights of the people.

In the reign of Edward III. (1327-1377) the Normans and Saxons were fused completely, and created the English nationality; chivalry reached its highest exaltation; but the court and the upper classes were morally rotten. The laboring classes rose during this reign, and compelled their employers to pay them just wages, and rent to fragments the despotic edicts that effected them; just as the "Common People" will ever do, whether the attempt is made to beguile them by the cry of Protection, Free Trade, Force Bill, or other distracting exclamations.

Richard II. (1377-1399) was a tyrant, with neither the capacity nor courage of his father and grandfather. He lost all the respect and admiration with which the people of England had ever regarded his father and grandfather. One of Richard II.'s tax-gatherers insulted the daughter of one Watt Tyler, at Dartforth on Kent, in exactly the same manner as "Chappie" feels at liberty to do, by his glances, the daughters of the laboring men to-day. Watt Tyler, the wrathful father, killed the man with one blow, and a formidable revolt sprang at once into being.

The shouts of about 100,000 "Common People," gathered on Black Heath, June 12, 1381, reverberated through the valley of Richard II. The vast horde poured into London, seized the Tower of London, put to death the Archbishop of Canterbury and others, and spared the cowering and cowardly King Richard II., only on his promise to abolish slavery and grant their demands.

That, my good and would-be lords and barons, is but another evidence of the Anglo-Saxon blood and its resentment of insult when offered to the female members of the race. Women ever have occasioned, in the Anglo-Saxon bosom, just and righteous indignation when insulted. The slights, sneers, and snubbing of the women of America by the snobs and sham aristocrats produced the reappearance of the same traits of character as led Watt Tyler and his horde of peasants to London. The women of America had become Democratic, and the result of their influence upon the voters of our country was revealed, November 8th, in an unmistakable manner.

James I. (1603-1625), the first Stuart to reign in England, was stubborn, conceited, weak, slovenly, dissipated, and cowardly. In his reign was first heard the prattle about "the divine right of kings, and the passive obedience of the subject." He ostentatiously opposed his will to that of the people, and during his reign was in constant conflict with Parliament. He was obliged to beg the House of Commons for money, and that body adopted the principle, now one of the cornerstones of the British Constitution, that "a redress of grievances must precede a granting of supplies.

Charles I. (1625-1629), the son of James I., was more refined and held more exalted ideas of his prerogatives; he repeatedly broke his promises made to the people; his reign was one long struggle with Parliament.

He was not as frivolous and false as his son Charles II., but James I., his father, had brought the idiotic doctrine of the divine right of kings into England along with the rest of his peculiar Stuart eccentricities,—for eccentric it was to the Anglo-Saxon people, who had forced from John the Magna-Charta at Runnymede before the amalgamation of the Norman and Saxon into one homogeneous race had been completed; who, while there still existed internal dissensions and race distinction, had been united upon the one great subject for which the Anglo-Saxon people, best and bravest representatives of the Aryan race, have ever fought—the equality of man in the representation in the legislation of the people.

Strange to the ear of the masses was the doctrine of the Stuart, that the king was one of the Lord's anointed and could do no wrong. They had seen kings do wrong when cursed with a wrong-doer as king, and supported any aspirant to the crown of England, no matter how slender may have been the thread of his claim thereto. Richard II. had played the autocratic ruler. Englishmen had resisted by espousing the cause of the first claimant who appeared upon the field. The assumption by the Stuarts of a divine right was the first stab that they gave to their own existence as the ruling House of an Anglo-Saxon people. Charles I. reaped where James I. had sown. The English people had forgiven before the bad faith of their sovereign, as they have since. They have endured the waste of their money because the Anglo-Saxon, whence we Americans derive the source of blood and laws, has not his tender spot upon the pocketbook, but in his heart, his home, his pride, believing himself, each man, equal to any other man.

In 1628, Parliament wrested from Charles I. the famous Petition of Rights, the second great charter of English liberty. It forbade the kings to levy taxes without the consent of Parliament, to imprison a subject without trial, or to billet soldiers in private houses. As usual, Charles disregarded his promises, and then for eleven years ruled like an autocrat.

During that period no Parliament was convoked, a thing unparalleled in English history.

Buckingham having been assassinated by a Puritan fanatic, the Earl of Stafford and Archbishop Laud became its royal advisers. The Earl contrived a plan for making the king absolute. All who differed from Laud were tried in the High Commissioner's Court, while the Star Chamber Court fined, whipped, and imprisoned those who spoke ill of the king's policy or refused to pay the money he illegally demanded. The bitter persecution of the Puritans drove them to America. In Scotland, Charles carried matters with a high hand. Laud attempted to abolish Presbyterianism and introduce a liturgy. The Scotch rose *en masse*, and signed (some of them with their own blood) a covenant binding themselves to resist every innovation directed against their religious rights. Finally, an army of Scots crossed the border into England, and Charles was forced to assemble the famous "Long Parliament" (1640), which lasted twenty years. The old battle was renewed. Stafford, and afterward Laud, were brought to the block; the Star Chamber and High Commissioners' Courts were abolished, and Parliament voted that it could not be adjourned without its own consent. Charles attempted to arrest five of the leaders of Parliament in the House of Commons itself. They hid in the City of London, whence a week later they were brought back to the House of Commons in triumph. Charles hastened Northward, and unfurled the royal banner. For a time his supporters swept everything before them.

Then arose Oliver Cromwell, a man of the "Common People," who, with his Ironsides regiment at Marston Moor (1644), drove the cavaliers pell-mell from the field. Nasby (1645) was the decisive contest of the war. Cromwell swept the field, and the royal cause was irrevocably lost. Charles fled to the Scots, who gave him up to the Parliament; but the army of the "Common People," led by Cromwell, soon got him into its possession, and he was condemned to death on the charge of treason, and was beheaded.

Thus, as has ever been the case when the "Common People" have been goaded by insult into a furious state of temper, some leader has aptly sprung, like Cromwell, from their ranks, and carried them triumphantly to victory. In the same way George Washington, Thomas Jefferson, Andrew Jackson, Abraham Lincoln, and Grover Cleveland have each in turn led the hosts of the "Common People" to victory in their battles against "divine rights," injustice, "caste," and "sham aristocracy."

England, by the execution of Charles I., was without a king. The authority was vested in the House of Commons (diminished by Bride's

Burge the expulsion of the Presbyterian minister) contemptuously styled "the Rump." Cromwell, the man of the "Common People," and his terrible army, composed of the "Common People," were the actual rulers. In Ireland and Scotland the Prince of Wales was proclaimed as Charles II., whereupon the grim Ironsides—those representatives of the people, and their terrific earnestness when aroused—conquered Ireland as it never was conquered before. Crossing then to Scotland, the covenanters were routed at Dunbar, and again at Worcester.

Cromwell, while he had the power of a king, like Cæsar, dared not take the title. He recognized, what it would be well for the sham aristocrats to attentively regard, that the people MAKE and UNMAKE ; hence, he did not dare offend the "Common People" by assuming the title of king, though exercising all the powers of a king. Under Cromwell, England's glory became greater than under Elizabeth. The Barbarian pirates were punished ; Jamaica was captured ; Dunkirk was received from France in return for help against Spain ; protecting the Protestants everywhere, Cromwell compelled the Duke of Savoy to cease persecuting the Baudois. The very name of England became terrible to the oppressor of the poor in every land. The people, in their might, were ruling England ; because, even though

Cromwell was styled "Lord Protector of the Commonwealth," he still understood that his greatest power rested upon the will of the "Common People" as a foundation.

Upon the death of Oliver Cromwell there was no hand strong enough to seize the helm of the ship of State. His son Richard, who did not inherit the genius of his father, and did not hold the confidence of the "Common People" of England, was quickly put aside. And the English people—the "Common People"—casting about for an executive to place at the head of the nation, selected Charles II., whom they called to England to rule them, but not "by divine right;" simply as their king.

The popularity of Charles II., the most profligate, the most licentious and immoral ruler that Great Britain has ever had, arose because he was the people's king. They had called him from over the sea; he ruled by no divine right, but through the affections of the people. He was to them *their* king, and though he sinned, erred, and wasted the money of the nation, he was *of* the people, and they forgave him. When James II. attempted to revive (as the people feared he would, and hated him in consequence, even before his succeeding Charles II.) "the divine right ot kings," and the privilege of doing anything, the idea that nothing that he did could be wrong, the people resented it. It was not Catholicism. Dear as religion may be in the heart of man, there is one thought that is dearer: it is his right to be man, and equal to any other. Had James II. been a people's man, as was Charles, his brother, it is quite possible that the House of Stuart might now reign in Great Britain. William of Orange was beloved by the people, because he was so thoroughly a people's man, that even the proud Anglo-Saxons preferred to submit themselves to his rule, joined with a daughter of the House of Stuart, rather than to the legitimate successor of Charles II. The mighty voice of the people was heard resounding in the selection of the Prince of Orange with the same notes that marked the music of the march of a triumphant Democracy, on November 8, 1892 ; like the grains of wheat taken from the tombs of the Pharaohs, though gathered in a harvest of fifty centuries ago, when planted will produce the same crop as to-day.

History repeats itself continually, and nowhere more obvious is the repetition than in the record of the Anglo-Saxon race. The same causes which occasioned the unpopularity of Charles I., the popularity of Cromwell, the popularity of Charles II., were working to create Cleveland's tremendous popularity and the overthrow of the Republican party November 8, 1892.

CHAPTER XVI.

THE GERMAN EMPIRE, 1520—1525.

GERMANY does not present a fruitful field for examples of popular uprisings and the exhibition of the indignation of the people when crushed by the oppressors of the upper classes. Germany to-day, even in the last decade of the nineteenth century, presents a picture of the only government in Europe which pretends to have a representative form of government, where the chief executive, the Emperor, can speak of himself, or would dare to do so, as the "war lord," to whom absolute obedience is due by the citizens of the Empire. The Anglo-Saxons, while a branch of the great Teutonic race, seem to have acquired, by their being transplanted to the British Isles, a greater spirit of independence than the other branches of the German race that have remained on the continent of Europe.

Otho I., son of Henry I., the mighty Saxon duke, was the founder of the German empire (936–973), and remorselessly crushed the rising opposition of the princely aristocracy. Mutterings of discontent, ominous of coming revolution, began to be heard throughout the whole of South and Central Germany, in the early years of the seventeenth century. The social position of the peasants was of the most degrading character. They were serfs; or, in other words, belonged to the soil on which they were born, and through that to the lord who owned the soil.

The miserable peasants had no right to move from these lands; there was no appeal from the authority of the lord. When he appropriated for his own use the common pasture grounds of the village; when he forbade them to fish in the streams, or to hunt in the woods; increased the ground rent; tithe socage service, according to his own need, they had to submit or revolt.

Thomas Münzer was an earnest, advanced preacher at Zwichfau, in Saxony, in 1520 and in 1523. He was expelled from Allstadt by the government, and went first to Nuremberg, and then to Schaffhausen, returning soon to Thüringia, and settled at Mülhausen. There he succeeded in overthrowing the city council and appointing another which was completely under his control.

Götz von Berlichingen was a famous German knight, surnamed "The Iron Hand." He was born in 1480, at Berlichingen Castle, in Wurtemberg. He lost a hand at the siege of Land Shut, and replaced it with an iron one. He was a daring and turbulent subject, continually involved in feuds with neighboring barons.

Thomas Münzer and Götz von Berlichingen were the only leaders who took part in what is known as "The Peasants' War," in Germany. This was an uprising of the peasants, which first manifested itself January 1, 1525, by the capture and looting of the convent of Kempton. This served as a signal for general uprising of the peasantry from the Alps to Havz, and from the Rhine to the Bohemian frontier. Münzer quickly persuaded the whole population in and around Mühausen and Laugensalza to rise in revolt, and Götz von Berlichingen hastened to place his skill at the service of the infuriated peasants.

Unfortunately, however, the uproarious hordes were without other leadership, and lacked discipline and effective weapons. They gathered in throngs of from 5,000 to 10,000, and ran hither and thither, with clubs, stones, and perhaps a few firearms, burning castles, destroying monasteries, plundering villages, towns, and cities, and committing ferocious outrages. Before the regular armies, these multitudes were scattered like chaff in the hurricane. They fought with the fury and courage of tigers, but it availed them nothing; they were routed, dispersed, and massacred, and effectually crushed in a few months. Münzer was tortured and beheaded. Von Berlichingen was placed under the ban of the empire by Maximilian

I., his exploits serving as the subject of Goethe's drama of "Götz von Berlichingen."

While unsuccessful, this uprising of the peasants demonstrates that the inherent love of liberty has a place in the hearts of the German race, and should furnish to Emperor William a warning note that there may be a point where, in spite of the Germans' love for Fatherland, and pride in the glories achieved by the Empire, they may resent expression of autocratic authority on the part of their Emperor. When the German becomes an American citizen—and there are no better citizens of America than the Germans— the spirit of equality, which has lain dormant in the Teutonic blood for centuries, immediately asserts itself. Under the wise guidance of Bismarck, German unity was made possible, and the glory won by united Germany has influenced the Germans in Europe to submit to heavy taxation, and the continued assumption of social superiority; but the time is rapidly approaching, which it would be well for Emperor William to consider, when the German people of Europe will exhibit the same love of liberty and equality that the children of the German race exhibit as citizens of the American Republic. It is to be hoped that the German empire will not sustain the severe shock in the latter part of the nineteenth century by which the whole social system in the kingdom of France was rent asunder, in the latter part of the eighteenth century.

CHAPTER XVII.

SWITZERLAND, 1424.

THAT little dot on the map of Europe, situated among the Alps, called Switzerland, has always formed an attractive and pleasing object to lovers of freedom and equality. Surrounded by powerful neighbors, the mountaineers of these little cantons seem to have imbibed, with the purer air of heaven in which they live on the mountains, that degree of stern courage, determination, and love of liberty which enables them to resist the pressure of the great nations by which they are surrounded. Switzerland, like the wedge of steel, tempered by the spirit of republicanism, has formed one point of pressure which the monarchies around her have been unable to resist. The love of liberty with which the Swiss are endowed, and their hatred of "caste," are best typified by "The Gray Leaguers" and their story:

In the green valleys of Eastern Switzerland, on almost every hill that juts out from the gray mountain walls of the Alps and commands the fertile fields and villages of the upper Rhineland, there stands a ruined castle. And in that castle, in the early Middle Ages, there dwelt some little local princeling who lorded it with almost unquestioned power over the peasantry around him.

These feudal nobles had held sway, with no right save that founded on might, for generations, before the subject peasants, weak, scattered, and resourceless, were at last driven by the intolerable arrogance of this dominant "caste" to combine for mutual defence. Some of the leaders of the movement met in the little hillside chapel of St. Anna, still standing near the town of Truns, in March, 1424, and took solemn oaths to respect their own and all the people's rights, and to wage war upon those who would not respect them.

Johann Caldar—a name revered in his district as is that of William Tell in the scenes of his legendary exploits—gave the signal for the first attack on the oppressors. Caldar dwelt in the upper Rhine valley, not far from the baronial castle of Fardun. The Lord of Fardun entered the peasant's cottage one day at noontide, and in wanton token of contempt spat into the soup that was boiling for the midday. Caldar seized him, and crying, "Eat the soup thou hast seasoned!" thrust his head into into the pot, and held it thus until he was choked. Then he went forth to bear over mountain and valley the banner of a revolt that forever annihilated the nobles' tyranny and left their strongholds in ruins.

For three centuries and a half the Gray Leaguers, as the victorious peasants called themselves, met every tenth year in the chapel of St. Anna, where their first oaths had been taken, and renewed the pledge of popular liberty. At length their territory became the fifteenth canton of the Swiss Republic, still retaining, as it does to-day, its old name—the Grisons, as it is in French.

The American traveling in Europe may view with delight scenes upon the beautiful Rhine; his artistic eye may be delighted by the art treasures of Italy; memories made dear to him may be recalled as he visits England; but in Switzerland he seems to fill his lungs with kindred and familiar air. This little oasis in the desert of monarchies, surrounded by worshippers at the temple of "caste," is to the American an Alabama, "Here we rest."

Until the overthrow of the Third Napoleon and the establishment of a republic in France, nowhere else in Europe did the American feel himself so much at home as in Switzerland; and to those rugged mountaineers of the Alps is due the credit of keeping alive the spirit of liberty almost submerged beneath the flood of monarchical ideas which inundated Europe. Every republic on earth, and each republican, should feel indebted to little Switzerland that the fire of freedom was not entirely extinguished.

CHAPTER XVIII.

RUSSIA.

AT the very name of Russia a kind of horror fills the souls of those who love liberty, equality, and detest "caste" and oppression. Russia is a veritable blot upon the civilization of the nineteenth century. She furnishes an example of all that was horrible under the old monarchical governments of Europe. Russia's social life is honeycombed with anarchy, nihilism, and hatred. Beneath the surface, made smooth by military despotism, there burns the fierce fires of inextinguishable hatred. The people are deprived of those rights and liberties enjoyed by the citizens of even those monarchical governments by which Russia is surrounded, curtailed though those privileges may appear to the free American citizen. Germany, Austria, Hungary, and Italy are almost respectable in comparison with Russia. There can be, of course, but one end to such a condition—we can hardly call it civilization—in that tremendous empire. Revolution and anarchy in its worst form will sooner or later drench the soil of Russia with blood.

Unfortunately for the future welfare and happiness of the Russians, their autocratic master, the Czar, permits no existence of a vent-hole or crater of the volcano upon which the nation slumbers. An election like that of November 8th in America relieves the pressure. In Russia, the discontent of the Common People, and all expression of it, are suppressed by the iron hand that controls the vast horde of soldiers of which he is master. Russia's history and record present not one shining spot to relieve the dark picture of crime, ignorance, oppression, intolerance, and the suffering of the Common People.

Briefly, Russia contains one-sixth of the land of the entire globe and one-quarter of the inhabitants. The government is an absolute and strongly centralized monarchy. It is one of the most arbitrary and merciless despotisms on the face of the earth.

As the positive and negative poles of an electric battery, or as like and unlike attract, there has long been a strong friendship between Russia and our country. The two represent the antipodes of government.

From the period of the appenages (small, petty States, 1054-1238) the enmity has been in a state of smothered or open revolt. It was overrun by the fierce Mongols and held under their

RUSSIA. 317

iron yoke from 1238 to 1462. During that period Moscow and many other cities were burned and the country devastated.

Ivan III. (1263), during his reign of 43 years, did much to consolidate the empire, and introduced the knout as an agent of civilization.

Ivan IV., known as Ivan the Terrible, was a ferocious monster (1533–1584), who first assumed the title of Czar (a Slavonic form of the Latin Cæsar), committed numerous atrocities, and killed his eldest son by a blow in a fit of anger.

Peter the Great (1689–1725) was remorseless in his punishment of those who revolted, as in the case of the streltzi; the rebellion of the Cossacks of the Don; that of Mazeppa, the hetman of the Little-Russian Cossacks; he inaugurated serfdom, and tortured his own son, Alexis, to death.

The rule of Paul was intolerable; he was won over by the artful diplomacy of Napoleon, and assassinated in March, 1801. In the Polish insurrection of 1831 the people were ground to powder.

Alexander II. (1855–1881) emancipated the serfs in 1861. It was freedom only in name. Nihilism sprang up and flourished frightfully. Where his father daily walked unattended, Alexander was in hourly peril. April 16, 1866, he was shot at by a Pole; the following year another Pole shot at him while visiting Napoleon at Paris; April 14, 1879, another Pole attempted to kill him. The same year saw the first attempt to blow up the United Palace and to wreck the train upon which the Czar was riding from Moscow to St. Petersburg. A similar conspiracy was successful, March 13, 1881. Five of the conspirators, including a woman, were executed. Alexander ruled twenty-six years, and left Russia exhausted by wars and honeycombed by plots.

He was succeeded by the present Alexander, whose reign has been characterized by conspiracies and the constant depredations of suspected persons.

The mines of Siberia have been the living death of hundreds of thousands of patriots. More than 50,000 Poles were transported thither after the insurrection of 1863. Since the opening of the present century more than 600,000 men, women, and children have been sent to Siberia. All are in the depths of utter misery and despair. Out of 200,000, more than one-third have disappeared without being accounted for. From 20,000 to 40,000 are living the life of *brodyaghi*—that is, trying to make their way through the forests to their native provinces in Russia.

And yet nihilism, socialism, the spirit of revolt, are more powerful than ever, and ere long will come the upheaval, when all shall be overturned and "the old shall pass away and all things become new."

The Russian nobility, with the Czar at their head, as the high priest of "caste," are solely and entirely responsible for the spirit of anarchy and nihilism which is abroad in the domain of immense Russia. It is a fashion and the fancy of the sham aristocracy in this country to inveigh against anything like socialism, nihilism, and anarchism in America. Should the presence of this dread monster, called nihilism, ever be felt in America, the blame would rest entirely upon the shoulders of the sham aristocrats, just as the Czar and his nobles in Russia are responsible for its presence in that country. There must be a vent for the pent-up indignation of the people; this is, happily for us, found in the ballot-box. It is to this source of relief that we are indebted for the non-existence of socialism in America. It has not been the prudence, wisdom, or consideration of the sham aristocrats which prevents the growth of nihilism here.

CHAPTER XIX.

PATRICIANS AND PLEBEIANS IN ROME.

THERE is a striking historical parallelism between the Anglo-Saxons in modern history and the Romans a thousand years before. The Romans conquered the world as the Anglo-Saxons are conquering the world. The Romans were the first race to found and maintain an empire as wide as the bounds of western civilization. Their characteristic qualities were, like those of the Anglo-Saxons, their supreme sense of duty, their respect for law, their great natural aptitude for government, their earnest practicality, their somewhat deficient sense of the beautiful, and their high military skill and discipline.

But before Rome could begin her march toward her later position as mistress of the world she had to rid herself of the domestic incubus of an internal oligarchy. The authentic history of Rome—for the earlier annals of her seven kings are little more than legends—opens with the struggle of the Plebeians—the mass of her people—to break down the hereditary domination of the privileged "caste," the Patricians, who had a monopoly of political power, had appropriated the whole of the public land, and by unjust laws had burdened the Plebeians with taxes and debts, and reduced many of them to actual slavery.

In the year 495 B. C., there one day rushed into the crowded forum an old man, ragged and emaciated, his back covered with bloody stripes. He loudly proclaimed his history, which was thàt of hundreds of others. He had done service in several wars; his farm had been ravaged and burned, and his cattle driven away; to pay his taxes he had been forced into debt; his Patrician creditor had demanded a usurious interest, and had finally compelled him to work as a slave.

The occurrence created great excitement among the Plebeians, and would have provoked an outbreak had not messengers entered the city bearing the news that a Volucian army was marching to attack Rome. With their stern sense of patriotic duty, the disaffected citizens prepared to meet the foe, it being promised that their wrongs should be investigated after the war. They met and defeated the enemy, but the promise of the Patricians was not kept.

In despair of obtaining justice, the Plebeians decided to secede from the Commonwealth and to found a city on the Sacred Hill, three miles from Rome. This brought the Patricians to terms.

Rather than lose the working force of the community, they agreed to release all those enslaved for debt, and to authorize the appointment of magistrates, called Tribunes, who should be chosen from the Plebeians, and should have the right of forbidding any act of oppression.

From that beginning the Plebeians advanced to full political and social enfranchisement, after a struggle that lasted for two centuries—a stern and bitter struggle, although it was waged "with a perseverance, forbearance, and moderation, of which there is scarcely a parallel in the history of the world."[1] The next step was a law to compel the Patricians to pay rent for the public land they occupied. It was disregarded, and the Tribune Genucius, who attempted to enforce it, was murdered. Then by mutual agreement a body of commissioners (Decemvirs) was appointed to draw up a revised code of laws for all classes. Again the Plebeians had been deceived; the commissioners seized the executive power, and held it illegally and tyrannously until the Commons ended their usurpation by a second secession to the Sacred Hill.

The agrarian question remained a burning one until the Tribunes Licinius and Sextius forced a settlement of it by stopping the whole machinery

[1] Dr. Schmidtz's History of Rome.

of government until their propositions were accepted. The procedure was constitutional, but for ten years (376 to 366 B. C.) Rome was in a state of anarchy, and the fact that actual civil war was avoided testifies strongly to Roman self-restraint.

The legislative power was now the only one denied to the Plebeians. The Publican law was passed to give it to them, but the Patricians prevented its enforcement until by a third secession the Commons again carried their point, and at last secured final and complete equality between the classes. (286 B. C.)

Rome, once the mistress of the world, retained her grandeur only so long as the principles of true democracy pulsated through her body politic and nerved her every action. When prosperity, corruption, and abuse blinded the rulers to the claims of the Plebeians, then came revolution, civil war, decline, and finally the fall of the proudest empire known in the history of man.

So, the mightiest empire the world ever knew declined and fell before the power of the PEOPLE, who, outraged in their most sacred rights, revolted again and again, until, as may be said, the fabric, whose shadow reached to the uttermost ends of the earth, was torn asunder, and so went to fragments that not one stone was left upon another.

CHAPTER XX.

GREECE—VENICE—THE RULE OF "CASTE."

ALTHOUGH ancient Greece was divided into many small countries, yet they were united by bonds of union, of community, of blood and language, of religious rites and festivals, manners and character. In these respects they were distinguished from all other people, whom they called barbarians.

A thousand years before the Christian era the Greeks were divided into the nobles, who were powerful and wealthy; the freemen, some of whom owned estates; and the slaves.

But the manners of the highest class were simple. The nobles were proud of their skill in the manual arts, and their wives and daughters ably discharged their household duties.

Two hundred years later (B.C. 800) most of the states and cities of Greece became democratic. One uniform method characterized the change from monarchy to democracy. An oligarchy of nobles would overthrow the monarchy, and then some one noble would overthrow the oligarchy and establish the cause of the people.

Sparta was the highest type of oligarchy; Athens of democracy.

Ever since Aristotle distinguished them, there have been three recognized types of government —monarchy, oligarchy, and democracy—the rule of one man, the rule of a few men, and the rule of the people.

That the last is the just and the true form of polity, the enlightened opinion of the world has long ago irrevocably decided. Of the other two, experience shows that monarchy is more tolerable. A Nero may have stained the pages of history by the diabolic cruelty to which autocratic power gave free scope; a Napoleon may have poured out half the life-blood of his country to further his selfish personal ambition; yet, on the whole, the evils of one man's rule have been more endurable than those of the domination of a class or "caste." In latter days the sovereign has come to be looked upon less as a personal ruler than as an abstraction—an embodiment of theory expressed in the old maxim that "the king can do no wrong"—a conception far less offensive to the innate democracy of all manly peoples; or, he is regarded as a mere figure-head, as may be said to be the case is England, whose nominal monarch has far less practical influence upon the executive and legislative departments than has the President of the United States.

An oligarchy is the worst of all governmental systems. It has never made a people truly great. Wherever such a government has existed its record has almost always been dark and its end bloody.

Look, for example, at two of the most successful obligarchies of history—ancient Sparta and mediæval Venice. Sparta was, as Bulwer justly observes in his "Rise and Fall of Athens," a "machine wound up by the tyranny of a fixed principle, which did not permit it even to dine as it pleased; its children were not its own—itself had no property in self. So it flourished and decayed, bequeathing to fame men only noted for hardy valor, fanatical patriotism, and profound but dishonorable craft—attracting, indeed, the wonder of the world, but advancing no claim to its gratitude and contributing no single addition to its intellectual stores."

Such was the state that was ruled by the privileged "caste" of the Spartans and its administrative committee, the Ephoræ—a state remembered only for its brief military supremacy over her Grecian neighbors. Contrast her with one of those neighbors—Athens, the most typical and the most democratic of ancient democracies.* "The people of Athens," says Bulwer, "were not, as in Sparta, the tools of the state—they were the state! In Athens the true blessing of freedom was rightly placed in the opinions and the soul. This unshackled liberty had its convulsions and its excesses, but it produced masterly philosophy, sublime poetry, and accomplished art with the energy and splendor of unexampled intelligence. Looking round us, more than four and twenty centuries after, in the establishment of the American Constitution, we yet behold the imperishable blessings which we derive from the liberties of Athens. Her life became extinct, but her soul transfused itself, immortal and immortalizing, throughout the world."

Venice was another such oligarchy as Sparta— ruled by a small patrician "caste," who chose an all-powerful Senate from their own number; and from the Senate was selected an Executive Council of Three—a name that has become proverbial for a body of secret and irresponsible tyrants.

* In the best age of Athens, life was marked by a dignified and elegant simplicity. Every free citizen was one of the rulers of the state, through his vote in the assembly and the law courts; and, consequently, there was little exclusiveness in social life. An Athenian might be poor, but if he had general ability, wit, or artistic skill, he was welcome in the best houses of Athens.—*Sanderson's Epitome of History*, p. 169.

Venice's strength was in commerce, in finance, as Sparta's was in war. Her rich trade with the East and West made her seem

> The pleasant place of all festivity,
> The revel of the earth, the masque of Italy.[1]

But her internal government was one long reign of terror. The Council of Three met at night, masked and robed in scarlet cloaks, to judge those against whom accusations had been thrust into the yawning "Lions' Mouths"—two slots in the wall into which any might thrust an anonymous denunciation of his enemy. And from the Council's sentence there was no hope of appeal; its victims were hurried across the Bridge of Sighs to vanish forever from human sight in the awful torture chambers to which that melancholy passage led.

The ending of most oligarchies has been a violent one, as was that of the Thirty Tyrants at Athens, or that of the Decemviri at Rome. At Venice the sway of a "caste" lasted for centuries, and was ended only by a foreign conqueror—so complete an ascendency had the privileged patricians gained over the fettered populace. The wonderful mercantile prosperity of the community

---

[1] Childe Harold, Canto IV.

stifled the sentiment of popular liberty—a notable warning to mercantile and materialistic America!

No oligarchy, and nothing of oligarchic tendencies can be endured in this country. We must not and will not have a dominant "caste."

CHAPTER XXI.

EGYPT, 4235 B. C.

EGYPT, the cradle of civilization, had its Democrats, who struck resistless blows for equality, freedom, and fraternity for the race. So accustomed have we become, in thinking of Egypt, to be struck so forcibly by those evidences, the pyramids, of slave labor and the oppressed condition of the large portion of the ancient population of Egypt, that the existence of democrats in Egypt seems totally inconsistent with our preconceived idea of the ancient civilization of that country. Yet, we find, during the fourth dynasty —4235 B. C., the pyramids were builded, and the great Sphinx at Gizeh. The wealth and splendor of Egypt were unapproached elsewhere; civilization, the arts and sciences, reached a height which, in some respects, the world has never known since that time. The civilization of to-day is unequal to the task of rearing such structures as the pyramids, over which more than fifty centuries have rolled without displacing a stone or crumbling a corner of the prodigious masses of granite, hewn from the distant quarries of Asswan, Mokattam and Tarah, and transported by means beyond the skill and comprehension of the science of the nineteenth century.

But with all its splendor, wealth, magnificence and culture, the kings and rulers of the Fourth Dynasty became corrupt, oppressive and tyrannical. The Common People, as they were called, revolted, and a revolution of fire and blood extinguished the dynasty, 3951 B. C.

Heedless of the immutable law that only in union is there strength, Egypt not only became corrupt and tyrannical, but divided into two kingdoms, who warred furiously against each other. Then it was that the nomadic hordes of Arabia and Syria saw their opportunity, and, swarming over the borders (2114 B. C.) and overflowing the valley of the Nile with a human flood a thousand-fold more destructive than the turbid inundation of that great river, they crushed the struggling legions like worms in the dust, and became the masters of the country.

They were the Hyksos, or Shepherd Kings, who stamped their rugged individuality on that wonderful land. They ruled for four centuries, forming the fifteenth, sixteenth, and seventeenth dynasties. Their last king was Apepi, who reigned sixty-one years, and is believed by many to have been the Pharaoh ("Pharaoh" was the general name for kings) in whose reign Joseph came into Egypt and was made governor over all the land.

The Shepherd Kings gradually succumbed to the civilization, culture, and manners of the Egyptians, and vanished from history by absorption among those people.

CHAPTER XXII.

CHRISTIANITY.

ASIDE from the fact of its divine origin and inspired teachers, the doctrine of Christianity, the advent of the Messiah, was so opportune that, even had he not been the true Saviour, but taught as he did and as his disciples did, Christianity, by reason of the condition of the civilized world, would have made rapid and permanent progress among the "Common People." Rome was at that time mistress of the world. Her empire extended over the whole of Western, and a large portion of Eastern civilization. Her conquering legions had carried their eagles to the utmost confines of the then civilized portion of the Western world.

The cultured Greek and the barbarous Briton, the learned Egyptian and the warlike Teuton, alike felt the Roman yoke. Palestine was a province of the great Roman Empire. Roman officials, Roman representatives, and Roman soldiers ruled the people of Palestine with a rod of iron. It had once been said that "to be a Roman citizen was to be a king." While the Roman Republic had ceased to exist, and the Cæsars ruled in place of the old republican form of government, creating, as a result of a monarchy, a nobility, class distinction, and "caste," still the traditions and the feelings of the Roman citizen remained with him. He was a king in comparison with the conquered people of the provinces which had been added to the Roman Empire.

The Romans were essentially warriors ; cruel and oppressive, merciless and masterful, at every period of the existence of the Roman government, whether monarchical or republican. But under the Cæsars there had sprung up a privileged class, the nobility, who had accumulated vast wealth, surrounded themselves with an army of retainers and servants, through whom they imposed upon the "Common People" every kind of oppression imaginable.

This was not so much the case where the nobility came in contact with only Roman citizens, but in every conquered province or country the arrogance and cruelty of the representatives of the nobility of Rome made absolutely wretched and hopeless the lives of the conquered people.

The Jewish people had become almost accustomed, as a race, to the yoke of a conqueror. So often had they been oppressed, and so long, they had learned that the ark of their hope and comfort lay, not in temporal power, but in that hope of everlasting happiness which the Word of God, delivered to Moses, insured them hereafter. This had resulted in the creation among the Jewish people of a priesthood and a religious order almost as powerful as the priesthood of ancient Egypt, which exerted, with regard to spiritual and social affairs, though not in conflict with the power of Rome, almost the same tyrannical power as Rome did by the might of her legions in temporal affairs.

Between the grindstones of military despotism and priestly despotism the poor Jew was ground until his very soul cried out in anguish. The true religion, given to his forefathers, through that great teacher, Moses, by God Almighty, had ceased to afford him comfort. "Caste" had crept into the temple, as well as into the Roman government, destroying, as it ever will, peace and happiness at home, security and prosperity abroad. Therefore, when a voice was heard "crying in the wilderness, Come, ye who are heavy-laden," the ears of the Jew, the Gentile, the barbarian, all the world over, were ready to listen and follow the sweet music of hope created in the breasts of the oppressed, which Christ brought.

The persecution of our Saviour and his sufferings arose and were occasioned by the priestly "caste," and executed, in that scene on the cross, by the military "caste"—the Roman soldiers. "Caste," and the crime of it, is responsible for the crucifixion of our Saviour, the Son of God.

The "Common People," in multitudes, followed Jesus, and listened in rapt attention to the loving words of peace and hope he brought them. It was the high priests of the temple who accused him; it was the Roman governor who had him crucified, by reason of the accusations of the priestly "caste."

No fair-minded man, examining into the beautiful story furnished by the existence of the Son of God on earth, can fail to recognize that the loving, peaceful, kindly mission of our Saviour was made wretched, resulting in his suffering and death, by reason of the *crime of "caste."*

Aristocrats and aristocracy have occasioned, from the beginning of the world, nearly all of the sins, wretchedness, and misery of the children of God; and when He sent His Son to save us, they crucified Him. In the coming of Christ, the "Common People" of Palestine saw a gleam of hope, a star to guide them to that haven of rest where neither priesthood nor Romans ruled; that province where all should be bright, where all should enter into perfect bliss. This sensation among the "Common People," starting like the ripples created by casting a stone into still waters, extended and widened until it permeated every province of Rome, making converts of the "Common People."

The conquered provinces had felt the severity of the iron heel of Rome upon their necks. The Roman nobles had driven so deeply into the hearts of the conquered the idea that "to be a Roman was to be a king," and that the subjugated people, though morally and mentally often the superiors of the Romans, were, by the power of the Roman legions, the inferiors of the followers of the eagles of the Cæsars. The utter uselessness and impotency of any outbreak upon the part of the subjugated people, where resort to arms would be sought, was so apparent, the futility of contending with the might of Rome was so great, that the civilized world at that time was hopelessly suffering. To contend with the trained and masterful soldiers of the Cæsars would be productive of but one result—destruction, suffering, and humiliation.

To the world, so bereft of all hope for relief from their sufferings, from the oppressive Roman "caste," His words and His teachings came like the sweet, refreshing breath of heaven, bringing a salve to the wounded spirits of the hopelessly oppressed masses. Christ, the Son of God, was of the people. The earthly parents selected by the All-Wise Almighty for the Son that He should send to save His people, were of the lowly. Christ himself learned the trade of His father, and was a carpenter ; His every utterance, His life, the selection of His disciples, was, like the Truth, democratic. In fact, Christ would to-day have been pronounced a socialist. In the nineteenth chapter of St. Matthew, twenty-first verse, we read: "Jesus answered, If thou wilt be perfect, go and sell that thou hast, and give to the poor." In St. Mark, tenth chapter, twenty-first verse: "And Jesus, beholding him, loved him, and said unto him, One thing thou lackest: go thy way, sell whatsoever thou hast, and give to the poor." In St. Luke, twelfth chapter, thirty-third verse, we find Jesus saying: "Sell that ye have, and give alms."

Imagine a minister of to-day, a teacher of the doctrines of this same Jesus, rising in some good Episcopal church with the would-be noble Astors seated in front of him, and proclaiming to them: "One thing thou lackest: go thy way, sell whatsoever thou hast, and give to the poor." Think of a Baptist minister, before permitting John D. Rockefeller and William Rockefeller to partake of the Holy Sacrament, commanding: "Sell that ye have, and give alms." Imagine the outrage, indignation, of these many-millioned moneyed lords, if the son of a poor carpenter should suggest to them, as Jesus did of old: "If thou wilt be perfect, go and sell that thou hast, and give to the poor." That meek and lowly Jesus who came as a panacea for all sorrow, selecting fishermen to abide with Him and be His associates, sitting at the table and breaking bread with these fishermen, making of them "fishers of men," teaching to the world the equality of man by His actions and His life ; He who was in the beginning the God, the Saviour, could sit at the table and live in close communion and association with fishermen. Will you, Mr. Rockefeller, will you, Mr. Astor, good Christians that you are ? Are you following the doctrines of Him in whose praise you raise your voices, Sunday after Sunday, in a hundred-thousand-dollar church, before an aristocratic, well-bred, genteel, ten-thousand-dollar-a-year clergyman ?

Would you, fair dames of fashion, assist at the coming into the world of a child in a stable, whose cradle was a manger, whose curtain was the straw thereof? You ladies of America, whose crests adorn your carriages, affect to view with adoring eyes a hundred-thousand-dollar painting of the Madonna and her child, yet gaze with contempt, and avoid with averted glances, contact with the pure but poor wives and mothers of our land.

St. Paul, who, of all the early teachers of Christianity, was probably the "most respectable," as soon as the angel of God appeared to him, became converted to the doctrines of Him who was Truth personified, and threw "caste" to the winds. In the seventeenth chapter of the Acts, St. Paul, upon Mars Hill, at Athens, proclaimed the equality of man ; in the twenty-sixth verse, he says : "And hath made of one blood all the nations of men for to dwell on all the face of the earth." As God has made us all of one blood, how contrary to the teaching of Him whom you say you follow, to endeavor to establish a theory that birth makes a difference and inequality, that there is any peculiarity about one drop of human blood that makes it better than another. The teachings of the divine philanthropist, the Saviour of mankind, took deep and permanent root in the minds of men, because the very essence of it was that no matter whether the believer in those teachings be a poor, oppressed Jew, or an outcast Gentile, or a Roman Cæsar, he stood only before his God as an equal of any other of God's children. It was the leveling, the equalizing of rank and power that gave the impetus, at first, to those truths which are the pillars of the faith of the Christian nations of earth. "Come, ye who are heavy-laden," is the doctrine that appealed to the "Common People." As lasting and as abiding as the faith that we have in the Christian religion, so long and enduring will be the sentiment of the human soul believing in the equality of man. It has been so from the beginning, and will be to the end, and surprise and astonishment at each fresh evidence of its outburst is unnecessary. The plebeians of Rome, before the coming of the Lord, asserted the same right, and would have sought the Sacred Hill to establish a city of their own had not the patricians made concessions. It is the same spirit that cost Charles I. his head, Louis XVI. his head, the British Government this vast empire, and the same spirit that, November 8, 1892, cost the Republican party its hold upon power; because, in the minds of the people, that party was thoroughly impregnated with the much-hated principle of the inequality of man.

The rich and powerful were the last to be converted to Christianity. They trembled and said, as the Roman Governor did, "Almost thou persuadest me to be a Christian," but not quite, because the very fundamental principles of the Christian religion are Love, Charity, and Equality. Their conversion would mean the surrendering of their cherished claim of "caste." Many a conversion among the mighty, when at last effected, was the result of policy upon the part of the converted, who had commenced to feel the power of the "Common People" who had listened and become imbued with the divine teachings of the doctrine of Christianity.

Had it been necessary, as now, to pay salaries of from one to ten thousand dollars to those teachers who, in the early age of Christianity, promulgated the doctrines of their God, how few conversions would have been made at all. These wayfarers, obeying the divine injunction of our Saviour, to "go and teach all the people of earth," took no heed of the morrow. They did not teach in temples which required thousands of dollars to build; they did not find it necessary to be surrounded with luxury; they needed no vacations and excursions to recuperate their exhausted natures. Had it been necessary for those "fishers of men" to have carriages, temples, and salaries, the Christian religion would have made exceedingly slow progress. There were no Astors, Vanderbilts, Rockefellers, in the congregations that surrounded the early teachers of the doctrine of the meek and lowly Jesus.

We hear on every side (when this idea is advanced), proclaimed by the gentlemen of the clerical profession, that "the conditions have changed." If such be the case, then history is terribly misguiding. We are told of the luxuries that surrounded the rich of the Roman empire. We read, in the Scripture, of Dives, and the rich men of that day. We know—unless history is entirely in error—that Astors, Vanderbilts, Rockefellers, existed then. But the early teachers of Christianity loved their Lord and followed his footsteps, in that he came to give hope, comfort, and rest to those who were heavy-laden.

The meetings held by the early followers of Christ were not "club meetings," at which expensive music entertained the audience. The audience was not addressed by high-priced elocutionists, nor entertained by the mental gymnastics of some word-painting acrobat.

Humbly and meekly, hopefully, trustingly, the people sought the presence of that Teacher whose earnestness and faith was evidenced in His life and manner of living. His words were blest, all untutored as he was, with the eloquence of that truth with which his soul was filled. He did not say to the people, "Give alms," and at the same time live in a brown-stone front. He did not say, "Take no heed of the morrow," and keep a bank account. He did not preach to his cold and hungry brother that the Christian religion would give him comfort, and keep the warm overcoat on his back while doing so.

In their very lives the early teachers of Christianity made the truth of their own convictions apparent. Is it any wonder that in this, the nineteenth century, doubt arises in the minds of the people? They doubt the doctrine because they doubt the sincerity of the teacher. It is so utterly inconsistent in a man to preach, "If thou wilt be perfect, go and sell that thou hast, and give to the poor," while his hearers know that within a few blocks of where this teacher lives in comfort and luxury, some poor family is starving.

Let us find men to teach us, who, when they find a poor, shivering wretch, but a brother, on the streets, will take off their warm coats and throw them round his shoulders. Let us find our leaders in the path made plain by the divine Master, taking off their shoes to clothe the benumbed feet of the outcast tramp. Then, and when that day arrives, there'll be no such thing as "caste" and class distinction in the house of God. Then will the house of God be sought by the multitudes, as of old they sought the mount whereon the Lord did preach. When the privilege of entering the house of God and occupying a seat therein is not sold to the highest bidder, to furnish the ten-thousand-dollar salary for the teacher of the doctrine of that lowly Master, who had nowhere to lay His head, then will the multitudes gather to do the bidding of the teacher. When there are no high places in the temple to be sold to the representatives of "caste" and sham aristocracy, then will the house of God be a home and refuge for the people. When the charities of Christ's church on earth are not controlled by snubbing, scornful, shoddy aristocrats, when the wife of the poor man shall feel welcome to give her mite, along with the contributions of the rich, without enduring their scornful glances, and subjecting herself to the insult of their assumed social superiority, then will the people become charitable. The church, the Sunday-school, the church society, the charitable committees, have all become impregnated with this crime of "caste," which crucified the Saviour.

CHAPTER XXIII.

NOT A DEMOCRATIC PARTY VICTORY.—DEMOCRACY IS
NOT THE NAME OF A PARTY, BUT OF A PRINCIPLE.

THE endeavor has been made in the preceding chapters to furnish examples of the uprisings of the people from the time of ancient Egypt to the present day.

The endeavor has been made to place before the thinking men of the wealthier class parallels, in ancient history, of great political upheavals in the past history of our own country, as well as in the history of foreign countries and nations—exhibitions similar to the powerful protest made by the people on November 8, 1892.

The object to be attained by such an arrangement of facts as will impress the wealthier classes, is that a change in their methods and manners may be brought about. No one can pretend to contradict that the people with incomes less than $5,000 a year could, if they saw fit, cause such legislation as would relieve them from the burden of the expenses of the government. It is almost incredible that a journal as preëminent in the Democratic campaign as was the New York *Sun*, should publish an editorial, as late as the 10th day of December, as follows :—

NOT DEMOCRATIC.

"Various propositions for an income tax come from Democratic free-traders, who are ready for any scheme for raising revenue that doesn't depend upon a protective tariff. Then there are the Populists, Nationalists, and divers miscellaneous cranks who object to wealth on general principles. Other men's wealth, of course. To these powerful thinkers an income tax is a penalty to be inflicted upon the plutocrats, a discouragement to the acquisition of money. There is much flabby talk about plutocracy, and a good deal of the talk in favor of an income tax is of that nature.

"With the opinions of the Populists we are not concerned, except as students and observers of the political curiosities of the time. It is proper, on the other hand, to remind Democrats that an income tax is undemocratic. Undemocratic in principles, because it is an interference with individual business and a premium upon perjury. Undemocratic in precedent, because the imposition of such a tax was unanimously and strenuously opposed by the Democratic party, and because the extension of the life of that tax from 1870 to 1872 was likewise opposed, with substantial unanimity, by the Democratic party.

"The only excuse for the income tax was that it was a war measure. What excuse can be given for reimposing it? Is there a war against money or against common-sense?"

Democratic free-traders, so obnoxious to the New York *Sun*, by the suggestion of an income tax, are merely seeking for means whereby the expenses of the Government may be defrayed. They know that something is the matter with the Democratic masses, who have shown their dissatisfaction with the existing state of things. These Democratic free-traders (and they fairly represent the doctrine proclaimed as a principle of the Democratic party, and adopted as a platform in the Chicago Convention) know that if they are to be consistent they must abolish, to a great extent, the duties upon imported articles. They also know that if they abolish duties, there will not be sufficient money paid into the treasury of the United States to defray the current expenses of the Government. They have realized the powerful current of public opinion, which demands the equalization of taxes between those who enjoy the benefits of living under the government of the Federal Union. The tariff duties do not fall with the same proportionate weight upon the rich and the poor. The rich derive greater benefit from the security offered their property than the poor, as the amount qf their property is greater than that of the poor; yet a Vanderbilt consumes no more sugar, and therefore pays no more duty, than the Homestead striker.

The Democratic free-trader, "with his flabby talk of an income tax," is merely seeking for a means to furnish, upon something like an equitable basis, the money necessary to run the Government.

The "Populist, Nationalist, and divers miscellaneous cranks" (referred to in the editorial quoted) call to mind the Abolitionists of 1856, who were spoken of with so much contempt, and yet who, four years after, as the Republican party, with Abraham Lincoln as their candidate, swept the country. If "flabby talk" means a demand made by the people upon the wealthier class to render unto the Government in proportion to benefits conferred by the Government, then let "flabbyism" continue to characterize the talk of our legislators, because it would be, with all of its "flabbiness," a welcome doctrine to the "Common People."

The editorial under discussion goes on to recite the fact that the opinions of "the Populist are not worthy of concern, except to those students and observers of the political curiosities of the times." Again is called to mind the studies and observations made concerning "curiosities" that existed in the political firmament in 1856, and resulted in the AURORA BOREALIS in 1860.

This editorial, which is worthy of great attention, emanating from the source that it does, reminds the Democrats (meaning the Democratic party) that an income tax is "undemocratic—undemocratic in principle," because the Democratic party strenuously opposed the life of that tax from 1870 to 1872. There is *not* a shadow of doubt that an income tax is *not* in accordance with the principles of that party which bears the name of the *Democratic party;* but that *it is in accordance* with *democracy* and the *feelings* that fill the breasts of the masses who voted last November for Grover Cleveland, and no one better understands the fact that the victory of last November was not won by the Democratic party, as a party, than the one man most benefited and elevated thereby; that is, the President-elect, Grover Cleveland.

The howl that one thing or another is "not according to the principles of the Democratic party," ought to have but little effect upon him; and, judging from the editorial of November 21st, which appeared in that other journalistic pillar of the Democratic party, the New York *World*, Grover Cleveland appreciates the exact position of affairs, and how and why he was elected.

THE FRUITS OF VICTORY.

"Mr. Cleveland's speeches since the election are even better than those which he made in the campaign. There is an advantage in perfect freedom.

"No truer or more philosophical statement of the causes that underlay the recent political revolution has been made than was contained in Mr. Cleveland's brief speech at the Manhattan Club. 'The American people,' he said, 'have become politically more thoughtful and more watchful than they were ten years ago. They are considering now vastly more than they were then political principles and party policies, in distinction from party manipulation and the distribution of rewards for partisan services and activities.'

"During the campaign, it was a common remark that so quiet a Presidential canvass had not been seen in many years before. But the result showed that the people had been thinking, and that they knew what they wanted. What they want, and what they have demanded, they must be given, if the Democratic party is to remain in power. And what the people ask and expect, Mr. Cleveland clearly indicated in this earnest and elevated passage in his speech:—

"'In the present mood of the people, neither the Democratic party nor any other party can gain and keep the support of the majority of our voters by merely promising or distributing personal spoils and favors from partisan supremacy. They are thinking of principles and policies, and they will be satisfied with nothing short of the utmost good faith in the redemption of the pledges to serve them in their collective capacity by the inauguration of wise policies and giving to them honest government.

"'I would not have this otherwise, for I am willing that the Democratic party shall see that its only hope of successfully meeting the situation is by being absolutely and patriotically true to itself and its profession. This is a sure guarantee of success, and I know of no other.'

"Truer words were never spoken. The fruits of Democratic victory must be sought in lower and more just taxes, in lessened expenditures, in a better public service, in the reform of abuses and the remedy of evils from which the people are suffering, and, in general, in good and honest government. This is indeed the only vindication of the success that has been achieved, the only guarantee of other triumphs to come."

Grover Cleveland, better probably than any other man in the Union, appreciates the fact that his elevation to the Presidential chair was not secured because there are more members of what is known as the Democratic party in the Union than members of what is known as the Republican party. It must be apparent that many who formerly voted with the Republican party decided, for some good and sufficient reason, that they would vote for the nominee of the Democratic party, in the last Presidential election, and that they did so vote on the 8th day of November is evidenced by the fact of Grover Cleveland's large majorities, and the increased vote for the ticket bearing his name, even in States whose electoral votes will be cast in the Electoral College for the nominee of the Republican party.

It is impossible to ascribe this change to increased emigration and the fact that recently naturalized citizens voted the Democratic ticket. In the first place, there is no such unanimity of love for the Democratic party, as a *party*, in the breasts of the emigrants who have been recently naturalized, as to account for their voting unanimously the Democratic ticket. Again, the number of foreigners who have been made, by naturalization, citizens of the United States within the last four years is not sufficient to account for this tremendous revolution; and, further, the greatest gains made by the Democratic nominee were not made in those sections wherein the greatest flood of emigration has poured. Therefore, it seems conclusive that the nominee of the Democratic party received the support of Americans who had formerly voted with the Republican party.

Now, upon what ground can this general conversion rest? It was not done by the flaring of trumpets, by oratory, or reasoning upon the issues as set forth in the platforms of the two parties. It is hard to imagine many voters being convinced of the advantages that would arise under a system of State banks. It would seem that that would convince few, if any, that the Democratic party was more desirable than the Republican party, to have in charge of the finances of the nation. That, as an abstract principle, "Free Trade," or "tariff for revenue only," converted this large number of former Republican voters, is a statement not justified by the vote cast in different States, nor is it possible to find one man, in each hundred who voted the Democratic ticket, who can intelligently discuss the subject of Protection and Free Trade and give satisfactory reasons for preferring Free Trade. The subject is a perplexing one, even to those who have devoted much time and study to political economy.

To show a lack of unanimity among the high priests of Democracy on the subject of Protection and Free Trade, one has only to refer to the record of the late and eminent Samuel J. Randall, who was a most pronounced Protectionist, yet a sterling member of the party known as the Democratic party. On the other hand, we have the Hon. John G. Carlisle, Senator from the State of Kentucky, who represents ultra Free Tradeism. Even the same difference exists between those two great journals, in which are supposed to be mirrored Democratic doctrines and principles: the New York *Sun*, whose editorial is here quoted, which is an absolute Protection organ, and the New York *World*, whose editorial is also quoted, the last-named paper being an absolute Free Trade organ.

It would seem perfectly apparent to even the most benighted mind that, with such divergence of opinion among the old-line Democrats, a doctrine not believed in unanimously by them, could make but few converts from the ranks of the party pledged to Protection.

Free Trade and State banks were the two leading cries in the campaign of the Democrats, joined to which was occasionally heard the cry of fear of a Force Bill.

The worthy New York *Sun* would, doubtless, attribute largely the victory to its efforts in calling the attention of the public to the Force Bill and the danger of its passage if the Republicans should gain the control of the Federal Government. As a matter of fact, however, the people of the Union had seen the Republicans in power, controlling both branches of the National legislature, and also the executive department of the Government; yet, the people have seen the Lodge Bill, known as the Force Bill, pass the Republican House of Representatives, and die a doleful death in the Republican Senate, killed by the votes of Republican Senators. Therefore, that part of the Democratic policy which indicated a strenuous objection to the passage of a Force Bill, if put in power, could not possibly have a great deal of effect in the missionary work done by the Democratic managers. Those Republicans who voted for the nominee of the Democratic party, at the last election, could not have been influenced to do so by the arguments advanced with regard to the Force Bill.

They had seen Senators of their own, the Republican party, kill a Force Bill in the Senate of the United States, and they had no reason to believe but that a recurrence of murder would take place should another Force Bill pass the House of Representatives and be sent to a Republican Senate. These three leading features of the Democratic party appear most prominently in the campaign. Can any fair man say that any one or all of them influenced those Republicans who voted for Grover Cleveland to change from the Republican party and become members of the Democratic party? Is there anything in any one of them or all of them jointly to make a man forsake old associates, old ideas and faiths, and to associate himself, by reason of conviction, with things that are new?

It could not be a matter of reason. It was a matter of sentiment. And (again repeating) no one seems to understand that to be the case better than the President-elect. It was the sentiment of detestation upon the part of the masses—the "Common People"—for that assumption of class distinction, the attempted introduction of "caste" in our country by those who are allied to, or who had forced themselves upon, the Republican party.

The cold and clammy arms of "caste," in which the Republican party was encircled, doomed it to defeat. All of the great virility with which it was endowed when, as Abraham Lincoln's Republican party, it represented the "Common People," was crushed out of it by this venomous python, so that when it faced, in 1892, the arrayed resentment of the "Common People," it was but a shapeless, disfigured form, in which all the beauty, purity, and strength with which it was endowed at the time of its creation had ceased to exist. Had the Republican party retained the vigor that marked its young manhood before it became suffocated by this mass of putrid matter, called aristocracy, there would have been another story to tell of the election November 8, 1892

Had the argument been well defined, as it was in the last election, with parties of equal merit in the eyes of the people, possessing equally the virtues and spirit of the American people—had we arrayed upon one side the Democratic party, with its oriflamme of "Free Trade, State Banks, and No Force Bill," and upon the other side marshaled the Republican hosts under a leader like Lincoln, a man of the people, upon whose standard should be written, "Protection for American Industries, Sound Money Guaranteed by the Faith of the Nation, and Fair Election," can any one who is fair doubt as to what the issue would have been?

It was not, November 8, 1892, a battle between the Republican party and the Democratic party, and when journals like the New York *Sun* would attempt to yoke the people's will by party principles and party traditions, they are merely preparing a harness of cobwebs, which public opinion will tear asunder, and ring the death-knell of the Democratic party in so doing.

The New York *World*, November 10th, publishes a remarkable editorial, in which it recites, among other things, what this victory does *not* mean. The editorial is given, because, if it be correct—and the New York *World* is certainly good authority—then it surely does not mean a victory for the Democratic party, while it does mean a victory for the "Common People," the democratic masses, and such cries in future as that of the New York *Sun* against an income tax, because it is contrary to the Democratic party, will be meaningless, inasmuch as the Democratic party has not won this victory, and Grover Cleveland was not elected President by the Democratic party.

Quoting from the New York *World*, whose editorial of November 10th is printed herewith, these sentences occur: "This victory does not mean Free Trade." Then, does it mean " Tariff for revenue only"? which is an expression in the Democratic platform, adopted in Chicago, and, therefore, if this be a Democratic victory, it must mean what the Democratic party pledged themselves to in their National Convention at Chicago. "It does not mean," says the New York *World*, "the unsettling of industry nor the derangement of commerce." Well, but how can we have tariff for revenue only without unsettling industry and the derangement of commerce? And, if it be a Democratic victory (by Democratic victory is meant a victory of the Democratic party), we must have such laws made and executed as will create a schedule of tariff for revenue only.

Quoting further from this editorial: "It does not mean disturbance of what is sound in finance." Then how can that portion of the Democratic platform, adopted at Chicago, be made consistent with the legislation in the future regarding the finances of the country? If the tax of ten per cent. upon State banks be withdrawn, and thus State banks be enabled to issue their notes, how will it be possible to prevent "a disturbance" of whatever is sound in finance?

Now, if this be a victory of the Democratic party, such a repeal of the ten per cent. penalty tax upon State banks must be enacted—that is, if the Democratic party intends to keep faith with its constituents.

FOR THE GOOD OF ALL.

"If there are honest Republicans who really believe what their party journals and speakers have told them—who fear that Democratic success in the nation threatens danger or disturbance to business—to them we say : Your fears are idle.

"The majority of the people of the United States, represented by the great Democratic majority, do not mean injury to themselves. This country is their country. Its business interests are their interests. Its prosperity is their prosperity. Its honor and welfare are their concern.

"This victory does not mean Free Trade. It does not mean the unsettling of industry nor the derangement of commerce. It does not mean disturbance of whatever is sound in finance.

"The President-elect is the very embodiment of conscientious caution. He is preëminently conservative. His administration will mean economy, reform, retrenchment in every branch of the Government.

"The victory does mean putting a stop to the riot of extravagance, profligacy, and corruption. It means the end of the reign of Plutocracy. It means relief from the monstrous robbery of the masses by unjust and unnecessary taxation. It means a veto upon the looting of the Treasury and the hideous waste of hundreds—nay, thousands— of millions of dollars in the course of a generation by unmerited pensions. It does mean lower and juster taxes and larger freedom of trade. It does mean good money, and good money only.

Our party has triumphed under the happy union of a great issue and a great man. The Republic is stronger for this Democratic victory. The Republicans themselves will be more prosperous, and in the end happier because of it.

Government of the people is safe in the hands of a great majority of the people."

In the concluding paragraph of the above editorial of the *World*, we read (and those of us who live in New York State, with considerable astonishment) : "Our party has triumphed under the happy union of a great issue and a great man." To start with, the issue seems to have been, judging from all of the preceding, Tariff on one side, Free Trade on the other; National banks on one side, State banks on the other ; and Force Bill as a kind of " Flyer."

With regard to these "great issues," there was a lack of unanimity among even the great newspapers of the Union, at the head of which, justly and properly, we put the Free Trade New York *World* and the Protection New York *Sun*. With regard to the "great man" (and there is no attempt to disparage in any manner the Presidentelect of this nation), it seems somewhat peculiar to use the term "great" to designate that citizen of the Union who has been selected as chief magistrate of the nation, in view of the fact that he had been dubbed the "Stuffed Prophet" by that great organ of Democracy, the New York *Sun*, and was so heralded through the Union for more than a year before his nomination. And when four years ago, he sought re-election, the New York *World* killed this "great man" by faint praise. His popularity and greatness did not seem to be recognized by the seventy-two members of the Democratic National Committee who represented the State of New York, in the National Democratic Convention at Chicago, as these representatives protested against the nomination of their "great" fellow-citizen, declaring that he could not be elected if nominated ; and they represented the politics of the Democratic party ; and they told the truth as far as the Democratic party was concerned.

By reason of his greatness or his popularity, he could not have been elected. But when he came before the people, as representing the great mass of the " Common People," then he became great, but only great in so far as he represented the greatness of the people.

The politicians of New York State pronounced the verdict of all that which is controlled by politicians in the State of New York, when they declared it as their opinion that Grover Cleveland could not carry the State of New York. They were simply saying what they, the politicians, in their little political way, could do. But when Grover Cleveland became the representative of the " Common People," then the " Common People" made him great—far greater than could the politician have done—and he has sailed into office on the favorable wind of the opinion of the

"Common People." His greatness is only the reflected greatness of those whom he represents. Inherently, greatness in Grover Cleveland may exist, but certainly no evidence of it has yet been given. He is great to-day because of the great support that has been given him by the will and pleasure of the "Common People." He is no more great of himself and in himself than would be the rifle in the hands of an expert marksman. The masses, the "Common People," represent the marksman. Grover Cleveland is merely the weapon which they will use to bring down the animal which has been devouring their substance, destroying their homes and happiness. The weapon, even though it be the rifle of Davy Crockett, would become impotent in the hands of the weak and inexperienced. The people are powerful, and they will render great the weapon which they wield. The people are skillful. For many centuries, as the preceding chapters recount, in the history of all nations, the people have become trained and skillful in the use of their power.

The President-elect has it within his reach to achieve greatness as the willing and trusty weapon of the masses, the "Common People," by whom he was elected. And wherever the "Common People," the masses, have found a weapon untrustworthy, they have cast it aside as readily and quickly, and secured another, as the ordinary hunter of the wild animal would do.

The "Common People" have been engaged in a chase after this wild animal, this destructive beast, called "caste," sham aristocracy, and over-accumulation of wealth. They imagine that they have secured a good weapon in the man of their choice, November last. And, should it become evident that they have been mistaken, his greatness will cease to be as soon as the great power by which he is supported falls away from him.

It is not well to call a man great until he is dead. Had Benedict Arnold died after the Battle of Saratoga, he would have gone down in history as one of the great heroes of the Revolution.

Grover Cleveland was elected, contrary to the expectations expressed (and expressed honestly) by the seventy-two most influential Democratic politicians of the State of New York. He carried the State represented by these sagacious politicians by more than 40,000 majority. And it was all done, independently of the politicians, by the will of the "Common People"—not by the Democratic party. For upon what issue, possibly, could converts have been made by the politicians?

From the standpoint of politicians, and from past experience, that eminent Democratic orator, the Hon. Bourke Cockran, was perfectly correct when he stated in Chicago, in his famous speech before the National Democratic Convention, that Grover Cleveland was the most popular man in the country on every day in the year, except election day. This was said, honestly and sincerely, by a leading light of the political world of the Democratic party. Mr. Cockran could not foretell that the great Democratic masses, the "Common People," would utilize any one who might happen to be chosen as the weapon of destruction which the "Common People" would use in the chase after the object of their resentment, that brute, represented by "Chappie" on Broadway, the Astors, Vanderbilts, Rockefellers, and Goulds —the sham aristocracy.

Mr. Cockran has, since the election, doubtless realized that, as a politician of the State of New York, he is justly eminent for his sagacity and wisdom, as well as his eloquence ; but, as a judge of what the PEOPLE will do, he is as unreliable in his judgment as the veriest babe in swaddling clothes.

He was talking in Chicago, as was the honorable Governor of the State of New York, and others, for the Democratic party, which COULD NOT and DID NOT elect Grover Cleveland. When, therefore, after the election of Grover Cleveland, that Democratic party, as represented by the New York *Sun*, assumes to dictate to the party of the people, who, independently of the Democratic party as a political organization, but acting only as "Common People," have elected a chief magistrate and representatives to represent them, the "Common People," it is simply bidding for the extinction of the power of that political party known as the Democratic party, with whom, on this occasion, the " Common People " have acted, for purposes of their own, and to achieve ends which they consider desirable.

Should it be assumed by those elected November 8, 1892, to represent the people in the government of the nation, that they were elected because they were Democrats—or, rather, members of the Democratic political party—then it would become their duty, as honest men, pledged to support the views entertained and expressed by the makers of the platform of the Democratic National Convention at Chicago, to repeal all existing tariff laws, until the amount received from duties would only be sufficient to defray the expenses of the Government. In other words, having a tariff for revenue only, and not for protection ; but, inasmuch as the expenses of the Government are as great or greater to-day than its income, it would mean that the "Common People," who voted for the nominee of the Democratic party, have simply swapped horses in crossing a stream, without benefiting themselves in any particular. The Government must have money to defray its expenses, and if, practically, the present tariff is only furnishing a sufficient revenue to defray the expenses of the Government, where is it possible to reform it, so as to lighten the burden of taxation now imposed upon the "Common People"? This is all upon the assumption that the Democratic party claim that it was that peculiar plank in their platform, "Tariff for Revenue Only," that gave them the victory last November. Then the tariff would remain as it is, as we need every dollar of the income of the nation to defray its expenses.

Should the Democratic party assume that it was that peculiar part of their platform which demanded a repeal of the ten per cent. penalty tax for the State banks, then, by the repeal (to which they are pledged) of the said penalty tax of ten per cent., State banks would spring into existence, issuing their own notes, as was the practice before the National Banking Act was enacted. What great good to the "Common People" could grow out of this change in the currency of the nation (that would apparently be the only thing, if the Democratic party is convinced that its nominees were elected because of the virtues contained in their platform), that can possibly be carried into execution by the incoming Government? The suggestion of an increase in the internal revenue tax levied upon alcohol would not be productive of an increase in the revenue derived from this source, as past experience, both in this country and in Europe, has demonstrated that increased taxes upon any article decrease the consumption of said article, and, therefore, decrease the revenue.

The perplexing question, therefore, that will confront those who believe that the DEMOCRATIC PARTY was elected to power, is: How can we adhere to the platform of the Democratic party, and at the same time benefit, in the slightest degree, the people of the nation? For even the most egotistical Democrat will understand, and does understand, that the people of the nation, having placed in the hands of those men whom they have chosen, the entire control of the affairs of the nation; that they, the "Common People" of the nation, will not be satisfied with merely holding things as they are. That would be merely a shifting of scenes without changing the play on the stage of public affairs. Something must be done, in addition to the mere putting out of one set of office-holders of the Republican party and putting in another set of office-holders of the Democratic party. The "Common People" of America, the masses, are not office-seekers. They desire something more than the mere changing of the political faith of their Postmasters, United

States Marshals, and other Federal office-holders.

If the Democratic party, now in power, fails to do anything except shift the scene and change office-holders, then the Democratic party will be relegated to that dismal slough of despondency, at the next election, in which the Republican party is now submerged. The people will elect, by some political name, a party who will perform something for the people's benefit.

It is almost impossible to reduce the tariff without running the government into debt. It is impossible to increase the internal revenue tax to supply the deficiency. Then, if the Democratic party believes in lower duties and decreased tariff, what other course is open for it? What other course is fair to the poor " Common People" of America than to pass an income tax to supply the needs of the nation? It is perfectly useless to talk about abolishing the pensions to any amount sufficient to create any perceptible impression upon the decrease in the income of the nation, should the tariff be materially reduced. It is utterly worthless to argue the subject. The time is wasted. Pension frauds—if any exist—should be at once abolished. But any attempt to repeal any existing legislation with regard to the pensions of the old soldiers of the Union would simply be met by such a howl of indignation as to make a step of that nature impracticable. Whatever sums have been given, and whatever obligations have been incurred, by the Federal Government in the last four years (except frauds which may possibly have been perpetrated), must continue to exist until time shall have relieved the Federal Government from its obligations to the old veterans of the Civil War.

We must have money for internal improvements, for our navy, and for our pensions. We cannot procure the money if we materially reduce the tariff, except in one way, and that is by an income tax, which necessarily must be a graded one. The people of America will not stand a general income tax, wherein one man with an income of a million dollars per annum can pay two per cent., and the man whose income is only two thousand dollars per annum shall pay also the same percentage upon his small income. That would be obviously unfair to the poor man, to whom two per cent. from his small income would represent an inconvenience to him greater than fifty per cent. would to the man with an income of a million.

If the Democratic party assume to have won this victory, then let them proceed upon the platform adopted at Chicago, which will result practically in nothing being accomplished. If Grover Cleveland has been elected solely for his "greatness," and by reason of his immense personal popularity, then let him gather the Reform Club with one arm and Tammany Hall with the other. This trinity of greatness, purity, and brightness will be sufficient for his administration, but nothing will be done.

If, as the facts are, or seem to be—and the vote indicates the correctness of the position—Grover Cleveland and the Democratic party have been put into power by the "Common People" because they represented to the minds of the "Common People" the opposition to "caste," sham aristocracy, and great accumulation of wealth, and not by the mugwumps and the kid-gloved gentlemen of the Reformed Club or the Tammany Heelers, then, if Grover Cleveland and the Democratic party recognize their election to be the result of the votes, not alone of the faithful of the Democratic faith, but of the "Common People," let something be done that may enable the "Common People" to realize their hopes and expectations—then, at the end of Grover Cleveland's four years of administration, he having performed the wishes of the "Common People," let us pronounce him GREAT.

If the Democratic party, with the President at its head, will now utterly throw to the wind old traditions and principles of the Democratic party, and give no heed to the howling of the Democratic press, but comply with the mandates of the people, that they should be relieved from this incubus which is crushing them—over-accumulation of wealth, centralization of capital, and sham aristocracy; the only possible way, without resorting to measures obnoxious to the American mind—confiscation and like enactments—is by a graded income tax, which will throw the burden of the Government where it belongs,—*i. e.*, upon the shoulders of those who have become fat and lusty by feeding upon the blood of the nation. And, in proportion as the burden of taxation is laid upon those ample shoulders, it may be lifted from the crushed and suffering poor of the body politic.

The mere utterance and repetition of the word "reform" is meaningless. *Saying* the word does not make any reformation. When Grover Cleveland was elected eight years ago, he was elected upon the "Reform" cry. The people were then suffering from this "class" infliction, and they gave vent to their feelings by the election of Cleveland. It had been so often repeated that there was great corruption in the Republican party, that the people expected a wonderful exposure of corruption and a great reformation in the affairs of the nation. Nothing was done. No corruption was exposed. The ledgers of the nation seemed to have been accurately kept. No crime was unearthed, and nothing was accomplished. The very plausible excuse was offered that the Republican party still controlled the Senate of the United States, and made abortive any attempt at reformation, or the accomplishment of any relief for the "Common People."

Now, upon this occasion, Grover Cleveland, after a vacation of four years, has been called once again by the "Common People" to command the Ship of State. Both mates and the whole crew have been placed under his command. They believe of him what the New York *World*, November 13th, here gives us:—

THE "STUFFED PROPHET."

"The 'Stuffed Prophet'—that is the nickname bestowed upon Mr. Cleveland by the newspaper organ of plutocracy, which has for years professed Democracy for the purpose of betraying it.

"The name was bestowed in derision. It was the favorite invention of a malice which mistakes insolence for wit. It was intended for ridicule, but, rightly viewed, it is a title to be worn as an honor.

"It is an honor to Mr. Cleveland that he has never had or merited the approval of the New York *Sun*. It is a credit to him that that journal is chief among those to whom General Bragg referred when he said, 'We love him for the enemies he has made.'

"And there is fitness in the nickname, too.

"Mr. Cleveland was a true prophet when he set the face of Democracy towards reform, foreseeing that the country would in due time demand it. He had the gift of the seer, when at the Washington Centennial banquet, he avowed his unfaltering confidence in the wisdom of the people who had so recently overthrown his cause, and his assurance that they would soon come to a juster view, and vote down the policy of monopoly and class privilege and oppressve taxation. They have done it this year.

"And this prophet is stuffed.

"He is stuffed with the virtue which accepts public office only as a public trust;

"Stuffed with the honor which refuses to 'palter in a double sense' with words, or even to keep silence when—as at the time of the silver craze—frank utterance seems to promise only destruction for his own and his party's ambitions;

"Stuffed with sturdy common-sense which 'sees clear and thinks straight,' and so commends itself to the 'plain people' who love the right and seek justice;

"Stuffed with a foresight unsurpassed by that of any statesman of our time;

"Stuffed with a purity of patriotism which views place and power merely as opportunities to render service to the country;

"Stuffed with unprecedented majorities, the eager tributes of the people in testimony of their approval;

"Stuffed with the confidence of his countrymen, who have called him again into their service in order that wrongs may be righted, oppressions

overthrown, errant tendencies checked, and that government of the people, by the people, and for the people may not perish from the land ;
"Stuffed with the Democracy that means all this, for truly—
"The next President *is* a Democrat."

If, as we hope, "Grover Cleveland is stuffed with the virtue which accepts public office only as a public trust," then he will accept his office as President of the United States as a trust from the " Common People " of our country, and not from the political party who nominated him,—*i. e.*, the Democratic party ; he will accept the trust confided in him by the Democracy in its broadest sense—the "Common People " of the land.

If he be "stuffed with honor," in accepting that trust, he will do so with full cognizance of the fact that in honor bound he is to acquit himself in his high office to which he has been called by the "Common People" of America, as will best satisfy them, and remove those crying evils which call aloud from the hearthstone of every Common Man in America. The most objectionable of all the evils, and the one most prominently considered by the voter last November, was the existence of an attempted class distinction in our country.

If he is "stuffed," as God grant he is, "with sturdy common-sense, which sees clearly and thinks straight, and so commends itself to the plain people who love the right and seek justice," his sturdy common-sense will teach him that he has been elected by the "plain people," and he will "think straight," that the "plain people" want such legislation and the execution of such legislation as may relieve them—not in pocket-book, but in feeling—from the assumption of a superiority upon the part of the wealthy worshipers at the throne of "caste," and to that end a graded income tax will be productive of more good and be more efficacious in the accomplishment of an object so near to the "plain people who love right and seek justice," that it made the plain "Common People" forget old affiliations last November—old ties and associations—and vote for the President-elect and the political party by which he was nominated.

If he be "stuffed with a purity of patriotism which views place and power merely as opportunities to render service to the country," then when his term of office shall have expired, having rendered that service to the country, and the "Common People" of the country, to do which he was elected President by the "plain people," he will have endeared himself so to the patriotic "plain people" of the land, having faithfully kept the trust reposed in him by the people, that his name shall go down in the records of the nation associated with the names of Washington, Jefferson, Jackson, and Lincoln.

Grover Cleveland is certainly "stuffed" with the confidence of his countrymen, who have called him again into their service, in order that wrongs may be righted, oppression overthrown, arrant tendencies checked, and that "the government of the people, by the people, and for the people, may not perish from the land." Let us hope that this confidence is well placed, and that now, when he may call to his assistance both branches of the national legislature, he will right those wrongs, and overthrow the oppression of which the people complain; and the chiefest of these is the accumulation of vast sums of money in the hands of families and persons, which creates a danger to "the government of the people, by the people, and for the people."

The people do believe that he is "stuffed with true democracy, in its broadest sense," else they never would have elected him. And how can that true democracy be exhibited better than by suggesting such legislation as will cast the burden of taxation upon that class who can so easily bear it—that class which have rendered themselves so entirely obnoxious to the "Common People" of America, those "plain people, who love the right and seek justice," and who, loving the right, have sought justice by calling him to the position of Executive of the nation? How can Grover Cleveland better right the wrongs of the "Common People" than by urging, as chief of the party in power, the passage of a graded income tax, which would certainly meet with the approval of the "Common People," by whom he was elected, that thereby funds might be furnished for defraying the expenses of the nation, and thus relieving the burden cast upon the "Common People," at the same time preventing a continution of this much-to-be-feared accumulation of wealth in the hands of a few in our country.

A double object would be thus accomplished: First, the primary consideration for which they voted, the abolition of "caste," sham aristocracy, would be brought about by preventing vast incomes being enjoyed by individuals or families, and the consequent idleness, luxury, selfishness, sensuality, and snobbishness attendant upon the enjoyment of vast incomes, where the recipient remains in idleness. Second, it would afford a cure and relief for the present excessive system of taxation which falls so heavily upon the general mass of the people. Thus, at one time, and by one measure (perfectly consistent with the will of the people by whom he was elected), Grover Cleveland could right most of the wrongs, and give relief to the "Common People," the "plain people" (so called by the New York *World*), by whom he has been chosen as chief.

There is no need to mince matters upon this subject. It is plainly and obviously the duty of Grover Cleveland to give some outward and visible sign of the inward and spiritual grace which is in him. There is no time to waste in this matter. Grover Cleveland understands too well that he was not elected by the Democratic party; that he will have the support of the party of the people, call it by what name you will. The Populists, representing, as they do, some of the grievances of the "plain" "Common People," will act with Grover Cleveland's party, the party of the "Common People."

The New York *World* furnishes an admirable article upon the subject, " Why Are They Natural Allies?" speaking of the Populists. Because they are the party of the plain " Common People," who, along with the Democratic party, will control the legislation of the nation, Grover Cleveland represents this army of "Allies," as surely as did Wellington, at the Battle of Waterloo, and the "Common People" will expect him to defeat, "horse, foot, and dragon," the enemy—the sham aristocracy, the representatives of "caste," and the monopoly of money, who have, like Napoleon, carried devastation and destruction into our country ; just as Napoleon did into every country of Europe. Grover Cleveland will have the assistance of these "Natural Allies," the Populists, which is indicated in the timely article below, from the New York *World*, of December 15, 1892 :—

"The Populists in the next Senate will be the natural allies of the Democrats on the most important matters that will come before Congress.

"The Democrats and the Populists fused in several of the Western States. They will together control several of the legislatures. The third party has no affiliation with the Republicans. It is composed in the main of voters who have become disgusted with Republican rule.

"The Republicans cannot rely upon retaining their grip on the Senate by the votes of the men who have overthrown them at the West."

If Grover Cleveland and the party which nominated him will but once recognize, *and at once*, that they did not triumph by reason of the conversion of old Republicans to the doctrines enunciated in the Democratic platform, at Chicago, but will now promptly come to the conclusion, which is so obvious, that they were elected by the "Common People," for the plain purpose of righting those wrongs which the people have endured in silence, then it will be impossible for Republican newspapers to claim that they are "at sea without a chart." They are "at sea without a chart" at present, because the Democratic party, under the whip and spur of Democratic newspapers, driving them to cling on to Democratic principles, and to hold to Democratic doctrine, will prevent Grover Cleveland and the Democratic party from taking any action which would furnish relief to the people. The New York *Sun*, under the able and magnificent management of Hon. Charles A. Dana, cries for Protection and against the Income Tax; while that most potential newspaper, the New York *World*, also Democratic, under the control of the Hon. Joseph Pulitzer, inveighs against Protection and in favor of an Income Tax. Torn by the dissensions in its own ranks, the Democratic party, if it attempts to cling on to the old ideas, will simply do nothing; *and that is what the people fear.*

Now is the occasion for Grover Cleveland to prove himself to be a "great" man. Now is the time for those representatives, elected by the will of the people, to demonstrate to the people that they are willing servants, and that "public office is a public trust"; that, as trustees of the will of the people, they will comply with the request of the people. And the request has gone forth to give relief to the people from this tumor which has grown upon the body politic—"caste," snobbery, and sham aristocracy, and the attendant evil which was the cause of the tumor—excessive taxation and class legislation. Throw old doctrines and principles of the Democratic party to the winds. Cleveland, the next House of Representatives, and the Senate of the United States were not elected and selected upon old principles, which were part of the constitution of the Democratic party. They were elected upon a broad democracy, and if they will adopt the will of the people, their wants and needs, and apply such remedies as the people may demand, then will it be impossible for Republican writers, who wield a trenchant pen like that of the Hon. John A. Cockerill, to truthfully say: "The incoming party is at sea without a chart."

The New York *World*, of December 11th, says of Grover Cleveland's speech, that its generalities are eminently sound and patriotic, and that he asserts that the people can be trusted and that they know what they want, which is here given:—

"Those who looked for any definite statement of his policy from the President-elect in his speech at the Reform Club banquet last night will be disappointed. Mr. Cleveland evidently thinks, and probably correctly, that the time for this has not yet come.

"But Mr. Cleveland's generalities are eminently sound and patriotic. Especially excellent is his sturdy assertion of the good Democratic doctrine that the people can be trusted, that they know what they want, and are entitled to have their will respected. Contrasted with the current Republican talk that the voters have been befooled for three years and are bent on turning the progress of their country backward, Mr. Cleveland's robust patriotism and faith are eminently refreshing.

"The spirit in which he contemplates the responsibility soon to be placed upon him and his party is equally admirable. There is neither shrinking nor boastfulness, but a calm courage characteristic of the man and befitting the occasion. It is to be hoped that Mr. Cleveland's admonition to and defence of economy, as something about which "there is nothing shabby or discreditable," will not be lost upon the present Congress."

This fills us with hope, we "Common People," who regard the *World* as a leading light in the Democratic firmament of journalism. It is like a bow of promise set in the heavens of the future, and especially when, upon the succeeding day, the *World*, which voices the sentiments of the Democratic party, publishes the following :—

"A monopoly organ declares that an income tax is 'undemocratic.' It says that 'the only excuse for the income tax was that it was a war measure,' and asks: 'What excuse can be given for re imposing it?'

"The excuse of necessity. The government is confronted with the condition of an empty treasury and a demand for tariff reduction twice made by the people. Either one of these things may make new taxes necessary. Combined, they are almost certain to do so.

"With an annual expenditure of over $220,000,000 due to the war (for pensions and interest upon the public debt) a choice in war taxes would fall on a graded income tax upon every principle of economy and justice.

"It is surely Democratic to tax luxuries rather than necessaries, superfluities rather than essentials. As one of the speakers at the Reform Club said: 'Any tax on what men have is better than a tax on what men need.' It cannot be undemocratic to tax those who are best able to pay, to apportion public burdens in a manner to cause the least hardship to the greatest number.

"A graded income tax is the coming tax if the expenditures of the government are to continue anywhere near the present mark."

It is with hope and trustfulness that we regard the future.

Here is a spectacle presented before us by two of the Democratic newspapers of New York City—the stronghold of Democracy in the Union is New York City—one arrayed on the side of Protection and against a graded income tax, the other, of equal prominence and position, arrayed on the side of Free Trade and a graded income tax. Now, let the members of the Democratic party view this picture presented to the "Common People" of America, and ask themselves: For what did the people vote November 8, 1892? Did they vote with the New York *Sun* when they voted for Grover Cleveland, or did they vote with the New York *World* when they cast their ballots for the President-elect? Common-sense, common reason, would indicate to the most superficial that they voted neither with the New York *Sun* nor the New York *World*, nor the Democratic party. This is not a victory of the Democratic party! And it cannot be said too forcefully that this victory *does not belong* to the Democratic party! It is a VICTORY OF THE PEOPLE, who demanded a suppression and an extinguishing of the wrongs that had been inflicted upon them. They voted out West with the Populist party on the same basis as they voted with the Democratic party in the East and South. It was anything—call it by what name you please—so that that thing, when elected, should be a party of the people.

Don't insist upon a revivification of the doctrines of the Democratic party. The people have spoken for themselves, and their voices must be heard through the representatives selected by them in the halls of Congress. During the next four years, Grover Cleveland must execute the WILL OF THE PEOPLE. He has been elected by no party. The Populists will be his "natural allies," because they represent the People, as he does. He need not remain "at sea without a chart" one day or hour, only follow the will of the people! They have placed their heels of disapprobation upon "caste" and sham aristocracy and the attempt to engraft it upon American society. They have placed the nail erect and have given Grover

Cleveland the hammer. Now let him drive it home! And we will stud the coffin of dead "caste" so full of nails that the shaking skeleton, borrowed from Europe, will never have a resurrection in our country. There is only one effectual way to accomplish the end desired—the eternal entombment of this multi-lived creature—and that is by the infliction of such an income tax as will prevent the possibility of the existence of a thing like " Chappie" on Broadway, and make America an undesirable field for the coroneted sportsmen of Europe to hunt in for matrimonial game, and prevent the accumulation of fortunes that would arouse a feeling of cupidity in the weazen chests of the puppified lords and degenerate descendants of Europe's nobility, whose greatest pride is in the "Bar Sinister" in their armorial bearings.

Why is delay in the execution of the will of the people necessary? Grover Cleveland is thoroughly convinced that he was elected, not by the Democratic party, but by the people at large. The first step in the right direction would be this— as soon as Grover Cleveland assumes the office of President of the United States—(that is, President of the nation, by the will of the "Common People"), to then and at once take such steps as would quickly afford the relief the "Common People" expect of him and his administration. Will the cry of the Republican newspapers, that "the Democratic party will do nothing," prove correct? It is only for four years that this man of the people, Grover Cleveland, can occupy the position to which he has been called by the "plain" people of America. After his induction into office, the "Common People" will expect that not one single day will be wasted in the execution of their wishes. "Twice in the election of Congress the people have decreed a reform in taxation and other changes in the policy of the government." And the people will not permit any further delay in the matter. The people, in the most pronounced manner, have exhibited their determination to bring about certain changes and a certain kind of reformation. Every hour that it is delayed is pregnant with danger to the Democratic party.

The closing sentence taken from the New York *World*, of December 10th, seems full of meat—"The way to reform is to reform." All the platitudes and promises ever uttered would not be a reformation. The people, by an overwhelming majority, have decreed that there shall be a reformation in taxation, and with regard to the social life of the American people, which has been made unhappy by the introduction of foreign mannerisms. The way to begin is to *begin*, and the sooner the better.

The calling of an extra session of Congress is but a minor detail where the will of sixty-five million people has been expressed in the positive manner that it was on November 8th, 1892. The great Democratic dailies of the Union, like Kilkenny cats, are fighting over little matters, seemingly losing sight entirely of the truth of the case, *i. e.*, that this is not a Democratic victory, but a victory of the people. And the sooner the wrongs of which the people complain are righted, so much sooner will end the sorrow, sufferings and the oppression of the people. Whether there should be an extra session or not, it is hardly worth while for two great dailies like the New York *World* and New York *Herald* to quarrel over. The people have said: It is well that certain things be done. "Then, if it be well that it be done, it is well that it be done quickly."

In concluding this chapter, it is desirable to have it distinctly understood that this volume was not written or intended as a Democratic aftermath campaign argument. If it be incomprehensible with the mass of the people who may read this book, that it was written from a broad democratic standpoint, and not from a Democratic party standpoint, that it is to be regretted. It has not been the aim of the author to fall prostrate at the feet of the Hon. Grover Cleveland, the President-elect of the nation, further than to believe and trust in his promises and integrity, and his manliness of character, and to await the result of his actions, with regard to the will of the people, pronounced the 8th day of November, 1892, in their selection of him as their representative. Should the Hon. Grover Cleveland, President-elect of the Union, by the will of the "Common, 'plain' People" of America, prove himself to be all that the people believe, should he fulfill the trust reposed in him, as did Thomas Jefferson, Andrew Jackson, and Abraham Lincoln, then with earnestness and sincerity would the author lend his voice to the anthem that would go up in his praise from the mouths of the "Common People," saying: "Well done, thou good and faithful servant; great hast been thy trust, and in such manner hast thou executed the trust that thy name shall be handed down, in the records of history, to be read by future generations of Americans as THE GREAT GROVER CLEVELAND.

CHAPTER XXIV.

NOT A DEFEAT OF ABRAHAM LINCOLN'S REPUBLICAN PARTY.

THE "Grand Old Party," which sprang from American intelligence and the advancement of civilization, fully armed, like Minerva from the brain of Jupiter!

That transcendant glory which will ever surround the name of the Republican party with a halo, was not forever submerged beneath the flood of indignant votes, November 8, 1892. That party which, by its deeds, shall ever live in the grateful recollection of the American heart, was not vanquished in the fight November last.

The symmetry, beauty, and virtues so preeminent in the party of Abraham Lincoln in 1860, will ever present a spectacle for the admiration of the "plain" "Common People" of America. They loved the Republican party in 1860, and cast their votes for it because it represented them—the plain "Common People"; because the candidate of the Republican party, Abraham Lincoln, was one of them, the "Common People"; because in the right hand of the Republican party was carried the standard of *equality and emancipation;* because in their standardbearer, Abraham Lincoln, the plain people recognized a typical man of the "Common People." "Mudsillism" was synonymous to them with the term "Common People." The industrial and laborial North was aroused to righteous indignation by the assumption of a social superiority on the part of the cavaliers, the believers in "caste," in the South. The Republican party, led by that wonderful creation of the American soil and the air of freedom, Abraham Lincoln, won the battle of the equality of man in 1861-65. Following still the guiding star which had left its reflected glory upon the horizon even after it had descended into the tomb made by the assassin, the people of the Union elected the victorious general, Ulysses S. Grant, to the office of Chief Executive of the nation. Believing in and trusting the man who had been a friend to Abraham Lincoln, when he was surrounded by a multitude of dangers, they cheerfully re-elected the victorious General Grant to be the President of the people for a second term.

Slowly, but none the less surely, had been going on, during General Grant's administration, the disintegration of those principles that made the party of Abraham Lincoln *great* in the eyes of the "Common People" of the Union. After twice enjoying the exalted position of Chief

Magistrate of the nation, General Grant was called upon to surrender his office to a successor. So great had been the inroads of decay upon that sterling honesty of the Republican party—that Republican party which had been planted by the loving hands of Lincoln in the breasts of the American people—that President Hayes succeeded General Grant, as a Republican President, only by concessions made in the interests of peace by a great statesman, Samuel J. Tilden.

The weakening influence of the barnacles growing upon that stalwart tree of Republicanism, and which had been washed there by the ocean tide of prosperity that had surged upon our nation, was felt in the campaign between Hayes and Tilden. And let all good Americans, Republicans as well as Democrats, uncover their heads in speaking of a man like Tilden, who was a man of the people, thought of the people, and of the horrors of civil war. Each succeeding administration tended but to weaken the hold of that good old Republican party, that Grand Old Party! (and it gives us pleasure to say it) upon the hearts of the American people, because the barnacles which had clung on to the life-giving roots of the stalwart oak of Republicanism and the Grand Old Party—those barnacles of sham aristocracy, believers in "caste" and class distinction, the wealthy—had managed to sap the strength of the vigorous young tree planted by Abraham Lincoln, until, deformed, it presented a spectacle obnoxious to the eyes of the "Common People" of America.

The first decisive evidence of the dissatisfaction of the people was given in the election of Grover Cleveland in 1884.

While Burchard, with that remarkable alliteration, "Rum, Romanism, and Rebellion," is accredited with having caused the defeat of James G. Blaine, the impression made upon the "Common People" by the spectacle of that dinner of millionaires, called the "Belshazzar feast," at which the nominee of the Republican party, James G. Blaine, occupied a seat, was much greater than the howling of "Rum, Romanism, and Rebellion," by an obscure preacher.

The Republican party had ceased to represent to the minds of the plain "Common People" what it had originally represented. There had grown upon that party the fruit of evil, in the shape of a moneyed class, who assumed to be better than the plain "Common People" of America. Hence, James G. Blaine, with all his personal popularity, magnetism, and magnificent record, was unable to secure, from the ranks of the "Common People," the votes necessary to elect him President.

The defeat of Grover Cleveland by President Harrison was brought about (and there can be no doubt of it) largely by the use of money, secured as contributions from the moneyed class to perpetuate the control of the Republican party in the Federal Government, thinking that by so doing the power and assumption of social superiority upon the part of believers in "caste," who cared nothing about the principles of the original Abraham Lincoln Republican party, and who were as far beneath it in patriotism, honesty, and truth as the earth is beneath the heavens, would also be perpetuated.

There is not a shadow of doubt, and even the most prejudiced slave of political "bossism" will be forced to admit, that President Harrison has filled his high office with dignity; that he is an honest, patriotic, representative American. He has kept faith with the American public, as far as was possible for him to do so, in the execution of the laws enacted by the legislative bodies of the nation. His renomination was but the natural consequence of his administration.

The Republican party certainly entered the campaign of 1892 opposed by a divided Democratic press, a divided Democratic party, upon the supposed and alleged great issue of the campaign —that is, Protection and Free Trade.

To illustrate that point, compare the New York *Sun*, believing in Protection, with the New York *World*, believing in Free Trade.

The American people for intelligence will average as highly as the people of any other nation, but they are not all political economists. They had not, even during the four years and with all "the campaign of education," become sufficiently instructed to form a decided opinion upon the information acquired by them with regard to the questions of political economy involved in the discussion of Protection and Free Trade.

It is perfectly ridiculous to hear it asserted that the people of the United States voted against the Republican party in sufficient numbers to create a political revolution by reason of the fact that they had learned sufficient to become convinced, founding their conviction upon information and reason, that Free Trade was preferable to Protection.

The average American voter would be as lost in an argument upon the subject of political economy as would a disputant regarding a legal proposition who had never heard of Blackstone or Kent, because the average American citizen has never read one line of Adam Smith, John Stewart Mill, or, in fact, any of the hand-books of political economy.

The conclusion to be drawn from the assertion that the people of the United States had become convinced that it was beneficial to them to have Free Trade is groundless. The Republican party had certainly the advantage in the argument, because, under the existing state of our tariff laws, the country is and was prosperous, wages were higher, a greater sum of money was deposited in the savings banks by the laboring classes than ever before in the history of our country. Now, these good things, representing a prosperous condition, actually existed and do exist under the Protection policy of the Republican party. It is hard to believe that the mass of our fellow-citizens would be led away by the simple desire for an "experimental change." It is hard to convince any man (when you select an individual) that he shall forsake a business or occupation which he knows furnishes him with a competency, to embark into some new and untried venture, forsaking that which he already knows furnishes him with a sufficiency, for that which is speculative.

Now, this is exactly what the Republican party, as represented by the Republican newspapers, is trying to preach as the cause of the defeat of the Republican party last November. In other words, the press of the Republican party assumes that, collectively, the people of the Union are more utterly ignorant, stupid, and absurd than they would be when acting as individuals, which, of course, is ridiculous.

It was not a question of the pocketbook with the masses. It was not a question whether they were doing better by reason of the Protective policy of the Republican party than they could hope to do under the Free Trade policy enunciated by the Democratic party. It was a clear-cut proposition : Shall we allow longer the accumulation of money in the hands of a few families, who are assuming before us and flaunting in our faces their claim to a social superiority, making a sham aristocracy, "caste," in our country? It was not the pocketbook, for with regard to that proposition there can be no doubt that the American characteristic, "shrewdness in business," would have inclined every voter to let well enough alone.

The Republican party and the principles enunciated at Minneapolis with regard to Protection had certainly the best of the argument. From a business standpoint, what was and is, is well. What may be in the future, under the Free Trade theories of the Democratic party, from a business standpoint, is problematical. But the voter remembered the snubs, sneers, and insults inflicted upon his wife and family by would-be social superiors, whom he associated in his mind, in an unmistakable manner, with the Republican party.

It was not a defeat upon the principles of the Republican party. It was a defeat of *class*, "caste," and sham aristocracy. It was not a defeat because of the pocketbook.

On November 5th, the *Mail and Express*, of New York City, published the following editorial, which is absolutely truthful :—

BUSINESS AND POLITICS.

"Here it is the last week before the Presidential election, and so sound are all the conditions that people seem to have little time to talk politics. Never before in the history of the country has business gone right on with so much more than usual activity for the season. Money has been easy and the volume of exchanges, as shown by the Clearing House returns, unprecedented for the season. Anxiety over the result of next Tuesday's election has neither interfered with the ordinary trend of trade nor has it checked its activity.

"The fact that wheat has this week sold at the lowest price ever known at New York (73½ cents) must interest the farmer in the cry of English cheap labor. If the Englishman comes to this country because he can live better here, he increases the demand for bread, and the farmer can certainly get a better return for his produce when he sells it to a workingman at home instead of sending it 3,000 miles across the ocean, paying freight room in a foreign steamship to support a foreign workman.

"It is rather surprising that this cry should have been raised just at this time. If the consumer and the producer are brought closer together, is it not better for both? They save the cost of the transfer from one to the other. If the English weaver can come to this country and work, so that his product does not have to cross the ocean, and then get his wheat, flour, and meal without having to pay the additional cost, do not both profit? The country is so large that we can well afford to increase its population when we can reduce to a minimum the cost of the exchange of necessary means of life.

"The market for iron is better all around, from the fact that stocks are being taken up faster than ever at this season of the year. This is due very largely to the even weather, which has been so favorable to building projects, the number of working days in October being probably more than in the same month for years, and now, in the first week of November, work is going on just the same.

"This will be apparent to every one who has watched the progress of work and seen new buildings reach the fifth or sixth story when, if the season had been adverse, they might not have been half as high at this time. The railroads have also contributed to consumption, for they are forehanded in placing early orders for the large increase in the equipment that they will have to have for next year.

"The voluntary advance in wages by the Fall River manufacturers is another suggestive indication. The South has had three years of steadily increasing cotton crops. The country has not only exported more than ever, but it has consumed more, and out of this great crop the proportion spun and woven in the United States has advanced even more rapidly. The figures will show that domestic consumption has increased proportionately faster than the crops.

"There is no better proof of prosperity than the ability of the people to buy clothes. Food they must have, but they can wear old clothes. Now, the woolen factories are full of work, and yet, thus late in the season, the orders are so large that the cotton manufacturers make a second advance in wages within three months. There is no idleness in the boot and shoe factories, and the rubber mills are as fully occupied.

"The country never was more prosperous on the eve of election."

It is impossible for a truthful man, who is not talking for the benefit of "the galleries," or as a political demagogue, to dispute the facts recited in the above article in the *Mail and Express*. That argument and the facts therein recited, ought to have had great weight; but did they? No! And the reason? The *Mail and Express* is owned by Colonel Shepard—doubtless a most worthy gentleman—but, unfortunately for any effect that might be created by the utterances of Colonel Shepard; unfortunately for the influence looked for by articles published in the *Mail and Express* upon this occasion, it is well and thoroughly understood that Colonel Shepard is a very wealthy man, a son-in-law of the Vanderbilts; that he represents the money power of the Vanderbilt family. The people of New York City (and Colonel Shepard and the *Mail and Express* is but an example) said to Colonel Shepard, to the *Mail and Express*, in no hesitating manner, November 8th, We will not dispute the facts that you publish concerning our prosperity and the advantages that we enjoy under the Protective policy. You appeal forcibly to our pocketbooks. But it is now the turn of the people to say to Colonel Shepard, the *Mail and Express*, and all the representatives of capital—The truth of your argument, so far as our pocketbooks are concerned, to the contrary notwithstanding, you, Colonel Shepard, representing that *class* of which your father-in-law was a prominent member, and to quote from his magnificent rhetoric—you, Colonel Shepard, *Mail and Express*, and representatives of "caste" and sham aristocracy, now in turn we say it, "You be damned!" as Vanderbilt a few years ago said "The public be damned."

We have been Republicans, we, the "Common People," until the party for which we voted in 1860, and which, under the leadership of that great Commoner, Abraham Lincoln, forever silenced the claim of the Southerner to social superiority. We have been good Republicans until *you* have fostered and aggravated the ulcerous sore of a sham aristocracy, defiling the healthy and vigorous body of the Republican party. You may have the best of the argument on Protection; it may benefit our pocketbooks, but we are not selling our birthright, the equality of man, for a mess of pottage!

The *Mail and Express*, at great trouble, and, doubtless, expense, furnished plausible excuses for the defeat of the Republican party, and disliking to admit the *true cause*, for in admitting that true cause, it would be necessary to hold the father-in-law of the proprietor of the newspaper responsible for his share of this "Waterloo." (In fact, W. H. Vanderbilt was to the Republican party what Grouchy was to Napoleon at Waterloo.) With great care did the *Mail and Express*, saving no expense, ascertain the opinions of the various newspapers in the State of New York, concerning the cause of the defeat of the Republican party.

Its columns were filled with the opinions of editors throughout the Empire State. Many and various were the reasons given. The defeat was blamed upon the "stay-at-homes"; the defection of the farmers on account of the McKinley Bill; the Saxton Ballot Law; a simple desire for a "change"; lack of organization; and a few correspondents intimated that the "Common People," tired of accumulations of wealth, voted the Democratic ticket in the hope of securing relief and equality thereby.

Could not one editor have been found by the inquiring representatives of the *Mail and Express* who possessed sagacity sufficient, coupled with enough frankness, to say, directly, that it was not against the policy of the Republican party, their platform, nor candidate, that the people voted November 8th, but that it was against that element in society which the proprietor of the *Mail and Express* represents so ably as the son-in-law of W. H. Vanderbilt, the sham aristocracy, snobbery, and the believers in " caste "?

It is not so much a matter of astonishment that the editors of Republican newspapers should have misjudged with regard to the cause of the social revolution as it is to find that eminently representative American, General Benjamin Harrison, the candidate of the Republican and the present President of the United States, giving expression to ideas so erroneous as those accredited to him in an interview published in the New York *World*, November 13, 1892.

The American people will always regard with kindly feeling the present President of the United States, General Benjamin Harrison, as a citizen of the Union, who was elevated to the position of Chief Executive of the nation, and who has kept faith with those by whom he was elected. It is well for a President, upon leaving the White House, to feel that he carries with him into his reabsorption in the mass of the people, the respect and confidence of his fellow-citizens. President Harrison, personally, has the respect and admiration of every patriotic American citizen in this broad land of ours. He may feel justly that satisfaction which is the reward of services well rendered to the Republic. Had his party, or, rather, the party which nominated him, the Republican party, not been cursed with the crime of "caste," doubtless he would have been re-elected, for he enjoys the confidence, irrespective of political affiliation, of each individual voter in the Federal Union.

In the day of disaster to the party by which he had been nominated, in the bewilderment arising from the overwhelming defeat of the Republican party, President Harrison may reasonably be excused for his erroneous judgment as to the cause of the disaster to the Republican party. That he should seek for an excuse, standing upon the vantage ground of truth itself, in the idea that the people of the Union had become Free Traders, possibly may be justifiable. At the same time, President Harrison is so thoroughly American that we would have expected a nearer approach upon his part to the real cause of the defeat of the Republican party.

That the Republican party had the best of the argument, so far as sound finance is concerned, there can be no question or doubt. There lingers yet, in the minds of many voters, recollections of the debased currency in use prior to the National Banking Act, passed by the Republican party. A bill issued now by a bank has the guarantee of the credit of the Federal Government behind it. Such would not be the case should the penalty tax of ten per cent. upon State banks be repealed. Every dollar of currency to-day in use in America is worth a hundred cents. And a lively picture to the contrary is presented by the experience of those older citizens who endured all the inconveniences of a State bank currency. The most ardent Democrat (meaning member of the Democratic party) would hardly have temerity sufficient to assert that the financial policy, as advocated by the Democratic platform, adopted at the Chicago National Convention, is superior to the sound money existing by reason of the législation enacted under the Republican administration of the finances of the Federal Government.

But the people said, November 8, 1892, it matters not whether the currency be debased or not. We, the plain " Common People," will not be debased into social inferiority! It matters not whether there be thousands of counterfeits in the currency of the community. We would rather have counterfeited currency than counterfeited aristocracy! The dollar to-day, guaranteed by the faith of the Federal Government, may be worth a hundred cents, and we'll make it worth only fifty cents, as guaranteed by each State in the Union, but the position, socially and otherwise, of each man and citizen of the Union must be worth a *hundred cents*. And we are weary at the attempt made by sham aristocrats to depreciate the value of that doctrine, which is dearer to the American than dollars and cents—the EQUALITY OF MAN.

With regard to the Force Bill, the Republican party had the best of the argument. Their platform, as adopted in Minneapolis, only indorsed the idea of a fair, free, and honest election, all of which was but the reiteration of part of that Rock of Ages for the patriotic American—the Constitution of the United States. Can any man argue that, as a good citizen of the Union, it is proper for him to believe in anything other than a fair, honest election? If there be such, he is not to be found in the ranks of the plain, common, honest people, who absolutely abhor any fraud upon their franchise as citizens of the United States.

So that, in point of fact, apparently the three great issues to be decided in the last campaign by the American people were: Protection *versus* Tariff; National Banks *versus* State Banks; Fair Elections *versus* Frauds on the Franchise.

Without a moment's hesitation, the American people would have decided that the Republican party should continue in control of the affairs of the nation, especially when that Republican party had for its standard-bearer a man who, like Benjamin Harrison, possessed the confidence of the American people—a man in whom the American people recognized every patriotic principle inherent in the breasts of the common, plain people of America.

But the Republican party of 1892 had become lost in the mist arising from the exhalations from the manure heap of sham aristocracy and "caste." Figures looming out of the gloom of the present, hardly compare favorably with those giants who cultivated the soil in which was planted the Republican oak tree.

Through the miasma arising from the rotting present of the Republican party, the picture of Thomas Platt appears. In the hellucid atmosphere of the Republican party of the past, we see the picture of Seward.

Amidst the odoriferous present we find the likeness of the skillful, the Honorable Matthew S. Quay. Upon the clear sky of the past is mirrored the majestic Roscoe Conkling.

Amidst the hurly-burly and charlatan parade of the present, we perceive that prince of clowns and jesters, Chauncey M. Depew, king of after-dinner speech-makers, the witty buffoon who represents the princely Vanderbilts, the man who was never heard of except when clothed, either in dress suit or imported English clothing. By the side of this figure of the present, look back and see the picture of that man of the Republican party who met Stephen A. Douglas on the stump in Illinois, whose jests were filled with the meat of common-sense, whose heart was an outgushing spring of kindness towards his fellowmen, the "Common People." Place the present picture, Chauncey M. Depew, in dress suit, supported by the Vanderbilts' millions, beside the long, angular figure of that Illinoisian, Abraham Lincoln, supported by the people—but pause; this is sacrilege!

Republicans, you know why your party was defeated. Be frank; be brave; be manly, and charge it upon the proper cause—"caste!" affectation! sham aristocracy! degeneracy!

CHAPTER XXV.

THE POPULIST: THE "ALLIES."—ELECTED BY THE PEOPLE; THEREFORE, WITH THE "COMMON PEOPLE."

It does not seem to afford any great amount of pleasure for the hide-bound members of the Democratic party, the thought that possibly the Democratic party may become but a fifth wheel to the coach, and they view with evident dislike the growing power of the Populist party.

Quoting from the New York *Sun*, of December 11th, that able representative, in a journalistic way, of the Protection Democrats, we print the following statements:—

WEAVER AND HIS MILLION VOTES.

"The Populists are naturally excited and encouraged by their demonstration of numerical strength at the election of 1892. The Populist view of the achievement, and the Populist interpretation of its significance, are set forth in detail in the very interesting summary of results printed in another part of this paper. In brief, the claim is this:—

"One million votes in the South and West for the Weaver electors;

"Twenty-three electoral votes obtained by fusion or otherwise ;

"Five Populist Senators and ten Populist Representatives in the next Congress ;

"Populist State Governments in Kansas, Colorado, and North Dakota, and greatly increased Populist representation in the legislatures of these and several other States ; "

Which evidently furnishes no great amount of satisfaction to that organ, which is essentially Democratic in a party sense.

Weaver, and his 1,000,000 votes, present the startling possibility to the organ of the Democratic party, that perhaps the people, who are members of that broader democracy, may be breaking away from the traces of the party harness. It is a little harder to prognosticate concerning future political events and manage the people, when they escape from party traces. The million votes for Weaver represent that part of the people who have become thoroughly exasperated by the manner of that excrescence, "sham aristocracy," on the Republican party, and who, at the same time, were still unwilling to become harnessed in the party-wagon controlled by the Democratic party. Thousands would have been glad to vote with the Populists had that party not been filled with all kinds of incongruities and "isms." There was a curse on the houses of both the Democratic and the Republican parties, and the people, exclaiming with Mercutio, in Romeo and Juliet: "I am hurt; a plague o' both your houses! I am sped," voted for Weaver and the Populists; because the plain "Common People," who were Republicans of the Abraham Lincoln school, had no confidence in the Democratic party as a party. They were plain "Common People," who wanted a party in which they would feel at home. They did not find it in the Democratic party, and, being absolutely disgusted with the degeneracy and social shams of the Republican party, they flocked to the party of the Populists to the extent of 1,000,000 voters, as presenting a haven—no matter how insufficient— in the storm created by the wrath of the people, caused by the idiocy and assumption upon the part of believers in "caste" in our country.

"The prestige of gains and achievements, indicating that the Populist party is destined to become one of the two great political organizations of the country.

"This last item is the deduction of optimism from the foregoing. The heavy popular vote for the Populist electors in some of the Southern States serves principally to show that under the conditions existing in 1892, the solid South would have been broken and its solid electoral vote lost to the democracy had not the Force Bill issue been put at the front. The twenty-three electoral votes credited to Weaver in the West and Northwest separate themselves, on analysis, into elements in which the Omaha platform and the specially characteristic features of the Alliance movement sustain a subordinate part. Colorado and Nevada went for Weaver because they were for silver, not because they were for Weaver. Kansas, Idaho, North Dakota, and the one vote in Oregon were gained by the acquiescence of the Democratic managers in a scheme of fusion obviously to the advantage of the Democratic national ticket. Weaver's proportion of the vote, either popular or electoral, cannot be accepted as a trustworthy measure of the growth of public sentiment in the West in favor of the general programme drawn up at Omaha.

"The first solid and effective achievement in the list is the direct gain of the Populists in their representation in the Congress of the United States. This means something. They must have Senators and Representatives if they are ever going to shape the legislation of the country; and until they can legislate, or muster sufficient strength at the Capitol to force legislation agreeable to their ideas of public policy, they have accomplished nothing. Now they turn up with five Senators, as they believe, and with at least ten Representatives, as they have reason to be certain. It is a respectable showing for a new party, even if we do not count the silver Senators as Populists out and out. But, as an indication of the probable strength of the Populists in the Fifty-fourth Congress, or in the Fifty-fifth, as a reasonable assurance of future progressive development, it is worthless. We need only remind the Populists that their predecessor, the so-called

National party, representing the greenback craze, and, in a measure, the dissatisfaction with political conditions that marked the period after the counting in of Hayes, went into the Forty-sixth House with fourteen Congressmen. The Greenbackers and Readjusters went into the Forty-seventh House with eleven Congressmen. In the Forty-eighth, their strength dropped to two. The Greenback wave had swept off and away; the two old parties confronted each other as before, and the phenomenon of a third party in Congress, mustering more than a dozen lawgivers, had disappeared as utterly as if it had never been.

"The same thing is true respecting the capture, with the aid of fusion, of some of the Western States. Nobody has forgotten the astonishingly sudden appearance and subsidence of the Greenback wave in the old and conservative New England State of Maine. In 1878, the Greenbackers cast about fifty per cent. more votes than the Democrats. In 1879, the Greenback vote was more than double the Democratic, and the election was thrown into the Legislature, which chose a Democratic Governor. In 1880, the Greenbackers fused with the remaining fragments of the Democracy, and carried the State and controlled its government. Where are the Maine Greenbackers to-day?

"The two great political organizations in this country have always been and must always be the party of centralization, paternalism, and meddlesome interference with affairs not belonging to the Federal Government, and the party resisting those destructive tendencies on the lines of

Jeffersonian Democracy and home rule. The issue is permanent and the same, no matter what the parties may call themselves. There is no chance for the Populists on the ground now occupied by the victorious Democracy. If they can crowd the Republican organization out of the special function which it has filled with distinguished ability for a quarter of a century, that is their business, not ours. The achievement would be much like Jonah swallowing the whale."

The Abolition party, which absorbed the old Whig party and made the present Republican party, had not nearly so respectable a beginning as the Populist party. With all the predictions of failure recited above, the Populist party has a name—and there is much in a name—which has already endeared it to the hearts of the masses to the extent of a million votes.

It was the suffering masses, the plain "Common People," who, under the name of Populist, voted for Weaver. There can be no doubt about the affiliation between the Democratic party and the Populist party in the next Congress of the United States. Every Representative elected by the Populist, every Senator selected as the result of their votes cast for the State legislators, will recognize that the Populist party contains the same elements, to the plain "Common People," as the Democratic party, and, therefore, faith will best be kept with the constituents by whom the

Populist Representatives and Senators were elected, by acting with the Democratic party, so long as it continues to wage war upon "caste" and class distinctions and the accumulation of wealth in a dangerous degree in our country.

The Populists have a mission in furnishing to the weary wayfarer a resting place. Many political wayfarers who formerly journeyed under the guidance of the Republican party, hesitate before seeking the protection of the Democratic party. To such the Populist party furnishes a haven of rest.

Should the Democratic party and Grover Cleveland, as representative of the party by whom he was nominated, fail to secure to the "Common People" those rights of which they deem themselves deprived by the Republican party; and should there be a hesitancy or neglect in righting those wrongs of which the "Common People" complain, then the Populists, if some of the "isms" be weeded out of its fair garden, would furnish the Eden for the "Common People." Should Grover Cleveland and the Democratic party neglect quickly and unhesitatingly to pass such laws, and execute the same, as will relieve the "Common People" of the burden that is cast upon them by ungraded taxation, then the "Common People," by the might that abides with them, may select the Populist party, freed from some of its idiosyncrasies, as the party of the people.

It is merely a question of whether the Democratic party and Grover Cleveland will perform the will of the people. If not, the people, by a reorganization of this, the Populist party, will secure a political organization which will perform the mandates of the "Common People." The "Common People" will thrust aside both the old parties and utilize that party which by the magic of simply a popular name was enabled to gain a million votes taken from both of the old parties.

CHAPTER XXVI.

"FLABBYISM" AND THE INCOME TAX.

Now, be it well understood that there is no attempt made, in commenting upon the article on the editorial page of the New York *Sun*, to disparage in any manner that worthy and eminent journal. It represents one part, or side, of that incongruous party, called the Democratic party, which presents phases as worthy of observance by the curiosity-seeker in the political field as the Populist party. On one side, Protection, endorsed by the New York *Sun ;* Free Trade, endorsed by the New York *World ;* a graded income tax, endorsed by the New York *World*, and even the suggestion of an income tax, dubbed by the New York *Sun* as "flabby talk."

Noah Webster defines flabby to mean, "soft, yielding, loose, easily shaken." Well, if the will of eleven million voters, as heard in the verdict rendered by the majority November 8, 1892, be "soft, yielding, easily shaken," then the talk of an Income Tax *is flabby*, then the talk of a Graded Income Tax *is flabby*. The will of the majority of the said eleven million voters made possible the election of Grover Cleveland and the other nominees of the Democratic party. Possibly the will of the people, so expressed November 8th last, may be "flabby"; but there will be another and fearful story to tell unless the will of the people, as expressed, be executed by their servants selected November last.

The New York *Sun* does not astonish the people—the plain " Common People "—of America when it announces a predilection upon the part of the privileged wealthy classes to commit perjury. The "Common People" of America have become accustomed to associate in their minds the worshipers of "caste" with every kind of crime which is consistent with their assumed superiority. It is only necessary to quote an article which appeared in one of the leading journals, to give evidence that, even under the present system of a tax on personal property, the inclination of these sham aristocrats, the would-be nobility of America, is to commit perjury. So worthy is the article of attention that it is given in *extenso*, that the people may judge of the animal they are chasing, and that the weapon, Grover Cleveland, may duly appreciate what efficiency is necessary, upon his part, as the weapon in the hands of the huntsman to destroy this beast of "caste" and accumulated wealth in our land :—

"Ever since the Comptroller and Tax Commissioners of the city declared war upon Lawyer H. Charles

Ulman for issuing his famous circular, offering legal services to those whom he believed to be grossly wronged by a wilfully corrupt administration of the personal tax laws, the enterprising counsellor has been hard at work accumulating evidence in support of the very critical attitude he has assumed.

"Mr. Ulman is a hard fighter and is determined to prove to the entire satisfaction of the public that the serious allegations he makes against our Tax Department officials are all true.

"Yesterday Mr. Ulman notified me that he had completed the compilation of a few statistics which he desired to submit to the HERALD for publication. I found him ready with his statistics and loaded to the muzzle with hot shot for the Tax Commissioners in general and Tax Commissioner Feitner in particular.

"'Let us get right down to business,' were the words with which Mr. Ulman supplemented the regulation greeting. "I have recently, as all New York is aware, challenged the methods of our Tax Commissioners as to personal property taxation. I now reiterate the challenge and desire to submit to public judgment a few figures taken from the personal tax records recently opened for inspection. These figures conclusively prove that our richest men are assessed for ludicrously small personal properties, so small and palpably unfair as to establish the conviction that falsehood and fraud are at the bottom of the ridiculous valuations. Here is the list :—

	Assessed for Personal Property to the Value of		Assessed for Personal Property to the Value of
Jay Gould...............	$500,000	George Kemp...............	100,000
George J. Gould............	10,000	Luther Kountz...............	10,000
Russell Sage...............	100,000	Augustus Kountz.........	15,000
Wm. Rockefeller............	50,000	Andrew Carnegie.........	150,000
C. P. Huntington...........	150,000	Addison Cammack.........	100,000
Henry Hilton...............	100,000	William Astor...............	500,000
E. S. Jaffray...............	100,000	W. W. Astor...............	4,311,400
Morris K. Jesup............	75,000	Henry Villard...............	25,000
Eugene Kelly...............	100,000	Jessie Seligman............	50,000

	Assessed for Personal Property to the Value of		Assessed for Personal Property to the Value of
James Seligman	$ 50,000	Robert Goelet	$150,000
I. Wormser	10,000	F. W. Vanderbilt	100,000
S. Wormser	10,000	G. W. Vanderbilt	100,000
D. O. Mills	50,000	W. K. Vanderbilt	200,000
Henry Flagler	25,000	C. Vanderbilt	200,000
John H. Flagler	10,000	T. A. Havemeyer	100,000
R. P. Flower	150,000	H. O. Havemeyer	120,000
Ogden Goelet	150,000	Wm. F. Havemeyer	15,000

"'Now,' continued Mr. Ulman, 'whether every one of these individuals appeared in person before the Commissioners, or whether the amounts were placed by the Deputy Commissioners, I cannot say.'

"The fact remains the same, that among all our very rich men there is but one—W. W. Astor—who pays taxes on anything like the amount of his actual personal property. Either the deputies charged with making the examinations have committed 'larceny,' or the wealthy citizens above mentioned have appeared before the Commissioners, 'swore off' as a matter of form, and been 'whitewashed' as a matter of course upon due exercise of 'influence.'

"'Let me tell you something that will surprise the public. The ladies of the city are its heaviest taxpayers. Every one of them who has personal property has an assessment levied upon her to the full amount of her possessions. In her case there are no votes to be considered, no political influences to be placated, and, as a result, no deductions are made, no scaling or estimating is allowed, but every dollar possessed is taxed. I have, practically, but just inaugurated this crusade against the corruption existing in the Tax Office, and I believe that a careful examination of the public records, backed by the logic of facts and figures, will enable me to expose a degree of rottenness more startling even than that of the old Tweed ring.'

THE BLAME.

"'Who is to blame for the state of things in the Tax Office?' I asked.

"Mr. Ulman pondered this question for some minutes before he replied, as though hesitating to convert his general charges against the Tax Department into a direct personality. But once having made up his mind, the counsellor sailed into the senior member of the Tax Commission—Mr. Thomas L. Feitner—with surprising vigor, handling him without gloves, and winding up with the suggestion of an appeal to Mayor Grant for his dismissal.

"'The fact of the matter is,' said the counsellor, "Mr. Feitner is the entire commission. The two gentlemen associated with him are comparatively new to the department, and are pushed into the background and kept there, by this all-wise Pooh Bah.

"'The Chief Justice and his associates on the bench of the Court of Appeals have had occasion to chide Feitner in their decisions, but Feitner will tell you that the Court of Appeals does not understand tax laws, and that its rulings are not good law.

"'Special capital is his special prey just at this time. Under the laws of New York it must be contributed in money and the amount advertised. This renders Mr. Feitner's raid upon it a matter of very simple procedure, and he levies his assessments upon it whether the status of the property in which the capital is invested is in Spain, Africa, or New York. Nor does it matter if the money is invested in imported goods in original packages, although, by the constitution of the country, such goods are removed from the jurisdiction of the State's taxing powers.

"'But this does not trouble Feitner. He puts his assessments upon capital so invested, compelling the owner to submit to a taxation of from ten to fifteen per cent. of his money or go into court by certiorari and obtain a release at an expense of more than the amount of illegal tax.

"'If Mayor Grant desires an equitable and proper administration of the Tax Office he will dismiss Mr. Feitner and appoint a man to fill his place who, to say the least, has a knowledge of commerce, the needs of business, and can understand the plainly written law when he reads it.

"'There is another point in this matter which furnishes food for reflection—namely, the very small number of persons in this city who are assessed for taxation —less than thirteen thousand out of a taxable population of nearly one hundred thousand.'"

After reading the above—and presumably it is correct—let us stand in holy astonishment that Jay Gould should suddenly have acquired over $65,000,000 of personal property, according to his will, since this schedule and assessment of personal property was filed, because this late lamented Gould was the possessor of personal property only, with the exception of his residence. Therefore it is obvious, since he swore to possessing only $500,000 of personal property, that he must have acquired, in some miraculous manner, more than $65,000,000 of personal property, which he bequeathed to his children, according to his will, recently filed in the Surrogate's office in the city of New York.

Mr. George Gould swears that he has only $10,000 in personal property. Now who believes it? Mr. Russell Sage has only $100,000 in personal property! and the Vanderbilts each have from $100,000 to $200,000 worth!

Poor men! Let the commiseration of the masses go forth. These gentlemen, who are accredited with the possession of millions, and who, when they die, find themselves suddenly possessed of the millions with which they are accredited by the public, are poor men while they live, and have to pay taxes!.

Right you are, New York *Sun;* an income tax would lead to perjury! Of course, not upon the part of the gentlemen named—for "Brutus was an honorable man"—but we will agree with you, after reading this schedule, that an income tax would lead to perjury. But let us suggest that we, the people, have elected a man as chief executive of the nation, who represents us, the "Common People," and will see to the execution of the laws of the nation—Grover Cleveland. To be an honest man and fulfill the expectations of the people, he will see that those who should pay the expenses of the Government by an income tax shall make honest returns concerning their possessions, and pay that sum of money to which the Government is entitled.

If he do not so, he is faithless, and the people will hold him accountable. The power of the Government will be in his hands—both branches of the Legislature. And should the National Legislature, selected by the people, deem it wise to furnish revenue for the Government, and pass an income tax graded according to the incomes received, then it will devolve upon Grover Cleveland, as trustee of the nation, to see that the will of the Legislature is executed. He has the power to appoint such officers as may be necessary to properly execute the laws of the Federal Union, and we, the "Common People," will expect a ratification of all the promises made by him to the people of the Union. The people of the nation, trusting and relying upon his honesty and integrity, selected him for the high office of Chief Magistrate of the GREATEST NATION ON EARTH. We have placed in his hands the power of the majority, and we shall expect the execution of such laws as the will of the majority may dictate; *the foremost of which will be an income tax*, whereby may be eradicated many of the evils of which the masses, the "plain people," complain.

Should perjury be committed—and it would not be astonishing, because the "plain people" of America are not apt to be astonished at anything vile that may be done by the sham aristocracy and worshipers of "caste" in our country—then let Grover Cleveland, as Executive of the nation, having the power of the people behind him, supported by the mighty voice of the broad democracy of our land, prosecute, by means of the officers of the Federal Government (paid by the people to punish crimes of the character indicated by the New York *Sun*, such as perjury), and, upon conviction, let the glorious sight be afforded to us plain "Common People," of a millionaire working in a shoe shop at Sing-Sing; let us see the stripes of the criminal adorning the backs of some of these good, my lords, the barons, who swear to lies and perjure themselves about their incomes; grab a dozen of them; convict them of perjury; make them appear before the people as criminals, as the people believe they are. One batch of a dozen going to Sing-Sing and Auburn—one batch of a dozen would-be Patricians breaking rock for the good of the public, would be a sight that would delight the very souls of the "Common People."

The people make the laws! Now, you millionaires, obey the laws; and a transgression against those laws, though you be worth $100,000,-000, will not be excused. The people believe that an income tax can be collected in spite of the perjury predicted by the New York *Sun*, because of the PUNISHMENT that the PEOPLE WILL INFLICT upon the perjurers.

The people have had enough, a surfeit, of this cry of immunity from the consequences of crime because the criminal happens to possess wealth. We are weary, tired of it. And the people have made up their minds that the wealthy criminals shall be brought to the bar of justice along with the poorest, pilfering thief of a penny loaf. There shall not be in our land one law for the rich and another for the poor. If these wealthy criminals perjure themselves with regard to their incomes, they must be punish d, and the people will expect the punishment and penalty to be inflicted by and through the administration of Grover Cleveland.

To cry out, with the New York *Sun*, that "If you pass a law requiring the citizens of the American Union to swear to the truth and record their incomes, it is but offering an inducement to perjury, and, therefore, is undesirable," is to admit that our Government is a failure, that a Republic is a failure, that the will of the majority shall not rule, that the American Constitution is a farce and a fraud, all of which the "Common People" will not believe to be the case. They demand the law! The enforcement of it rests with the Executive of the nation. The punishment rests upon the integrity and honor of the judiciary of the Federal courts. And there has been no evidence yet of a lack of honesty in the members of the Federal judiciary. The perjurers can and should be punished. If the Legislature of the nation, the Congress of the United States, will pass a graded income tax, as the people desire that they should do, the people believe that the law will be executed under the wise and honest administration of that Executive chosen by them November 8, 1892— Grover Cleveland. The people believe that, should any be accused of perjury and false return of their incomes, they will be prosecuted by the officers of the Federal courts, who will be honest, being appointed by Grover Cleveland, the representative of the people ; that, when so charged, perjurers brought to trial will be prosecuted fairly and ably by the representatives of the executive department, selected by the people November last, and, when so tried, the people, by twelve of their number, the jury, will decide whether the accused be guilty or innocent, and, if guilty, the people believe that the wealth and position of the accused will not enter into the consideration of the Magistrate representing the Federal Government, but that he will sentence a guilty man, even though he be worth a million or a hundred million, in the same manner as he would the commonest counterfeiter or petty larceny thief in the land.

Believing thus, the plain people of America see no good reason or argument in the cry that an income tax will be productive of perjury and that it is a sufficient reason to prevent its passage. And, therefore, a graded income tax becomes the most desirable measure possible to introduce for the advantage of the people who elected the incoming administration, November 8, 1892.

CHAPTER XXVII.

CONCLUSION.

IT would be with feelings of regret that this volume is brought to an end if the object for which it was intended could reasonably be expected to be in any way nearer of attainment. Unfortunately for the successful solution of the social problem in the United States, such can hardly be hoped for by the publication of one book, or as the result of one election; it will require the efforts of many skillful writers, a vast number of volumes, and it is to be feared many and more serious exhibitions of the indignation felt by the "Plain People" than that of the election of November 8, 1892, to convince the sham aristocracy of our country, that the existence of "caste" or privileged classes will not be endured in Free America. It is to be dreaded by all who love the Union, that the blinded believers in snobbery and imitation of European manners will not be warned by the positive, pronounced disapprobation exhibited last election day of the plain "Common People" with the conduct, lives, morals, and manners of the worshipers of "caste;" that these sham aristocrats will neglect to heed the signal of danger which their insolence and affectations have created in our loved Republic, until upon the next occasion the plain " Common People " may have become so incensed as to no longer exercise the great and good commonsense of the American people in dealing with questions of internal interest—but will throw to the winds moderation, and crush out the pretensions of that asinine part of the human family who believe in the possible existence of anything like "caste" in our country. To some of these shoddy aristocrats who have become absolutely intoxicated by their dreams of social greatness, this book will be unworthy of their condescending attention; they will dismiss the subject as the vaporings of a madman, without investigating the possible and more than probable theory expressed herein, that the result of the last Presidential election was produced, not by the fact that the people of the nation had become Free Traders and gone over to the Democratic party, *en masse*, but by the natural resentment felt by the democratic "plain" people of the country at the absurd and offensive pretensions of the wealthy classes who had fastened themselves like leeches upon the Republican party, and who, by aping the manners and morals of the aristocracy of Europe, had rendered themselves hateful in the eyes of the worth and merit of our land, the "Common People" of America. By the existence of this leech upon the body of the Republican party, all the pure patriotic blood had (in the opinion of the people) been sucked out of that Grand Old Party, leaving only a withered skeleton around whose fleshless form was twined in festoons the venomous serpent of "caste," imported, like the cholera, along with much else of evil that comes to this dear land of ours from Europe.

A small part of owners of villas at Newport and castles in Scotland will see in this book the expression of opinions which they dub as dangerous, and declare should entitle the utterer to the treatment accorded the private soldier who did not sympathize with the tyrannical Frick in his treatment of the Homestead strikers. This part of our would-be nobility have always ready in their throats the cry of "Socialist"—"Anarchist." With studious care has the author of this volume insisted upon the fact that the only practical and effectual method of ridding the land of the curse that would result from the existence of "caste" here, is by the ballot—by laws enacted to prevent the accumulation of menacingly large fortunes in the hands of a few citizens of the Union.

To this part of the pretended "Lords and Barons," who declare that truth is sometimes best left unexpressed, and that a man may become dangerous by giving utterance to the feelings that fill the breasts of other men, it would be well to consider which is the most efficacious method to be adopted in dealing with the bite of a mad dog, or a cancer. Is it by covering it with beautiful silken bandages, and thus concealing it from view, or is it by cauterization? Does concealment render the disease less dangerous or deep-seated? Recommending a cure, and not a curtain to cover the wound which festers all the more rapidly by the fact that it is heated by the covering, should be the line of treatment adopted by the good physician of the public body, as of the individual body. Every party slave may object to the idea of the victory of the "Common People," November 8, 1892, being considered in any light save that of a party triumph. The fact remains just the same, however; party machination had little to do with results produced by the people at the last election. There are such positive and unmistakable indications of the demand of the people for the passage of a Graded Income Tax, that silence any longer upon the subject is puerile.

When leading Democratic party newspapers, like the New York *World*, openly proclaim the necessity of such laws, it is useless to hesitate in meeting frankly the causes that led to the demand of the people for such legislation as a "Graded Income Tax." Since part of this volume was put in type, an American citizen has died, leaving an estate of $70,000,000, which tremendous amount consisted almost entirely of personal property, upon which practically no taxes were paid. This almost countless mass of the wealth of the nation is held entirely by the descendants of Jay Gould. Not one dollar was bequeathed to one single object of charity. Not one poor man calls to mind the name of Jay Gould with gratitude. The common, plain people of America have no desire to rob the children of Jay Gould of that $70,000,-000. "Enjoy that great fortune in peace and safety," the people say to the Goulds; but the people also add this : "We have now an opportunity to judge of the supreme selfishness and absence of charity in the hearts of the millionaires. As an object lesson, Jay Gould's will is valuable. In future give us a Graded Income Tax, and prevent the vast accumulation of wealth in the hands of the selfish and uncharitable."

We missed from the first great accompanying fracture and crack of ~~that the~~ landslide in Nov 1890 — Gippsland Stanleim — a few months after the passage of it's 35 acts! — When the word "Ill Kirby" was on everybody's tongue —

www.ingramcontent.com/pod-product-compliance
Lightning Source LLC
Chambersburg PA
CBHW020541300426
44111CB00008B/754